DIARMUID GAVIN & TERENCE CONRAN

OUTDOORS

THE GARDEN DESIGN BOOK FOR THE TWENTY-FIRST CENTURY

conran OCTOPUS

◄ Dramatic shoots of water tumble from stage right in this compelling climax to a garden. The tumultuous energy, zingy colours and a zigzag composition combine to create a bold, dramatic scene.

► Sculpture in nature: twisted branches of strawberry guava and rose apple saplings wind and weave their way through the trees in an intriguing form of contemporary art.

▶ Drought-loving succulents will thrive in a sunny garden, resulting in a dramatic and exotic show of foliage and flowers. These low-maintenance plants are the ultimate in garden show-offs, and can be combined to create a colourful and textural display.

Contents

◄ Planting has been kept to a minimum in this contemporary garden, allowing the clean lines of the design to go unhindered. The black bamboo, growing in super-smooth raised beds, forms a tunnel effect, making a visual connection between the glass extension of the house and the outside space.

▶ By creating a tunnel along a path, the garden designer has made the most of a distant view, drawing it into the garden. The tunnel acts as a picture frame but, rather than allowing us to see the view all at once, the designer has masked the edge with plants, forcing us to walk through to the other side.

Inspiration

Design itself is my inspiration...

I create gardens because I have to. Ultimately, it is a private endeavour; I need to do what I do for myself. I need to explore ideas and I need to work with nature to create. It's my form of expression. But I am constantly thinking, examining and reflecting on ideas, gardens made and gardens still to be created. It's my great joy and sometimes a huge frustration. The question I am most often asked is where do you get your ideas? I find it a frustrating one because the answer always appears glib – everywhere. I don't seek out ideas, I stumble upon them, I daydream and I question. When inspiration comes in this way, I'm delighted by its arrival, but I can also be frustrated because too much excitement about a new concept for a garden design or a planting combination can lead to a lack of sleep for a night – or even weeks!

As somebody who creates gardens in the contemporary age, my inspiration is split. It's about hard landscaping materials and plants. The unique thing to gardens is that the spark is often a particular combination of the two. Inspiration is a private conversation. Before I went to college to learn my craft at the age of 21 I knew exactly what I wanted to do. My desire was to create gardens, but I also had a huge need to examine what a garden was and to take influence from other disciplines, and incorporate different ideas and thoughts into this process. As I dug gardens, I spent years examining what I was doing and why. For a long time I was caught up in the 'traditional' and the twee. It seemed of prime importance to clients that gardens were pretty – pretty and colourful, pretty and tidy, and pretty and needing little work to be maintained that way. And it is extraordinary but nonetheless true that there was guilt involved in wanting to change things. Change not for anybody else – change for me. Why would you mess with tradition and why would you mess with something that worked, a venerable craft developed over the centuries and beautifully honed to sublime perfection? What would cause someone to question the English cottage garden? Why would I have a problem with re-creating Japanese-style gardens in the Irish countryside? And why would a Mediterranean pastiche garden be unsuitable for a London suburb? It would be wrong to suggest that there

wasn't a fairly dramatic movement towards the creation of new gardens. But growing up in an extremely insular world I wasn't aware of it. I ploughed my own furrow and then grabbed a book that was to become my outlet to a different world: Guy Cooper and Gordon Taylor's *Paradise Transformed: The Private Garden for the Twenty-First Century*. All around the world there were people with new ideas and genuine motivations for creating. Intellect once again was being harnessed and rules that I had grown up with had been broken.

So what were my inspirations? Well, I was never a fan of traditional gardening programmes. It was music videos, architecture, the changing face of my home city of Dublin, materials, furniture, the wild landscapes of the west and south of Ireland, a river close to my home and the woodland beside it – a strange combination. But, of course, inspiration is in a state of constant change. Now it extends to other areas – the desire to express emotions such as joy, fun, happiness or sorrow. The constant state of evolution of our planet leads to moral gardening issues. The use of water, power, natural resources and artificial fertilizers, and the extraordinary advancements in technology allow for fascinating gardening endeavours.

But the shock for me is maturity! From the age of 30 to 40, I was given permission and, indeed, challenged, mainly through television programmes, to present the new, to ask the questions, to dramatize. And, after a while, you question yourself and realize that gardening heritage isn't something to be torn up. All classic styles were innovative in their day, so it has been a great and recent joy to examine the works of Le Nôtre, Capability Brown, Gertrude Jekyll and Roberto Burle Marx to see what great innovators they were.

◀ This garden, featured at the RHS Chelsea Flower Show in London, combines the old with the new, with simple planting, made up primarily of lavender and clipped box, and practical, contemporary spaces, in this case a spherical concrete pod that acts as a potting shed.

One of the greatest pleasures in life...

… is gardening, or simply growing plants. Collecting seeds or cuttings from friends or from visits to foreign climes, then watching them grow in small damp pots of earth until they are big enough to be planted out in the garden… it's thrilling to feel the simple joys of creativity rewarded as you see seedlings and saplings develop into mature plants or trees with flowers, fruit or berries.

Give a child a packet of runner bean seeds (think of Jack and the Beanstalk), help him make a tower of tall sticks and just see him get hooked as the plants rush up the sticks, produce pretty flowers, then tiny beans that grow with extraordinary speed, ready for Sunday lunch. The child may never have enjoyed eating beans before, but I bet he enjoys these! To have a feeling of creative pride in helping to feed the family is the start; soon that child will move on to potatoes and even a herb garden.

I have always enjoyed vegetable gardening. During the war, growing your own was something of a necessity because food was so scarce, but now I am motivated by flavour: vegetables from the garden gathered and rapidly cooked are incomparable with anything you can buy in a shop. Vegetables and fruit really do have a fugitive flavour; if they come all the way from Kenya or Chile in gas-filled containers or are grown in water in Holland, the flavour will be long departed.

Vegetable gardens can also be very beautiful. In my garden, among the rows of vegetables, I like to grow tall frames of sweet peas and clematis, alongside towers of beans, climbing courgettes and cucumbers, which are decorative, easy to pick and not so prone to snails and slugs. As well as making a cheerful landscape, flowers grown in the vegetable garden can be picked for the house and are delicious for the kitchen. Nasturtiums grow very well up sticks and are colourful and flavoursome in salads.

Growing vegetables also makes you very aware of their seasonality. The excitement I feel cutting the very first asparagus is matched with sadness when relinquishing the knife. However, by then, the first tiny peas and broad beans will be ready, and the first crop of new potatoes… and how good are those tiny French breakfast radishes!

When I bought my 18th-century home in the country, the house was derelict and surrounded by desolate gardens. Somebody had thought they would make a few bob by growing Christmas trees in the beautiful walled kitchen garden, but thistles had outgrown the Christmas trees by several feet. The house sat in a rather barren landscape and looked like a large dolls' house that had been left in a field. I felt I had to do everything possible to anchor the house to the ground. This is a problem that I often see with new houses that have not yet settled into the landscape, so I built a raised garden in front of the house and planted wisteria, honeysuckle, clematis and climbing hydrangeas, hops, and a beautiful white rose against the walls.

The house is now covered with greenery and flowers, admittedly after quite a few years, and looks as if it is also growing out of the soil. The raised garden, with its herbaceous borders, provides a peaceful and rather private space, which is easily kept in order. I love to sit and read, sipping a glass or two of wine – if only the wasps would stop chewing the wooden frame of my chair!

Your garden does not have to be a flat, boring space at the back of your house. You can create different levels and vistas, which can make it much more interesting. As Sir John Soane suggested, invest in some hazard and surprise. The soil and the landscape, within reason, can be shaped to your command.

Terence Conran

◄ A towering hedge allows this neat and tidy formal garden to take centre stage, rather than the splendid natural scene that lies beyond the boundary of the space. The tall screen also has a practical use, protecting the plants growing within the space from being damaged by strong winds.

▶ Garden rooms do not just have to be functional – they can also be fun. Here, the garden designer has sought to make a literal translation of the term 'garden room', by making an outdoor room, complete with marble floor, and planting a large, multistemmed tree at its heart.

Diarmuid Gavin and Terence Conran in conversation

When did you decide to become a designer?

Diarmuid Gavin I knew when I was growing up that I wanted to do something creative, but I'm deeply impractical – I'm no good at DIY. My outlet was pottery, and I did this for seven years when I was at Trinity Art College in Dublin. I was no good at throwing pots – I didn't like the discipline of the wheel, so I made things by hand.

Terence Conran Like coiled pots?

DG That was a bit boring for me. What I enjoyed was being given the freedom with this lump of clay, working it and getting the air out of it. I was very prolific and had a whole production line going. I'd take everybody else's stuff out of the kiln and my work would dominate. I didn't do any pottery for a year and I became very depressed because I wasn't making anything.

TC That's a very strange coincidence because I was also a potter. I went to a public school in Dorset called Bryanston and was taught, funnily enough, by a man called Don Potter, who took us for sculpture, metalwork, woodwork and pottery. In the basement of the school there was a terrific pottery with enormous chimneys and kilns – I became absolutely hooked. On my holidays from school, I used to bicycle 17 miles from my home in Farnham, Surrey, to a pottery where I dug the clay by hand and prepared it. It was mainly a flowerpot factory and I spent my days throwing flowerpots. I was quite good at this and I got a penny for every 6in pot I made. I became so keen that I made my own pottery, making a treadle from the crankshaft of a car, and built my own wood-fired kiln in my parents' garden.

DG What was it like being a teenager and being interested in art? I bet your mates found it amusing.

TC You're right. When I left Bryanston in the 1950s, I went to the Central School of Arts and Crafts in London. My father, who had played rugby for England, was keen his son should also play. So I played rugby, but when my team-mates discovered I was at art school, they thought it was very funny.

DG I remember telling my art teacher in the early 1980s that I was going to study horticulture and I was looked at as if I was weird. This was the person I most associated with at school and I really thought that they would have had some affinity with what I wanted to do.

TC I was very lucky at Bryanston, as it was a very creative school. Music and the arts were very important. During the war years it was fantastic – many artists were conscientious objectors and we had a steady flow of really interesting people come to teach us.

What were your early influences?

DG There was a woman called Lady Valerie Goulding, who had an estate in County Wicklow and her son was a sculptor. He produced incredible stuff from coloured steel beams, the likes of which amazed me because I grew up in a very suburban household, with a suburban attitude on a very suburban road. Seeing this work had a strong influence on me, because when I left school I thought I wanted to design gardens, but had no interest in trying to emulate those I saw in Ireland – they didn't interest me whatsoever. I wanted to do something new.

TC One of my greatest influences was one of my aunts. She was an extraordinary woman who used to travel to the foothills of the Himalayas to find plants. She created a fantastic damp garden that sat just on the edge of the moors in Devon. I was sent to stay with her during the war, and she was the first person to really excite me about growing things. I also collected wild flowers and pressed them – moving to Devon introduced me to a whole mass of flowers that I'd never seen before.

What about the main influences on your work?

TC Have you ever been to Yves Saint Laurent's garden in Marrakech?

DG In terms of influence, I think his garden has been a massive inspiration for the last 11 to 15 years. A re-creation of the Majorelle Garden was built at the Chelsea Flower Show in the 1990s, and that shade of blue, Bleu Majorelle, which was used on the walls, had never been seen in this country before. I can remember shooting the pilot for *Home Front in the Garden* and we did an inspirational trip to see the garden – I came back and painted the walls of a garden with this colour. And then Alan Titchmarsh took it up, almost instantly for *Ground Force*, and that was when Barleywood blue was introduced.

TC The colour does make a fabulous backdrop for green plants. I heard the exhibition we had at the Design Museum on Mexican architect Luis Barragán had an influence on you.

DG Absolutely. It was a great help. I was making a garden for a Mexican lady in south London and was having trouble deciding what to do.

Themed gardens are always difficult because I don't think they travel well. I went to the exhibition, which was wonderfully set out, and took influence from that for the garden I was doing.

And the retro influence on design?

TC My first proper commission was working on the Festival of Britain, which took place on London's South Bank in 1951 – the festival was enormously influential on design.

DG And still is enormously influential on design in this country to this day. It is quite extraordinary that you can map so many things back to it.

TC It was the touch paper for the development of creative business in this country. It totally surprised people who saw it. It was so colourful and full of new architecture, buildings like the Dome of Discovery and the Skylon. It created a colourful, exciting, uplifting atmosphere. Most of the architects and designers that worked on the festival had been in the war and had travelled the world. They had been to Italy, France and Africa and their eyes had been opened. They came back and created an antidote to this dreary, grey, bombed, rationed city.

DG Was there a feeling of frustration immediately after the festival because people had been shown something that was magic, including the innovative gardens?

TC There wasn't really an immediate change. If you were running a factory at that time, making chairs, you could sell everything you produced, so why change? There was no economic reason to make a different kind of furniture.

DIARMUID GAVIN & TERENCE CONRAN

DG Pictures of the festival have certainly influenced me and sometimes my work, although when I was younger a greater influence was probably some huge big round ball-shaped containers in Dublin. I'm sure they came from the festival and as a trainee horticulturist with the Dublin Corporation Nursery, I'd fill them with bedding plants every year. They were a radical, retro shape and not the sort of thing you would have found in Dublin at that time. They really went against all the architecture and the way people lived. So that was an influence, and I loved the Skylon, and recently I've seen a picture of the multi-coloured metal spheres that formed an abacus-like screen on Waterloo Bridge. I take influence from all that 1950s work, and I went through a phase of getting that out of my system three or four years ago.

TC It's interesting because all of my furniture at that time, which was mainly constructed from welded metal reinforcing rods, the only metal you could get, always had a coloured wooden ball on the bottom of each leg so they wouldn't scratch the floor.

DG When I did the Hanover Quay garden at Chelsea in 2005, you said it was too retro for you. I wasn't devastated, that's not the right word, but when you say something, people listen. I was a bit crushed.

What are more inspirational – man-made or natural creations?

TC You can go for a walk in a bluebell wood and it is the most beautiful thing you have ever seen. You think: how can I find a way of re-interpreting the pleasure I am getting from this? When you've seen what somebody else has achieved, somebody like Capability Brown, or some wonderful way the land has been sculpted, you think, well if they did it, why shouldn't I?

DG That's very interesting. I've been out to Japan recently with the idea that I have to produce a garden. To start with, I was overawed by some of the gardens I saw. I went to Ryoan-ji in Kyoto, where 15 stones have been placed in a sea of gravel. It was designed five centuries ago and is the place where Zen Buddhism reaches its zenith. My wife, however, brought me back down to earth when she reminded me that the garden had been created by humans, not a god – she was right – I think it is important to maintain a sense of perspective and not to be overawed.

TC I've been around a lot of Japanese gardens and it's the architecture, things like teahouses, that I find awfully inspirational.

What is your experience of designing show gardens, particularly for the Chelsea Flower Show?

DG The first time I went to Chelsea, I went there with a plan. I wanted to make a garden that they would expect, and then they would invite me back and I could then create the garden I wanted to do. I made a romantic Irish scene, which won a bronze medal. The next garden I made at Chelsea was a contemporary garden with glass walls, so-called new exotic planting and glass slabs that lit up. It was terrible and didn't get an award.

The lack of an award didn't get me down. My attitude to flower shows is that the views of the judges are subjective and you'll never agree with what they say. So my approach has always been, go along, do your job, pack up and say thank you very much. You have to be gracious about it, there's no point having any arguments about the award you receive. Your drive should always be to do good work, be true to yourself and to learn.

TC There's a certain gimmick element to designing a show garden, which

we wouldn't naturally do in everyday life. It's an unreal thing, it's not really a garden, there's a lot of pot plants gathered together, so it's not serious gardening.

DG I think show gardens do have some things in common with real gardens. Shape, proportion, ideas and especially, in terms of the Chef's Garden that you created, a suggestion that people can loosen up their lives and live outdoors. I think this has been your essence, right the way through everything you have done.

TC It's a very unreal experience making a garden at Chelsea. I very much like things that get better as they get older and, of course, with any show garden, it's only there for a few days. You mentioned that your Colourful Suburban Eden garden is going to be remade in a forest glade. I thought it would make a wonderful children's garden – wouldn't it be fantastic to walk through a woodland, come into a glade and suddenly find this extraordinary garden?

DG That's where it's going. It's found a new home in a brilliant place in a woodland garden in Ireland.

You know, you have to accept Chelsea for what it is – the best horticultural show in the world. It's the Mecca for anybody involved in the horticultural industry. It is crammed with the best growers, the best breeders and the best merchandise. But it is not crammed with the best designers. You get the same people every year, with maybe five or six new faces. People do Chelsea for all sorts of reasons, but an awful lot of it is about ego and getting your name out there.

TC If your ambition is to be a garden designer, it's a very good place to advertise your skills. I do Chelsea because I quite enjoy that exhibition thing, and sometimes it is an opportunity to get my ideas in front of the public. With the Chef's Garden, it was an opportunity to show how to grow vegetables decoratively or the importance of vegetables. There is something exciting about the whole business of constructing a garden, getting it up and finished in a period of time.

DG Chelsea is definitely a place to have private experiments in a very public way – an experiment that a sponsor may commission. In my early days, it was an escape from the drudgery of creating pretty gardens in Ireland – nobody would commission anything different because they hadn't seen anything different. And it got me into a different place, it got me onto television so I was able to carry out all sorts of good, bad and ugly stuff.

Subsequently, I don't need the exposure from Chelsea and I don't need a show garden to lead to work. This means I can use it as a place to experiment and have fun – although as I'm getting older, my need to experiment is becoming less important.

TC I must admit I hadn't noticed that you'd toned your work down!

Is garden design inclusive or exclusive?

TC I think good garden design is open to everyone and not just the middle classes. If you look at allotments, some of them are absolutely beautiful. The plot holders have thought about how they want their patches to look and have gone to great trouble to carefully lay out their kitchen gardens.

DG Garden design must be open to everyone – particularly as these days many people are far more aware of design. That has been the big difference in the last ten to 15 years. It's gone from nobody caring about their homes, when, say, the curtains were changed once a generation, to a point where everything is style over substance. It's instantaneous, but I think it will eventually find a happy balance.

Where is garden design going?

DG Many prominent gardeners and garden designers will not acknowledge suburbia. It was something that I hated when I was growing up, but whether we like it or not, it will influence gardening greatly in the years to come.

TC Are you going through your Betjeman period?

DG I just think that with the Government's plan to build thousands of new homes across the south-east of England over the next 20 years, suburban gardens will have a major impact on design and designers.

If you build a show garden somewhere like the Chelsea Flower Show, do you approach it in the same way that you did when designing other products – is it your mission to bring it to the masses? In other areas of design you showed them how they could eat out, how they could cook, the furniture they could have and how they could appreciate quality on a different level. We're not good at that yet in gardens.

TC You mean there's no Ikea or Habitat approach to gardens? I think you're right.

DG Funnily enough, it was done in California during the 1950s. There were some exceptional designers who understood plants, who understood materials, who understood shape and form, but there wasn't the money around for it to become common at the time. I love the idea that really well-ordered gardens, which fitted a certain lifestyle, were built, and I want to see if I can unlock that secret.

TC I think it's good that there are lots of different designers doing different things. Creativity and competition keep the creative juices moving on and help to bring about something that is new and better. There's no point in doing a repetitive thing.

DG With any artistic endeavour or craft, you want to get better at what you do. From a personal point of view, that's the constant challenge and interest, and that keeps me excited. You're always striving to paint the perfect picture and to get it right.

What do you think of the rise in growing your own vegetables and vegetables as a major trend in gardening?

TC I think that vegetable gardens are just as beautiful as flower gardens and, to me, seeing a red cabbage growing is as beautiful as any perennial. I've always tried to get my children to grow vegetables, as I think it is something that gets their gastric juices going. To be present at the planting of runner beans and to harvest them several months later gives them a sense of achievement.

DG Growing your own vegetables is very important. It's a huge moral obligation when you look at how the environment is being damaged by things like intensive farming, the use of chemicals as pesticides and the amount of energy that is being used to fly beans half way round the globe to land on our supermarket shelves. Equally, we have to think about the way we grow plants. I meet the sweetest little old ladies who think they have the right to grow their hostas slug-free and don't question the quantity of chemicals they use to keep them this way. But we will have to,

and it is something that affects contemporary garden design. You have to consider ways of making your own compost, saving water, growing organically and many more things.

When I was growing up I didn't grow any vegetables until I joined the boy scouts and grew some cress on blotting paper. I don't feel there's any conflict with growing vegetables and other plants in the garden, and I don't think they need to be treated differently from any other plant in the garden. I think it's fine to have a vegetable garden in a contemporary garden, or to grow vegetables with other plants. You can have great fun with vegetables – contemporary thinking is that kids should know where food comes from, so fill some containers with peppers or tomatoes and display them on the patio. When I design a suburban garden for someone, I'm asked for a vegetable garden more and more.

What has the greatest change in garden design been since you started out?

DG Democracy. Gardening isn't owned by the establishment anymore and people feel like they can have a go themselves. That's really important and I'd put that down to one television programme: *Ground Force*. Whatever your view of it, when those three presenters appeared on our screens in the late 1990s, people could see gardens happening, and they could see that gardening was associated with fun. A while later, they did revisits to some of the gardens that were created and the plants were growing and, generally, the gardens had been very well looked after. OK, some of these gardens were the height of twee, but the people had had a go.

Is the vision of a designer hampered by technology or the materials available at the time?

DG It's not always possible to achieve what you want to achieve. I often look with frustration at the work of interior designers and the materials that they can use indoors. For instance, I could see something wonderful and wavy, and I look to re-create this in concrete or resin, but it's impossible. You speak to a million people to see if they can help and you just don't get there. But that's a wonderful frustration at the end of the day, as you are learning all of the time. It enables you to have an innate feel for a material, which is central to everything. You must know the feel and properties of a material, and have confidence in what you are using. You must push people, technology and materials to the ultimate, to try and find out if you can do something, or if it's worth doing.

TC If it's worth doing, yes. The first thing that I have to know with any project, whether it's inside or out, is how much it costs. You can go an awful long way with an idea and then suddenly find it's completely beyond your budget and not practical. I also try to work with materials that improve with usage, such as some stone and wood that get a beautiful patina after being exposed to the weather for some time.

DG I'm really amused that costs come first. That's the huge difference between you and me. But that's why you live in a lovely penthouse on top of your own office block, have an estate in the country, a house in France and probably a private jet. And why I live where I live. I don't think the price should stop things being done. Some things will always bug me until they are achieved.

► Mounds of clipped box and simple cool stone prove that a striking garden can be created out of very little. This garden, teetering on the edge of a dramatic precipice, illustrates the control that man can exert over nature, compared with the untamed natural environment beyond the garden boundary.

Rural

Mention rural gardens to many town or city dwellers and they will immediately think of a cottage garden, with prolific summer-flowering perennials spilling carelessly out over a white picket fence. Of course, this cliché does still exist, but rural gardens are as diverse in style as they are in size. While many are large enough to need a ride-on lawnmower, others are as small as the tiniest city gardens. Some have bucolic views over open countryside, while others may be bordered by woodland or neighbouring cottage walls.

Although there are exceptions, the key to making an attractive rural garden is to keep everything looking as natural as possible. The materials used for garden boundaries and surfaces need to be well chosen, and the planting within the garden will be at its best when allowed to grow with the minimum of maintenance. Letting the garden blend into the countryside allows it to become a magnet for wildlife and an idyllic oasis for the owner. What better way of whiling away a few hours than lazing on the lawn while serenaded by the soothing call of birds and the gentle buzz of bees flitting from flower to flower?

Boundaries

Boundaries help to define a space, and the materials you use will depend largely on what surrounds your garden. Solid boundaries such as walls or fences provide privacy and security, and can help to hide an eyesore or keep unwanted wildlife from entering your plot. Hedges and screens give structure to a garden, which is especially important in the depths of winter, and are perfect as windbreaks or for muffling the sound of traffic. Apart from making perimeter boundaries, vertical barriers of one sort or another help to define space within the garden. Generally, these are lower in height and can be used to create a number of different rooms within the garden or to introduce a sense of mystery and surprise, so the whole of the garden is not revealed at once.

▌ Walls

Walls are a feature of the countryside, whether the dry stone field boundaries of the Yorkshire Dales, the formidable stretches of stone wall surrounding large country estates, or the mellow brick of a country vicarage garden. It is unusual to build boundary walls today, as the cost is prohibitive but, within a garden, walls can be employed to divide different areas or levels, to create atmosphere and a sense of place.

It is best to hire a builder to construct any walls, and it is important to use local materials, either bricks the same colour as your house or stone quarried in the region. Dry stone walls can look wonderful if constructed by an expert; the cracks between stones can be planted with cascading

▶ Screens painted bright orange are perfect for a desert garden and echo the intensity of the sun. This striking colour is an ideal backdrop for agaves and other sun-loving plants.

▼ To blend in with a garden, dry stone walls should be created from local stone that echoes the colours used in paths or other buildings. Irregular chunks of rocks, carefully placed, give this wall an interesting texture.

alpine plants, or if nature is just allowed to take its course, self-seeded plants will soon appear. The choice of stone is largely dependent on locality, but could include slate, sandstone or limestone. Local stone can also be used in combination with a traditional brick wall – in some areas of England flint is widely used.

Not all rural garden walls need to be traditional in style. A clean sweeping surface of dressed stone or rendered, painted concrete in a simple, uncluttered space can bring elegance and style to the countryside.

▲ Boundaries do not just have to be functional – they can make wonderful garden features in their own right. Here, a shallow pool perfectly reflects an abstract design created on a screen.

◄ With age, dry stone walls take on a romantic air and gradually fall apart. In new rural gardens, this look can be replicated by leaving edges deliberately unfinished.

◄ Solid screens are like a full stop in the garden. This translucent fence, created from metallic ribbons, is a physical barrier but also allows the eye to see beyond.

▼ In summer, the scarlet stems of red dogwood are hidden beneath a cloak of foliage, but in winter, stripped of their leaves, they sparkle when backlit by the sun.

▲ Rectangular plinths make a clearly defined boundary but also allow the visitor tantalizing glimpses through to the other side. Their height draws the eye upwards into the trees.

◄ Tapestry hedges planted with native species are excellent for providing wildlife habitats. They also bring shape and colour to a garden when very little else is growing.

► Lengths of willow are the most sustainable of materials for making barriers and can be woven together successfully to create a variety of shapes. The diamond windows of this screen will soon be closed by masses of new foliage.

◀ Even harsh industrial materials, such as sheets of corrugated metal, can be turned into unusual architectural screens. The rigidity of this structure has been softened by cleverly knitting together a variety of ornamental grasses.

▦ Hedges

If there is a large area of garden to enclose, then hedges will be the ideal solution. Not only are they relatively inexpensive from the outset, but the right varieties will attract all kinds of wildlife. Mix native plants together, such as hawthorn, hazel and field maple, allow them to grow naturally with the minimum of maintenance, and you will soon create an informal boundary that blends in perfectly with its surroundings.

A more formal solution is to grow different plants together to create a tapestry hedge, clipping it to reveal the different colours or textures of the leaves. A fine example of this can be seen at The Gibberd garden in Harlow, Essex, which was designed by architect Sir Frederick Gibberd in the twentieth century. Another type of formal hedge, which looks best in larger rural gardens, is the topiary hedge. Yew is the perfect plant to trim tightly, and a hedge of crisply cut castellated shapes looks dramatic around the perimeter of a garden or as a backdrop to colourful perennial plantings.

Living willow sculptures are becoming a common sight in many informal rural gardens where they are used to make dens or shaped to resemble creatures. Unrooted rods of willow can also be used to make a fedge, a hybrid of a fence and a hedge. Sticks of willow are pushed into the ground at intervals, at a 45-degree angle to the ground, in a diamond-trellis formation. The rods soon root and the fedge will become thicker as the branches grow.

In a garden designed with a strong architectural backbone, a pleached lime screen would be ideal. These shaped trees, where the branches have been trained along horizontal supports on top of stilt-like trunks, are seen widely in continental Europe in both private gardens and landscape plantings.

▦ Screens

Hurdles of woven hazel or alder, or panels of split bamboo, can make an effective barrier when joined together by posts, but they are generally not robust enough to make a perimeter fence. They can be used within the garden to create different rooms, hide a composting area or act as a windbreak. With imagination it is possible to make a screen that is both contemporary and in keeping with natural surroundings: at the first International Garden Festival at Reford Gardens in Canada in 2000, the designers constructed a raised mesh screen that had been stuffed with the most rural of materials, hay.

▦ Fences

Most types of fence are suited to town gardens and would look completely alien in a rural environment; close-boarded panels should never be used in the countryside. A white-painted picket fence, however, is synonymous with the traditional cottage garden and makes a simple, effective boundary to a front garden. Although it will not offer any security or privacy, it does look pretty. Open fences, such as split chestnut railings and traditional iron estate fencing, mark a boundary without interrupting the flow of the scenery.

Views

Whether the focal point is a church, river or stately tree, if you have a wonderful view, it pays to make the most of it. Rather than block it with a solid fence or hedge, you can capture it like a picture so that it becomes a feature of your garden. Portholes or windows can be cut into hedges using a frame or a clair-voyée, or an ornamental ironwork window can be built into a wall.

In larger gardens, a moon gate can make an exceptional feature, either as a circular opening in a wall that can be walked through or as a freestanding circular sculpture. Moon gates can be made from stone, brick or other materials – an unusual one spotted in a private garden in California was honed from the timber of a redwood tree.

Exploiting views from the garden is important, but it is essential to maximize the view from the house. When designing a new garden, make sure that you consider the sightlines from windows and doors, and devise your plan from an upstairs window, so that you can see all of your space and the landscape beyond. Looking out over the garden you have created can be very satisfying, and it can be the best view of all.

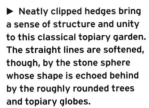

▶ Neatly clipped hedges bring a sense of structure and unity to this classical topiary garden. The straight lines are softened, though, by the stone sphere whose shape is echoed behind by the roughly rounded trees and topiary globes.

▲ Pergolas are a useful device for transporting you or your eye from one part of a garden to another. Here, the visitor is drawn through a climber-clad tunnel to admire at close quarters the statue set against the lush boundary hedge.

▲ Even a conical pile of locally quarried aggregate takes on a sculptural form when carefully placed in the garden. The success of such a display depends on using a mineral in the same tone as other features. Here, the light grey of the aggregate is echoed by the canal edging and the water.

◀ Garden art does not have to be permanent. These three 'house' sculptures created from straw, logs and twigs will decay over time, ensuring that the display changes on an almost daily basis.

◄ It is possible to give lawns a new lease of life with some careful trimming. In this garden, concentric bands of mown and unmown turf radiate from a specimen tree, transforming a horizontal surface into a 3-D feature.

▼ A flat space can be made more interesting by introducing different levels. This raised, grassy, serpentine path winds its way around the garden and acts as a viewing platform. If you stand at its base, the path becomes a barrier and you can see only parts of the garden.

▲ A narrow path through a dark woodland garden leads to a glade enclosed by birch trees, where shafts of light pick out a grassy labyrinth. For the grass not to engulf the path, it needs to be cut regularly or the path has to be filled with gravel or a similar material.

Art in rural gardens

Henry Moore's famous garden at Perry Green in Hertfordshire is probably one of the best examples of how art can be used in the rural garden. Here, many of his organic bronze sculptures complement the landscape rather than jar with it. While an original work may be beyond the pocket of most of us, modest pieces of art can be placed in the garden, immediately making the space more personal. Ignore the serried ranks of gnomes, animals and comedy characters for sale in garden centres and, instead, seek out a simple figure, a modern concrete planter or a mirrored obelisk. Larger pieces make wonderful focal points in the garden, while smaller sculptures or objets d'art can be hidden beneath a mass of foliage or hung from trees to surprise your visitors.

Turf landforms

A sea of horizontal turf can be pleasing to the eye, but to many it is simply monotonous. In recent years, turf landforms have become more widespread in both private and public gardens. Although this art form goes back centuries, today's designs owe much to designer Charles Jencks, whose work can be seen at his own garden at Portrack House, Dumfries, Scotland, and in the gardens of the Scottish National Gallery of Modern Art. Whether the design is an earth mound, terrace, amphitheatre or a serpentine wave pattern, by shaping the land it is possible to add texture and height to a flat level. As a work of art, a turf landform is forever changing, its appearance altering with the growth of the grass and the movement of the sun.

▥ Water

The sight and sound of water is the ultimate stress buster, and a must for any garden. Few of us are lucky enough to have a gentle stream or river running through or within sight of our garden, but if you do, make the most of it. If you need to, open the view so you can fully appreciate it. It is easy to bring water to a garden. A simple pool, planted with oxygenating plants to keep it crystal clear, is ideal, especially when it reflects surrounding trees or a carefully placed sculpture. Nearer the house, a classic geometric pool could be designed as part of a patio.

From the eighteenth century, many landscaped gardens featured rills, linear narrow channels leading into a pool. Today, rills are still an important design element, especially when given a contemporary treatment. A wavy-edged design will break the hard lines of a formal garden, while water will positively shimmer when flowing down a channel of highly reflective stainless steel.

In gardens built on hilly terrain, a water staircase is an attractive way to link several levels. Often found in Italianate gardens, they look very much like a normal flight of steps until a circulating pump is turned on and water flows continuously down the stairs. A stunning curved water staircase can also be seen at Longwood Gardens in Pennsylvania.

▲ Water features do not have to crash, splash or be built on a massive scale to bring tranquillity to a garden. This narrow rill slowly follows the rise and fall of a flight of stairs and is caught by the sun to add light to a dark corner.

▶ The heat of a garden created on the edge of the desert is tempered by the sight and sound of running water pouring from a contemporary water feature made of smooth stone.

▼ Water can be used as a low-level divider, separating one part of a garden from another. To be effective, a stream must be wide enough to be a feature in its own right, while allowing you to step across it easily. Here, the muddy banks have been replaced by random-sized pieces of smooth stone.

▲ In many historical gardens, fountains were an ostentatious feature created by the garden designer to show-off their engineering wizardry. Some water jets reached heights of over 80m (260ft), but this modest fountain is perfectly in tune with its compact setting, with the water only just topping the aquatic plants.

▼ This huge raised pool makes an artistic and cooling focal point for a long double border in the height of summer.

▼ Reclaimed wood is an ideal and sustainable material for paths. In this coastal-style garden it has been used to build a raised boardwalk, which allows you to walk among the planting schemes.

▼ A curvaceous path through a foliage-clad pergola has been designed to give a textured look to the garden. Gaps between the bands of timber have been filled with slate shingle, while the edges of the path are softened by billowing clumps of grasses.

⁞⁞⁞ Paths

Paths are an essential, practical element of any garden but, depending on the kind of materials they are made of, they can become a design feature in their own right. In traditional cottage gardens, grass or cinder paths were often used, as were brick paths, sometimes laid in an intricate herringbone pattern. They cut their way through billowing borders planted with flowering perennials, herbs and shrubs, where there was no lawn or paving. A contemporary version of the brick path is the wood block path, where short sections of wood are packed closely together on their ends. Depending on the kind of timber that is used, the path can be hard-wearing, and the grain on the cut ends also looks attractive.

In larger gardens it is possible to combine different types of path in the same space. Simple stepping stones create a route across a lawn, while a sinuous path of bark chippings is perfect in areas of woodland. As with all hard landscaping in rural gardens, it is important to use materials sourced locally.

◄ By mixing together large-leaved plants and exotic flowers, it is possible to create an exciting jungle effect. This is best experienced from a path that runs straight through the display, so you feel engulfed by the plants and are able to appreciate fully their form.

Bringing the Town to the Country

▲ Clear-stemmed trees with a light canopy are ideal in a sun-kissed garden - instead of blocking out light, they cast dappled shade, which allows many sun-loving plants to be grown at ground level. The trees in this controlled planting scheme are in contrast to the gnarled, native species found beyond the garden boundary.

▶ Huge terracotta pots with a weathered patina, which comes only after years of standing outdoors, are home to clumps of healthy African lilies. A series of pots stands along the edges of a pool, as well as throughout the garden. The repetition helps to pull the scheme together.

◀ In the late afternoon, the ochre-tinged walls placed at the head of an ingenious water feature take on a new intensity – the setting sun washes the smooth surface of the stone with a dazzling colour wash of orange. Close up, the rough surface of the floor provides a dramatic contrast with the smooth walls and crisp lines of the metal lining the rill.

▼ Water is used in this garden to provide a sense of movement. The eye naturally wants to follow the perfectly linear rill into the distance, while your curiosity urges you to find its source as you explore the different areas of the garden.

The idea of the ultimate garden, the true escape, means something different to us all. In towns and cities it can be easy to design outdoor spaces because you are surrounded by rules and regulations. Space is always at a premium, and there are inventive ways of squeezing in different features and dealing with privacy. Away from built-up areas, things are different, but the challenges of space and lots of it can be intimidating. Creating a contemporary garden in open countryside may be difficult. It requires dedication and bravery, as well as an understanding of the locality, of light and shade, and of the architecture you are dealing with. Good local horticultural knowledge is, of course, essential.

How about Le Jardin de la Noria depicted here for rural magic with a French slant? Many people's idea of the perfect location for a garden would be in open countryside in an area that enjoys a good climate, where it is possible to grow large amounts of trees, shrubs and perennials. The views beyond would be of gentle, pastoral landscapes with, of course, some paddocks with grazing horses thrown in for good measure. Heaven.

So the location is perfect. How has it been tamed and developed? How has a beautiful garden been created that integrates the dwelling and its setting? An intriguing mix of styles that seem to marry perfectly is the answer. There's a good appreciation of the space and its possibilities, an understanding of proportion, an ability to create intimate areas, a good use of the concept of borrowing from the landscape, treating fields beyond as the final scene-setter and a confidence regarding the use of materials.

There is also evidence of historic design meeting bluntly and yet wonderfully with a contemporary use of materials. Islamic-type pools, simple tanks of water with adjoining rills, create a cool feel on scorching days.

RURAL

UZÈS
FRANCE

| CASE STUDY #1 CONTINUED

DESIGNER
OSSART & MAURIÈRES

▼ Tall walls create a powerful presence in the garden. They reflect the light and form a canvas against which dramatic shadows are cast as the sun starts to set.

▶ This complex water feature consists of a series of rills on a number of levels, fed by tanks of water. It produces a gentle yet refreshing trickle of water as it cascades gently down and comes to rest in a still pool.

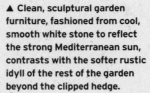

▲ Clean, sculptural garden furniture, fashioned from cool, smooth white stone to reflect the strong Mediterranean sun, contrasts with the softer rustic idyll of the rest of the garden beyond the clipped hedge.

▶ As if propping themselves up against the supporting wall, these throne-like seats, which flank the formal lines of the rill, are less about taking the weight off your feet and more about injecting humour into an otherwise serious garden. Their rigid, disciplined lines contrast with the informal foreground and background planting.

Compartments have been created through the use of poured concrete walls. Seating pavilions designed for relaxation frame views, and the pools are edged with magnificent terracotta pots filled to the brim with African lilies. The water is fed through a series of mini canals that appear to travel down the top of the modernist wall, which is both practical and humorous. Either side of this vertical water channel, two sculptural seats, reminiscent of Tutankhamen's throne but not actually designed to be sat on, complete the scene in a restful way.

Wide pathways of light-reflecting gravel lead through tree-framed avenues, bringing the eye or, indeed, the visitor to open areas of lawn. The main planting is striking, with trees that create structure and provide shade but, pruned into lollipop forms, they also have a distinctly humorous edge. Low flowering beds edge all the major areas with lavender, rosemary and verbena, creating a colourful symphony among the many shades of Mediterranean greys and silvers.

This is a garden that is also a journey. It is full of walks, formal avenues and open spaces. Views are continually framed, and materials have been chosen for their reflective qualities and strength. Great attention has been paid to natural sunlight – in the evening sun, the walls seem to glow as if they are on fire. The combination of hard and soft is carefully balanced. Much of the planting appears to float in a colourful and frothy way, and yet the furniture, low walls and bridges in sheer natural stone or concrete are uncompromising.

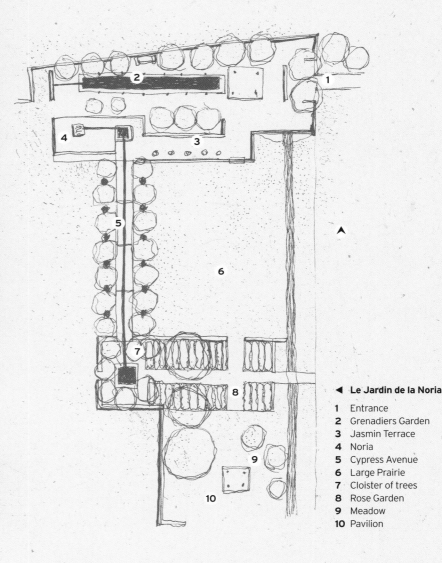

◄ **Le Jardin de la Noria**

1 Entrance
2 Grenadiers Garden
3 Jasmin Terrace
4 Noria
5 Cypress Avenue
6 Large Prairie
7 Cloister of trees
8 Rose Garden
9 Meadow
10 Pavilion

Garden Buildings

Whether it is for work, rest or play, a garden building is a practical and aesthetic garden feature. Apart from a shed, the most common kind of garden building is a conservatory, which is usually built on the side of the house as an affordable way of extending the living space. If you have a large garden, why not opt for a freestanding conservatory constructed largely of glass to allow in the maximum amount of light? Choose a classical design or go for something that is organic or contemporary, such as a cube shape with a frame of green oak, which will weather slowly and gracefully.

Alternatively, if you work from home, consider finding space for an outdoor office. Built at a distance from the house, an outdoor office is the ideal working sanctuary for anyone who is easily distracted by his or her possessions or who finds it difficult to concentrate when enveloped by the noise of family life.

An office should be big enough to house the tools of your trade, whether that is a computer or a potter's wheel. It will also need to be insulated, heated and supplied with electricity and a phone line. A water supply might also be an advantage. Off-the-peg wooden offices in a variety of different sizes, designs and materials are also available. Alternatively, if you are a whiz at DIY, you could create one to your own design. Generally, you should not need planning permission for this kind of garden structure, but it is always worthwhile checking with your local council to be sure before you make any commitments .

Not all garden buildings have to be useful. Follies and grottoes have no purpose other than to be fun and intriguing, and they can be used as a focal point in a large garden, or hidden among foliage as a visual surprise. A variety of traditional materials are used to create classic folly designs, such as sham medieval ruins, temples, shell seats, rustic huts, towers and belvederes. But by using easily malleable materials, such as metal and concrete, it is even possible to go beyond the traditional and create follies using curved, organic shapes.

Perhaps the first garden building we all remember from childhood is the tree house – a few simple boards lashed together that became a place to play throughout the long summer holidays. Today, many companies specialize in building and installing tree houses that are several light years away in terms of design and construction from those of our childhood. If you have the space, it is possible to build a vast, waterproofed tree house that may come complete with a living area, kitchen and dining room. These buildings, which look like they are straight off a Tarzan film set, can even be constructed on hefty poles – perfect if you do not have a tree big enough to support a tree house.

▲ Tucked away in a copse of trees, this open-sided pavilion makes a useful resting spot in a large garden, where you can quickly shelter from a passing shower or sit and enjoy the sylvan scene that opens up before you.

▶ Built on huge wooden stilts, this garden room in the sky is the perfect place to survey the garden and enjoy distant mountainous views. In a large garden, a room such as this, equipped with a cooking device and a bed, and built far from the house, becomes a sanctuary from everyday life.

▲ Standing at the foot of a raised pool, this summerhouse clad in shiplap boards makes a focal point at the end of a rectangular garden, the edges of which are defined by rows of neatly maintained trees. The close proximity of the pool allows the garden building to be reflected in its still waters.

▶ Traditional candlelight is the perfect antidote to electric lighting. Sustainable and eco-friendly, this candle-powered lantern is perfect for hanging from a pergola, where the gentle flicker of the flame will become more apparent as dusk falls. Although modern lanterns are widely available, you are likely to find a second-hand one full of character at a junk shop or reclamation yard.

Structures

A garden with no change in level can be given a lift by adding various structures, such as pergolas, arches, obelisks and tunnels. These decorative features have been built in gardens since Egyptian and Roman times and, apart from providing vertical space to grow climbing flowers, fruit and vegetables, give interest and structure to the garden over winter. Pergolas can be used to cover a patio area, draw the eye into the garden, shade a path or, if the uprights are wide enough apart, frame a view.

By using different materials it is possible to build pergolas that suit both traditional and contemporary rural gardens. A rustic pergola, popularized by the Arts and Crafts movement, looks at ease in a garden with billowing borders. Typically, these are built using brick pillars and chestnut poles overhead that have been stripped of their

bark. In a modern rural garden, a geometric wooden pergola or even one built from metal, such as steel girders, makes a bold statement. There is no reason to restrict yourself to a traditional shape – why not build a curved tunnel of thick steel rods, or even a row of freestanding hoops clad with hardwood?

Made from similar materials to pergolas and tunnels, a single arch makes a visual entrance to a garden or to a room within a garden, or it can be placed against a dark hedge to create a frame for a seat or piece of sculpture.

Simple but extremely effective, obelisks are the punctuation marks in a garden. They can be placed like a full stop at the end of a path or make their mark as a comma, dotted around a bed to break up the flow of planting. A variety of materials can be used to construct obelisks, such as glass, reflective and matt metals, wire or

◀ Scrambling emerald-coloured ivy has quickly engulfed a dome-shaped frame to create a quirky, cave-like garden structure, which looks as if it has been a part of the garden forever. This shadowy room would make a suitably mysterious feature in a woodland or shaded setting.

▼ The vibrant explosion of summer flowers dominates this colourful space, but walking through the deep borders does not allow you to appreciate fully the spectacle either side of you. A well-placed gazebo is the perfect place for you to take the weight off your feet and enjoy the floral display.

timber, which can be painted to blend or contrast with your planting scheme. In a relaxed country garden, a few obelisks used simply in a bed would be ideal, but if you have a large space and fancy a formal look, make a strong statement with a row of obelisks flanking a path.

Lighting

In a rural setting it is important to keep lighting simple and understated, creating a magical ambience that is perfect for entertaining or relaxing after dusk. In the past, solar-powered lights have been criticized for their pedestrian looks and feeble glow that was about as powerful as a torch running out of batteries. Fortunately, today's models are stylish, efficient and environmentally friendly. They are also perfect for anyone who wants instant lighting – there are no wires and no need for an electrician

– all you need to do is take them out of the box and position them. Most are spike-mounted and have a small solar panel on top that powers them for up to eight hours at a time. Try placing them along the route of a path.

Low-voltage lighting is another good choice, especially if a light can be fixed high up to shine down through a tree, rather like moonlight. Or use a single spotlight to pick out a specimen plant, tree or piece of sculpture.

Although subtle lights can be used in many parts of the garden, they are most effective when adding atmosphere to outdoor dinner parties. A simple way of doing this is to encircle the dining space with low-voltage ground lights, which can be sunk into stone or wood to sit flush with the floor. Alternatively, hang tea-light holders from a tree or shepherd's-crook-style stakes. The gentle flicker will create a relaxed, romantic mood.

Planting

Borders bursting at the seams with hollyhocks, lupins, daylilies, delphiniums and roses is what automatically comes to mind when we imagine a cottage garden. Nothing is prettier than a mix of these perennials gently jostling together, creating magical combinations in a rather unplanned way.

More restrained than a cottage garden are traditional herbaceous borders, although after they have been planted, it is a good idea to take a back seat and allow nature to take its course. Within reason, try not to interfere with the plants and let them spread or self-seed. By doing this, you will end up with some amazing combinations that you could never plan yourself.

A good alternative to the traditional border is prairie-style planting. To achieve the look, perennials, such as sedum, achillea, rudbeckia, helenium and echinacea, are planted in bold blocks with swishy grasses, such as stipa and pennisetum, to create a textured display with lots of movement. For maximum impact, this needs to be created in a large garden, as it looks rather pitiful when attempted in a small space. For inspiration, visit the prairie borders created by Piet Oudolf at the Royal Horticultural Society Garden at Wisley, or at the Dream Park in Enköping, Sweden.

If you have lots of space, consider allowing plants to ramble into trees. This can look amazing, especially when the climber produces its flowers before a deciduous tree is fully clad with leaves. A particularly memorable sight was a beech tree that had *Clematis montana* planted beneath it – in spring the tree was filled with starry white flowers. Roses, honeysuckle and some hops are other climbers worth trying and, although many plants will get a foothold naturally, do not be afraid to give them a helping hand and train them by tying in branches. Apart from ornamental trees, a mini orchard or nuttery can be planted

▼ Planned planting schemes can look extremely artificial, but although this colourful show of poppies, grasses and other sun-lovers was originally orchestrated by the hand of the garden owner, self-seeding and the careful editing of the many varieties has given rise to a natural-looking display.

► It is possible to create a beautiful garden in the most inhospitable of environments. Here, in the menacing shadow of a volcano, the garden designer has worked solely with native cacti to create an artistic display that will flourish under the blazing sun. Despite being placed in carefully curved sweeps, the appearance of these drought-tolerant plants looks strangely natural.

▼ Salt-laden winds would batter many taller plants into submission, but on a craggy cliff in a seaside garden, tough, low-growing plants spread happily by finding protective pockets and clinging close to the surface of the rock. Their neat hummock shapes perfectly complement the silhouette of the cliff and echo its shape.

► A traditional double herbaceous border is a brilliant sight when in full flight and always works best planted against a tall hedge. A dark green backdrop, such as yew, which is shown here, makes the perfect foil for many flowers, as well as providing an evergreen structure when the perennials die back over winter.

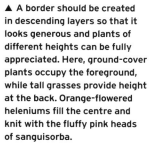 

▲ A border should be created in descending layers so that it looks generous and plants of different heights can be fully appreciated. Here, ground-cover plants occupy the foreground, while tall grasses provide height at the back. Orange-flowered heleniums fill the centre and knit with the fluffy pink heads of sanguisorba.

▼ Informal drifts of pink cone flowers have been repeated throughout this huge prairie planting scheme to create a sense of unity. For even greater impact, the same style of planting has been used for the other varieties of flowers and grasses. This display is at its best in late summer and into the autumn.

► Dwarf box, yew and box-leaved holly respond well to tight clipping. To appreciate your topiary creations fully, place them where they can be easily seen from the house, especially an upstairs window. From here, the shapes appear quite different from how they are at ground level.

in a larger rural garden. Nothing beats picking fresh filberts, walnuts, apples or pears. Fruit can also be grown in more formal gardens: the branches of apples and pears can be trained as espaliers or along horizontal wires to make an attractive living barrier that has the bonus of providing good things to eat.

Ornamental plants can be mixed with attractive vegetables and herbs, such as black Tuscan kale or purple basil, to create a potager. Traditionally seen in French country gardens, such as the famous one at Villandry, potagers have made a comeback, thanks to an increased interest in growing your own crops and in the gardens of working chefs, such as Raymond Blanc's at Le Manoir aux Quat' Saisons in Oxfordshire. A potager works exceptionally well if it can be treated as a separate garden room, rather than as a solution for the whole garden, because for many months of the year this area would be lacking in colour or interest.

Topiary spirals, balls or cones are often seen as sentries guarding the front doors of town houses, but in a rural location they really come into their own, providing structure and year-round interest in a garden. Hedges can be castellated or shaped, while box clipped into different shapes and sizes looks dramatic planted en masse to create a textural display that really takes your breath away when crystallized under a layer of hoar frost.

Designing for wildlife

Gardens in the countryside have a head start on their town cousins when it comes to being attractive to wildlife. Situated close to fields, hedges, woods and rivers means that there should be an ample population of native creatures within close proximity. But even in rural areas you can make your garden more, not less, attractive to desirable insects, birds and mammals, even if you have the most minimal of gardens.

A pond or water feature of some kind is essential, and will be quickly discovered by frogs and toads, together with birds and hedgehogs who will visit for frequent drinks. Nesting boxes for birds and beneficial insects, such as ladybirds and lacewings, can be placed on trees or hidden beneath a cloak of foliage. But beware – there is a bewildering choice of these available, and too many wildlife-friendly devices will clutter the garden: the adage that less is more certainly rings true here.

In a spacious garden, it may be possible to have a wild area where native flowers, grasses and bulbs can grow unhindered, which would be perfect surrounding a log pile. A simple arrangement of logs can be allowed to rot naturally to provide the perfect habitat for insects, toads and hedgehogs. In a contemporary garden, substitute a log screen or log wall – this striking feature is constructed by arranging pieces of log, cut to the same size, between two book-end-like supports.

When designing a garden for wildlife, choose your plants carefully. Palms, bamboos and other exotics that are becoming increasingly popular have little merit when it comes to enticing wildlife, whereas native plants, especially those that bear nuts and berries, sustain many creatures. The solution when making a garden is to use a combination of both.

▲ A tightly knit nest of twigs sits securely in the branches of a tree, making an enticing shelter for many garden birds. Surprisingly, it was not created by birds but by the garden owner. The nest becomes visible only when the deciduous shrubs have dropped their leaves.

◄ Making a topiary garden allows the gardener to be creative by combining a variety of shapes that contrast perfectly with one another. In this garden, cones, domes, obelisks, pyramids, balls and plate shapes are mixed together without fear to create a topiary forest that shows its full potential in the depths of winter.

◀ Neutral colours have been employed throughout this Scandinavian garden to give the space a cool, contemporary look. The pale tones are used for the surface of the floor, benches and walls to draw the whole scheme together, and are even echoed in the ghostly white stems of the perfectly straight birch trees.

▼ A semi-transparent screen stands between two large wall panels and allows light to filter through the gauze-like material, revealing the silhouette of a fern frond. Up close you can see through the fern pattern to the trees in the distance, but from further back the screen becomes part of a cleverly designed room set.

A Place to Think

Contemporary gardens can sometimes look out of place in a rural location, the clean lines and architectural style clashing with the natural surroundings. However, the Skogens Trädgård (Gardens of the Forest) in Sweden is ample proof that a modern garden can be married to the countryside perfectly. The garden was designed by Ulf Nordfjell in a very remote part of his homeland. It is a 225-km (140-mile) drive north from the country's capital, Stockholm, in a densely forested, sparsely populated region near the small town of Ockelbo.

The garden has been built at the heart of the Wij Trädgårdar, a sprawling rural education centre where the region's agricultural heritage is kept alive. The centre holds demonstrations on how to grow vegetables and encourages visitors to attract wildlife into their gardens.

When he was commissioned to design the garden, which opened in 2002, part of Nordfjell's brief was to ensure that the garden was sympathetic to the wooded environment that envelops it. His design achieves this triumphantly and draws upon many elements of the natural environment.

Nordfjell has built a long, linear garden, measuring 12 x 108m (40 x 355ft). It has been broken into a series of seven interlinking, open-plan rooms that meld harmoniously into each other. The use of neutral shades in the walls, paving, benches and even in some of the plants helps to unify the whole space.

As well as forests, the area has many natural water features, and Nordfjell has echoed this in his garden. A series of crisp granite cubes has been turned into low-level fountains, with the water soaking away into a moat of pebbles. Another room has been dedicated to a long raised bog, its sides made from double steel walls – the black water of the bog has been edged by a rectangular

◄ Towering panels enclose a room in the garden but they avoid being claustrophobic, thanks to the generous gaps between them that allow you to see far beyond into the nearby woodland. This natural feature is aped in the garden by a geometric copse of trees.

▼ **Skogens Trädgård, Sweden**

1   Entrance of Birches
2   Entrance building
3   Clipped hedges
4   Clipped Malus
5   Granite water feature
6   Perennial border
7   Steel screen

▲ Water bubbles slowly from a pipe drilled into a crisp cube of granite before soaking away into the moat of pebbles and then recirculating through the water feature again. The use of water in this garden is a reflection on the natural pools found widely in this part of Northern Europe.

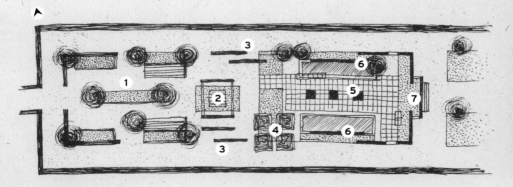

▲ Trees are essential ingredients of a rural garden, but although the trees used here are mainly native species, they bear little resemblance to those found growing in the wild. The clear, straight stems and neatly maintained canopies let you pass easily underneath, while plenty of light is allowed to filter through.

◀ Planting is kept to a minimum and largely consists of foliage varieties, the texture and form of which help to soften the clean lines of this architectural garden.

band of moss. Conifers enclose the space, and a pair of curved benches make it the ideal place to relax.

To make the garden blend into its environment, the designer has made use of local materials. Swedish granite, which is used for the foundations of local houses, is employed widely, and there are links to the area's industrial past in the steel chosen to create gabions and benches, and to form the structural parts of some heavy-duty walls.

Unlike some rural gardens, there are no exuberant displays of flowering perennials here. The designer has used a limited palette of shades, predominantly grey, green, purple, brown and red, with the odd hint of blue. Nordfjell has also brought the forest into the garden by planting a copse of sparkling white-stemmed birch trees.

The designer has created a magical space that has been skilfully executed to ensure that you never lose the sense of the location; the garden is only loosely defined around its edges by grasses, panels, a knee-high run of pebble-filled gabions or short lengths of wall, placed to allow the visitor frequent views across the mown grass into the nearby woodland.

◄ Standing like a crowd of commuters at a railway station, these topiary specimens are a dramatic feature that, once seen, will never be forgotten. The myriad fantastic shapes illustrate the seemingly endless possibilities for topiary designs that can be sculpted from fast-growing yew.

▶ A series of spotlights, like an airport runway, leads the eye into this modern office atrium, but it is the up-lit birch trees that give the courtyard its life.

Urban

The nature of gardening is changing in quite a radical way for all sorts of reasons, mostly to do with contemporary living. Society is increasingly being urbanized, with people living gathered together in large areas. There is a high rate of house building, even in today's high-density developments; most of the new dwellings have their own gardens, allowing more people than ever before to become gardeners. Of course, people have different attitudes to these spaces – some people do nothing with them – but there is a universal awareness of the value of outside space both in monetary terms (seeing gardens as another 'room') and in health terms (people enjoying the outdoor exercise of gardening). In addition to the housing principles of local government, there is also an increased encouragement of individuality in terms of design, and the conversion of underused spaces such as roofs for rooftop gardens. We have left behind the days of the vast Georgian or Victorian estate and villa-type gardens, and have entered a new era. Gardens today have to work for their householders – gardens in built-up areas, gardens that will add value, excitement or create a retreat. What we should avoid is a garden with a loss of identity, a garden that pretends it is something else.

◀ Shafts of sunlight create bold geometric shapes across the garden. The composition is confident and maintains interest in a small area.

▲ Heat emanates from the yellow brick terrace and walls, which soak up the sun. Terracotta pots and the burnt sienna walls add to the warmth.

pokes fun at dry, formal planting schemes. As the grouping is evergreen, it will create a year-round picture.

A bed to the front of this area is planted simply with iris, festuca and lavender. A bubble fountain sits here, making good use of an old millstone. Opposite the bay trees, a rendered wall stands starkly but, again, with a floating wooden seat. The whole scene is amusing, cheeky even. The stark modernist elements contrast successfully with the original yellow stock brick wall and are all linked together by very understated planting.

This garden could have been pretentious but, instead, it emerges as uniquely successful, and it certainly needs little regular maintenance. The rendered walls and terracotta pots absorb the heat from shafts of sunlight, and even in cool weather give warmth from their rich colour, and the mature trees in surrounding gardens top off the scene.

Suburbia

Suburbia is taking over the world – its relentless march is staggering. In the grander strata of society, the very mention of the 's' word brings sneers, sniggers and derisory comments about being bourgeois – smart houses in town, and properties with land are traditionally the only way to live if you are somebody. But there is a growing realization as the suburbs evolve and age, as they mature and settle, that there are great joys to be had from this type of community living. If local planners get it right and facilities – recreational, shopping, schooling and transport – have been provided, the suburbs can be the perfect place to live. And this is especially so when children are involved. Suburbs are the new villages. People grow up together and interrelate on a very personal level. And the key to their success is the use of plants, the greening of the outdoor spaces, the gardens. When the builder leaves, the harsh lines of any new development are omnipresent. Three or four years later, it is the planting – carefully planned or haphazard – that will blend, soften and give the environment character.

Suburban gardens divide into two groups. At the front of the house, the space creates an image, makes a public announcement, is sometimes regarded as communal or park land. But back gardens are the real havens – family-centred plots away from the restrictions of public acceptance where individual thoughts can be developed – the place that gardens are mainly built today. Again,

they are smaller than before, although houses of long-established suburbs are often greatly prized for the amount of outdoor space they have. But even the smaller plots will generally be the single biggest area available to a family, bigger than any room in the house and often bigger than the complete floor space of the house. Increasingly, they are the backdrop to the house, thanks to the relegation of net curtains to the bins of history and an increasing amount of well-insulated glass. These gardens become a view for the family all year round. And with the growing interest in garden design, there is a great public awareness of potential and possibility, and gardens are often an expression of individual style. Most, if not all, members of the household now seem to have an opinion: they have likes and dislikes and take a keen interest. With global warming, soil temperatures in many parts of the world do not cool down so much in the winter months, which allows us to use our gardens more.

So the suburban garden is the garden of the future. It is the one garden where standard rules will apply. It is also the place within your property where you can break the rules and create a sense of the individual. This is happening more and more. And whether you live in established suburbia (usually a green oasis) or barren, new, windswept suburbia (usually defined by boundary fences), consider what you have, look at your options and then drive forward an ambitious plan to carve out from the already green, or introduce from the start, your dream garden.

▲ Even a small green space allows you to experiment with plants, materials and sculpture, and you can be as adventurous as you like.

◄ Well-chosen plants can mature into a beautiful canopy in a relatively short space of time. The use of more tropical plants is possible in warm areas and in cities, where the concrete tends to hold onto the sun's heat.

◄ By dividing your space so that not all is immediately visible to the eye, you introduce a sense of mystery and intrigue. Be sure to make the final destination wonderful to avoid any disappointment.

▼ Shades of orange bring a sense of heat to this cool stone area. Tactile grasses and flowers soften the space, while neatly clipped pleached trees unite the space.

▶ A decked path is a guide through lush planting, inviting the visitor to explore different areas of the garden.

▲ An unusual curved wall provides a fun seating area, especially for children.

▶ The structure in this garden has been provided by plants, stone and brick, to create a design that is lasting and special. Mature hedges act like towers, shaping and dividing the space.

▼ Slopes and changes of level in a garden can be used to your advantage. Short rendered walls retain soil and provide wonderful backgrounds for planting. This slope is defined with parallel railway sleepers, which enhance its appearance and also make it safe.

Boundaries

What defines any person's property is its boundaries. Visible or invisible, you can be sure they will be mapped out somewhere. They are the cause of more disputes between neighbours than anything else. With luck, you will have good neighbours but you must always let them know when you make decisions that will affect them. If you behave decently towards your neighbours, it makes things easier and, more often than not, they will be thoughtful in return.

What do you want to achieve with your boundaries? At the rear of your property it is most likely that you will want to mark out your space, make it safe and enclosed so that children and pets cannot wander, and strangers cannot intrude. It is a matter of defining your castle. The options are – quite simply – walls, fences or hedging plants. It may depend on how much you can spend or how much time you have. A beautiful wall of warm-coloured reclaimed brick or natural stone will cost more than a wooden fence, but both will provide privacy and shelter quickly. But, over a period of time, a beech hedge laid down very cheaply as young saplings will probably be the most majestic option. Think of your budget and think of the greening of your environment. If you can make do with a chain-link fence, while at the same time planting up a hedge or a variety of species to create a well-planned structural mixed border, this could be your best option.

There are, of course, planning and legal issues relating to boundaries. They vary according to where you live but, running alongside the legal requirements, there are the neighbourly values of sharing light and views, and possibly the odd conversation. Planting a fast-growing conifer hedge and allowing it to grow without restraint will be self-defeating – think how it will look in a decade. Put some work into choosing the right species for you.

Hard landscaping

The texture and colour of paving set the tone for the garden and must be well thought out, as it will be costly to replace. Brick paving flows well from the house and brings warmth to the garden; sandstone is extremely durable, available in different shades and can sit well in both traditional and contemporary gardens. Cobble stones create a country garden feeling, and terrazzo tiles can be used to highlight outstanding features to great effect.

Walls within the garden can contribute to a garden in terms of design and texture. There are many materials to choose from, which will determine the required style: painted walls, the very adaptable concrete, toughened glass and drystone walling are just a few options. Rendered retaining walls are fantastic solutions for level changes, as they can also become useful low seating for enclosing a space for dining or wonderfully colourful foils for planting. Concrete walls can be formed off site – ready-shaped with doorways for entering the next part of the garden and with cut-out shapes that may highlight particular views of the garden. Always ensure that you have a definite design plan before any construction work begins and that these more permanent fixtures complement the garden as a whole.

Steps lead between levels, across water as a bridge or simply from the house down into the garden. They must be in keeping with the rest of the garden and also safe and comfortable for their particular use. The gradient is important – a wide tread and low riser create a more relaxed, slower slope and is much more pleasurable in a garden, provided there is enough space. Use materials that complement the surroundings – wood, tiles, brick and even grass will produce very different looks.

Water

Water should be used with care in the suburban garden where children will be playing. Large, flowing water features are only appropriate for grandly designed gardens and tend to look out of place in suburban situations. A narrow rectangular stretch of water running across the width of the garden does wonders to make the garden appear wider, and brings softness and flow, but the water must be kept shallow. If you are lucky enough to have an acre or two, swimming pools are a consideration. Natural swimming pools are very much in vogue for an integrated style of pool; specialist companies can advise on installation and maintenance.

Placing a pond towards the back of the garden in more relaxed areas of planting will attract wildlife and allow you to experiment with aquatic and semi-aquatic plants. Water-adapted plants offer fantastic forms, flower and texture, which will contribute greatly to the garden.

Furniture

For a well-used family garden, the most vital consideration for furniture is how you will use it. If you regularly dine out on the patio, you will need a robust, permanent seating area that will not need to be covered over but is still comfortable to use. A simple garden bench and table painted in your desired colour always works well, but if you have the space, stone seating set into a defined wall can create a wonderful retreat in which to relax and entertain friends and family alike. Cushions can be used to soften and warm up the area.

For the more flexible option of tables and chairs, the market offers a massive choice covering all budgets. Choose sun loungers for relaxing on Sunday afternoons, and for visitors use fold-away directors' chairs that can be easily stored away when not required.

▲ Beautiful and perfectly placed white stones appear to float above a small pond, creating magic and excitement. The combination of plants and water introduces a feeling of serenity.

▼ The warm-coloured gravel and aged furniture suggest a hot tropical location. Plants enclose the space, for privacy and relaxation.

◄ Building a framework to ensure that all available space is used, however awkward, can create an interesting and fun garden. This well-constructed lower level is an amazing hideaway for children and adults alike.

▲ Life on Mars meets modern abstract art. This daring experiment with colour, geometry and minimal planting creates a lasting impression.

▼ Gorgeous herbaceous planting softens the straight lines of the garden architecture. A haze of delicate flowers creates a semi-transparent screen so that whatever lies beyond remains a mystery.

▶ Create your own tropical rainforest using bamboos and the dramatic foliage of exotic plants. The jungle atmosphere is heightened by the lush planting and green canopy.

Wildlife

At a time when the demand for new housing is at an all-time high, much of our green space is being eaten away, so suburban gardens are increasingly important as wildlife retreats and green corridors. A huge number of insects, birds, mammals and amphibians can be found in gardens if they are provided with a suitable environment. The biodiversity can be enhanced by growing a mixture of cultivated and native plants, which will provide food, shelter and breeding sites. Flowering plants that offer nectar for bees, insects and butterflies, as well as trees and shrubs that produce berries for birds, are integral to a wildlife-friendly garden, and wonderful from an aesthetic point of view. Late-flowering types that produce vital nectar when other flowers have passed extend the feeding season, and an area left to become overgrown will provide a habitat for insects and small mammals. Bird feeders, nest boxes and ponds are also a consideration, as are various other specialized abodes for wild creatures – it all depends on how serious about wildlife you are!

Planting

The garden is an extra room outdoors; it is your chance to express your individual style. The planting is the life of the garden, it shapes the garden and it finishes the garden – the sky really is the limit. Once you have designed the space and decided on a style, it is relatively easy to select plants for your chosen palette. As there is space in a suburban environment almost anything goes, but it's also unlikely that there will be a strong vernacular style to fit in with. The best thing to do is look through your favourite gardening books and decide which types of plants you like, and what colour palette strikes you the most. A more restricted colour palette produces a stronger, more definite finish to the garden. For a planting scheme with flair, try to arrange plants of the same type in broad strokes rather than dotting them around, and group plants that perform at the same time to create seasonal areas of interest.

▲ Anything goes in this urban garden, where hardscape is turned into a lush landscape by a cascade of greenery. The plants are cleverly incorporated into what would otherwise be an uncompromisingly severe flight of concrete steps.

▼ Instead of resorting to lawn, the owners of this tiny space have opted to fill their garden with a mass of perennial plants, which look no less out of place in the city than they would in a rural cottage garden.

◄ Spectacular in its minimalism and cocooned by immense surrounding walls, this thoroughly contemporary garden is as much an extension of the interior – a room without a roof – as it is an outdoor space.

Roof Gardens

Rooftop gardens are the utopia for all city dwellers. It is a dream to tame an elevated outdoor space, to create an urban hideaway, a crow's nest over a busy city, a place that escapes noise and atmospheric pollution, high above everybody else. This is literally romantic gardening at its height. Imagine the sheer sense of excitement and delight of going outside having reached the top floor of the building. It would be a thrill to water the potted plants or, at the other extreme, to swim in your own lap pool 28 storeys up on top of a high-rise in Manhattan.

With property at a premium, people are beginning to open their eyes to possibilities, whether for added value or, for the less cynical, extending from inside to outside, no matter where outside is. And it is not confined to the Rockefeller Center, or Canary Wharf; it is not just cities. Roof gardens are valid now in suburbia. That flat-roofed concrete garage attached to your 1930s house, that space you look out on as you walk up the stairs in your creaky provincial office – we are beginning to see potential everywhere, and the planners and the designers are beginning to agree – there is no better place for getting away from it all than a garden where you least expect to find one.

This is one gardening scenario that you have to consider carefully before you start. There are plenty of problems and difficulties to overcome – it is not a task for the faint-hearted. There is the issue of whose roof it is anyway: you may have potential access to it and look at it every day, but it might not be yours. Structurally, is it sound? Would the roof take your weight, never mind the weight of plants, soil, water and furniture? And what about the safety aspects? By creating a garden you will accommodate

▼ Outdoor space in the city is always at a premium and it invariably has to serve more than one purpose. This roof garden has been turned into a green living room, with its sofa, armchair and coffee table flanked by containers planted with evergreen shrubs and miniature trees.

◄ If it weren't for the urban roofline in the background, the whimsical path of circular sawn wood could easily be mistaken for a rural idyll.

◀ A miniature outdoor plot should never be a restriction. By utilizing the available space efficiently, there should be plenty of room for plants and people. Here, tropical plants, which thrive in the urban microclimate, are contained in wooden raised borders, to be admired at close quarters.

▶ Plant lovers will put down roots anywhere. On this minuscule balcony buffeted by the wind, a collection of spherical pots contrasts with triangular and square containers.

▼ An intimate outdoor dining space has been created on this balcony by simply placing a table and chairs among large containers planted with box. Sculpted into strong shapes, the plants are reflected in the glass sliding doors.

▶ Plants that would never survive a more exposed rural situation often flourish in the shelter provided by a cityscape, where tall walls create warm microclimates and protect vulnerable plants from damaging winds.

people of all ages, shapes and sizes. Whether you are elevated two metres or 20 storeys, you must create barriers to make people feel safe and be safe. You may want to achieve a lot in a small area. Space can be limited, and you may also need to include storage. Dwellings that rely on roof gardens for their only outdoor space will inevitably have little space inside for gardening equipment. So plan ahead, gather the experts, look at your property deeds, talk to the engineers. They will be cautious – it is professional indemnity as much as any lack of spirit of adventure, and sometimes they are right. From a design point of view, roofs are difficult; your options are limited and what you would really love to do will probably be too adventurous. But you can be safe and creative, and the potential is just waiting to be released.

We know the arguments in favour of a roof garden are endless, but what are the difficulties? Mostly they are obvious. It can be hard to grow plants out of the ground where there is no natural base, no natural soil structure for them to bed into. You have to create their living environment, which includes their soil or growing medium but also their protection, because they will be more exposed to the elements, especially battering by winds and being dried out. And you will have to provide irrigation, as there is unlikely to be running water. This new living space has to be safe, which means putting up barriers such as railings or enclosures: all this is expensive. But the engineer may well tell you that the roof is not load-bearing. New steels may need to be put in place, posted by walls that will take their weight. Over that you will need to create new flooring. If you are in an urban environment, you may be one house or office grouped with lots of others, and you may not own the walls you want to connect with – all sorts of permissions may be needed.

▼ The mass of beautifully maintained planting on this miniature roof garden has created a welcome oasis of greenery and a private retreat from the fast pace of city living.

▼ This roof garden makes the most of the borrowed views beyond, particularly at night when everything is illuminated by the city lights.

When all this has been achieved, cast your eye to design: what do you want your garden to look like? Innovation can be quite difficult in such a situation. Again, there may be planning issues as to what can be used. So a lot of your garden planning may come down to styling, which is easy to achieve. Pick a look that you like and try to find materials that go with it.

Take health and safety seriously. When the weather is hot, roof gardens are a great draw for groups of people to enjoy barbecues and beers. This is an invitation for accidents, considering your elevated position, so make your garden work easily, with no tripping obstacles (the classic hose left out) or tight spaces to squeeze through. If you are introducing tables, chairs and loungers, make sure you have space for them so everybody can move through the space easily.

Lighting

A roof garden can be transformed by lighting. Dramatic uplighting of bamboos as they tower out of their pots adds drama, and floor lights produce a warm moody glow. Go slightly wilder and for an edgier, urban feel introduce brightly coloured neon lighting, even commissioning your own neon sign.

Planting

Transforming a dead space into an urban oasis can be beneficial to the community. Glancing up and seeing trees on top of a building is a real joy. From ground level, the sight of a building with an unruly green hairstyle is fun. Being practical, think about what plants will thrive in such a situation: it is exposed and it can be very dry. There is a great amount of natural light available, so pick plants that are appropriate for the situation. It is true that there are exceptions and there are some delicate Japanese maples growing successfully on a 40th-floor garden terrace in Manhattan. Go with plants, however, that have a track record: ornamental grasses that take a battering and do not lose water easily, trees such as mountain ash or pines that you may find in exposed coastal situations, shrubs with waxy outer leaves, which stop them losing water so readily, like escallonia, or common low-growing varieties of plants such as ceanothus or cotoneaster that can grow below the shelter line. Use light compost but one that retains moisture. Do not add to your weight problems by using clay crocks or shingle for drainage; instead, use polystyrene beads (the type you find inside a bean bag), which will successfully trap oxygen in compost and yet allow for free drainage.

▲ Containers are the ideal solution to a small outdoor space. Play with shapes, texture, colours and positioning to achieve a stylish effect – it's a movable feast that can be changed as and when the mood takes you.

▼ Plants will adapt to the most challenging of conditions. Here, a relatively small container plant sits on an exposed rooftop and towers over the cacti and succulents at its feet.

Dramatic Gestures

Here is a turbulent scene, created in Australia by experimental landscape architect Vladimir Sitta. It is an extremely dramatic garden, making great use of limited space and selected materials. Imagine an earthquake has just taken place, or something has burst through the skin of the earth and we are faced with the leftover shapes. It is reminiscent of Hollywood movies where, after some catastrophe, inferno or disaster, slabs of motorway or bridges are left in incongruous situations. It is a dramatic if slightly unsettling creation, which ultimately engages the viewer with humour. The lovely thing about this garden is that it is a new idea in a relatively small space. It is not restful, indeed it is dramatically sculptural and slightly uncomfortable, and that feeling is magnified when it is illuminated at night.

The designer uses a very restricted palette of plants, and groups them in large blocks that successfully accentuate the geometric shapes of the hard landscaping. The plants will survive well in this arid climate and are used to great softening effect – the grey-blue of the *Festuca glauca*, the dramatic fleshy foliage of the agaves, and the sword-like foliage of the echeverias. Their cool greens make a refreshing contrast to the hot desert colour of the stonework. Bright orange bird-of-paradise flowers appear to flit through the scene. By keeping a dead dracaena tree, the designer makes a feature that serves to echo and heighten the feeling of nature's destruction.

A complicated garden design to construct, it certainly has the feeling of movement and energy. It is not sedate – you feel that this garden never stands still, that something

▲ In the baking Australian sun, this garden appears to be made up of randomly positioned raised borders. Built from blocks of stone, they are reminiscent of a shipwreck listing on the high seas.

◄ At night, the same scene is softened by lighting that has been strategically placed among the raised borders. The dead tree in the background turns into a mysterious natural sculpture, silhouetted against the white walls of the house.

URBAN

CASE STUDY #4 CONTINUED

SYDNEY
AUSTRALIA

DESIGNER
VLADIMIR SITTA

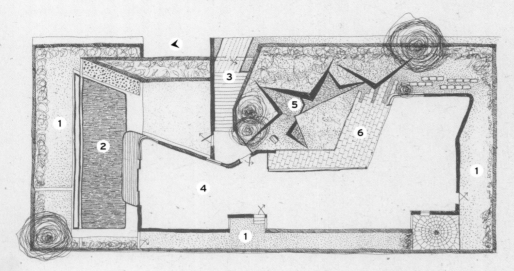

◀ **Sydney, Australia**

1 Gravel path
2 Swimming pool
3 Steps
4 House
5 Stone raised borders
6 Brick patio

▲ The monochrome planting has been carefully designed to demonstrate the contrast in texture and shape between the leathery sword-like foliage of mother-in-law's tongue (*Sansevieria*), the cup-shaped form of the agaves and the rounded, feathery hummocks of *Festuca glauca*.

▶ Agaves, succulents and blue-grey grasses spill from one border to another, creating a sense of undulating water that washes over the entire scene.

▼ The masculine, angular borders are built out of large, chunky blocks of stone – a deliberate contrast to the tiny pea shingle spread among the plants.

is about to burst through. It is a garden to be looked at – it does not invite you in and encourage you to wander about. With its hard edges and spiky plants, it is definitely not a garden suitable for children, although children would probably be fascinated by it. It is an unusual choice for a domestic garden where relaxation is important; it would work extremely well as a landscape to be viewed in a public space.

The use of local stone, in this case a wonderful burnt orange desert sandstone, and the exploration of the change of levels, done quite simple by terracing, show the drama that can be achieved through taking a basic idea and pushing it to its limit. Different textures have been achieved with the same stone – large slabs contrast with chunky chipped pieces, as well as gravel. By using the same material in different ways, a coherence is maintained in a complicated picture.

This is a garden with a big idea. There is a dramatic contrast in terms of the soft colours of the foliage, the borrowed landscape beyond and big open skies. The 'action' takes place so near the house that there is a sense of impending doom from certain angles. The inviting, low-slung furniture, which is somewhat reminiscent of the 1950s, contrasts with the unsettling images in front and gives a heightened sense of theatricality to the whole arrangement.

► Protected by tall rendered walls and shaded from the intense heat of the sun by the boughs of an ancient tree, this long trestle table is in the perfect spot for long, leisurely meals with family and friends.

Entertaining

When you are planning a garden, take into account all its uses and the various guises it will adopt. A large part of your enjoyment will be in scenarios that may not have been planned. So whether it is dance floors or decks, fire pits or chimineas, projectors or sound systems, always consider the possibilities and probabilities. When it comes to enjoying the garden with friends, people are more relaxed than they used to be. Over the past few decades, the vast class of home owners – and therefore garden owners – have realized the preciousness of outdoor space and have a desire to exploit it to the full. The new decklanders use the gardens as outdoor rooms. This does not imply that they exclude the traditional gardening activities, indeed once we have been drawn outside many of us realize the value of our views, our privacy; it opens our eyes to traditional gardening activities so we relish cultivating plants, erecting trellis, growing herbs and vegetables. But our opinion on how we use that outdoor space is very different from that of our forefathers. The net curtains have disappeared. When we look out from inside, we want to look at an inviting scene, a place that we are drawn to, whether it is simply to hover with a cup of coffee while standing in our dressing gown first thing in the morning or kicking a football with our kids on our return from work or at weekends. But most of all, we like to sit down and eat and drink, observe nature's work and relax.

Entertaining in the Garden

In recent years, the marketplace has responded rapidly. Every spring new ranges of patio plants, pots and containers – but most of all, furniture and barbecues in every style imaginable – are launched. The ephemera of gardening has taken on a must-have quality, with new collections by noted designers and established firms snapped up. While some regard this as nothing to do with real gardening or garden use, it is offering choice – market forces are providing what the consumer requires, and that is a nice outdoor lifestyle. People want to be able to throw open their doors from late spring to early autumn, to blur barriers between inside and outside and to have both areas reflecting their taste. Choice is always a good thing, and a selection of styles from which to pick can only add to the feeling of making one's own nest.

▦ A garden for alfresco dining

When summer arrives, rustling up a delicious meal alfresco becomes one of life's daily pleasures. There is nothing quite like the taste and aroma of food that has been cooked outdoors, whether on a barbecue or gas-fired cooker or over a simple fire.

Most alfresco dining tends to consist of a freestanding barbecue with a selection of tables and chairs set up nearby. If the predictions for longer, warmer summers prove to be true, however, more time will be spent outdoors, and the concept of a permanent outdoor cooking area will no longer be the preserve of countries with reliably hot summers such as Australia.

When planning a garden for alfresco dining, it makes sense to have a separate cooking and dining area. In a large garden, there is plenty of space to keep the two apart, but in a small courtyard garden it is not so easy. The aim is to create two visually defined areas. For instance, the

cooking area could be near the house, while a section further away could be raised up a level, like a stage, to become the place to dine.

Equipping your alfresco garden largely depends on how you are planning to use it. If it is mainly for intimate, romantic meals over candlelight, then a good barbecue may suffice, but if you have a large family or like to throw lavish dinner parties, then a state-of-the-art outdoor kitchen may be a worthwhile investment.

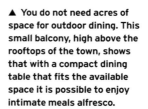

▲ You do not need acres of space for outdoor dining. This small balcony, high above the rooftops of the town, shows that with a compact dining table that fits the available space it is possible to enjoy intimate meals alfresco.

▶ An architectural sail stretched tight between lofty metal uprights makes dining under the sun on the ocean's edge a comfortable and memorable experience. Here, formal furniture has been replaced in favour of cushions and a low table.

A Place to Cook

Common in countries with a mild climate, the permanent outdoor kitchen is becoming more popular in the UK and can be built in gardens of any size. In a small courtyard garden, the entire space can be turned into an outdoor kitchen. If your indoor kitchen opens directly onto the garden, consider extending the worktops outside, using weatherproof materials and similar colours to those used indoors. Storage units that mimic those used in the kitchen complete the look and create a sense of cohesion.

There is no reason why an outdoor kitchen cannot be built further away from the house to make better use of a part of the garden that is rarely visited, such as an underused deck. Particularly suitable is the American idea of the grill island – a freestanding patio built using the same stone as the main patio or even the indoor kitchen – equipped with every type of unit you need to rustle up a great feast. This may be some way from the house, so it is important to make sure you have everything you need.

Outdoor kitchen units available include gas, electric and barbecue cookers, sinks, worktops, storage cupboards, and refrigerators. In countries where the weather is variable, such as the UK, buy units made from tough, durable materials, such as eucalyptus wood, galvanized steel and granite tops for cutting on. Unless you are planning to leave them in place permanently, buy units

fitted with castors, so you can relocate them around the garden as the mood takes you – a truly movable feast – or position them against the side of the house for protection over the winter.

Barbecues

You could spend a small fortune on a brushed steel unit with four burners, a temperature gauge and a special gadget that will smoke meat, but is it worth it if you barbecue only a few times a year? Spend a fraction of the cost on a smaller model that is easy to carry around the garden and can be tucked in the back of the car for days out at the beach or in the country. Standing on short, stout legs, these barbecues can be placed on the grass for informal picnic-style dining, or raised up to a comfortable cooking level when eating at the table. All models are compact enough to be stowed away easily, making them ideal for small gardens, rooftops and balconies.

For serious cooking, you need a bigger grill. There are hundreds of wheeled barbecue units available, from the simple kettle-drum barbecue to stainless steel models that look similar to an outdoor cooker. Kettle-drum barbecues have been popular since the 1950s and are the epitome of suburban outdoor living in the US. The classic, round bowl design has not changed much over the years,

▲ A wooden pavilion nestling among the leaf litter and trees, bamboos and tree ferns of a shaded woodland garden has been equipped with down lights to provide a warm glow, making cooking and dining possible in this most gloomy of spaces.

◄ After a great meal late in the season, nothing could be more relaxing than kicking back in front of an outdoor fireplace. Nearby, a covered garden room with glass walls is the ideal place to take in the views of the sea and also to retreat to should the weather take a turn for the worse.

▲ Large rocks have been roughly arranged in a circle to enclose a fire, making a simple cooking device that is almost primeval in spirit, especially when dusk falls and the glowing embers of the coals become an hypnotic spectacle for guests.

▲▲ An outdoor kitchen built under a sleek, modern pergola has been placed between the structure's massive pillars. This clever positioning in an area of dead space ensures that the maximum amount of paving remains free of clutter, so that parties are relaxed affairs with plenty of room to socialize.

▼ In countries where the weather is unreliable, it makes sense to create an outdoor kitchen that is protected from the rain or wind. This geometric room with sliding doors makes a contemporary feature for the space and ensures that meals can be cooked throughout the year, whatever the weather.

with only slight tweaks being made, including the addition of catch pans for the ash. They generally have porcelain-enamelled lids, and bowls come in a range of colours, including black, green, turquoise, blue and even pink.

Cart barbecues are more sophisticated and have lots of added extras, such as hardwood chopping boards, hooks for tools, a rotisserie, two or more grills, warming plates or even a swing-out holder for a wok. Beneath the grill is a storage area, sometimes enclosed by doors.

Should you go for a gas or charcoal barbecue? If you love the ritual of lighting charcoal and the leisurely wait with good friends for the coals to reach the right temperature, you will probably avoid gas at all costs. However, the convenience of simply being able to turn on gas and cook is appealing for those who often eat outdoors. In Australia, where the weather is perfect for barbecuing for much of the year, the vast majority of barbecues sold are run on gas. These barbecues also have very accurate controls for altering the temperature, so there is no excuse for burning a single sausage.

If you prefer to build a permanent barbecue, find a place in the garden that is as sheltered as possible. For a traditional look, use bricks; rendered concrete will create a more contemporary feel. Make sure you have surfaces to the side of the barbecue for stacking plates and dishes, and think about designing it to double as a fireplace to keep you warm when the temperature drops.

Tabletop devices

Cooking devices that would look lost in a large garden are ideal in a small space, for example tabletop grills such as the Spanish *plancha*, which heats up quickly and is easy to clean. Powered by gas, they have an enamelled metal, non-stick hotplate and a bowl that collects juices and fat. There are also gas-fired tabletop woks and paella sets, as well as compact ceramic pizza ovens, which are just big enough to cook a large pizza.

The ingredients

There is little point in having an outdoor kitchen if you spend most of the time going back to the house to fetch your ingredients; how much better it is to have a supply of vegetables, herbs and fruit to hand. You do not have to be an expert gardener to achieve this – simply buy some of your favourite vegetables as ready-grown plants and plant them in large troughs or pots. If you have a passion for a particular type of food, try planting with a theme in mind. For example, grow Italian herbs or plants used in Thai cooking, such as lemon grass, Thai basil and red chillies. As well as using herbs in cooking, sprinkle their leaves and branches onto the barbecue coals. The aroma is wonderful. When cooking outdoors, avoid complicated recipes. Keep it simple – eating a piping hot baked potato cooked to perfection in a fire is bliss.

▼ High walls washed with an
earthy colour, along with Ali
Baba urns in a descending row,
are typical of a traditional
Mediterranean patio garden.
Here, though, the designer has
brought the look up to date by
introducing the organic shapes
of a sleek dining table and
plastic moulded chairs.

▶ If you have a patio or deck,
choose garden furniture that is
easy to store when not in use.
Here, the trestle table and
benches are perfect for enjoying
an alfresco meal, but they can
be folded or stacked away when
the space is to be used for
other activities.

A Place to Dine

A simple blanket unfurled over the longish grass of an orchard or meadow is an idyllic place to eat a delicious picnic on a warm summer's day. Unless you have a very large rural retreat, it is unlikely that you will experience this kind of outdoor dining in the comfort of your own garden and, instead, you'll have to savour the experience on days out in the country. For many, alfresco dining consists of a table and chairs arranged under a parasol but, with a little bit of planning and time spent finding the right accessories, you can create a place to eat that will do justice to any meal you decide to rustle up.

If you have a big garden, hive off a patch to become a dining space that is far enough away from the cooking area so guests are not engulfed by smoke or cooking fumes, but close enough to save the cook walking too far. The location of the dining area is largely dictated by your garden; if you have a wonderful view of a lake, the sea, mountains or a forest, pitch your camp to make the most of the scenery.

Creating a dining area in a small garden is more challenging, especially in a courtyard garden where space is tight. An effective trick is to split the space into a kitchen and a dining area by changing the levels – not only to create two outdoor rooms, but to make a flat space more interesting. Ideally, the kitchen should be closest to the house and the dining area furthest away, but be guided by the aspect of your garden. If the bottom of the garden is permanently plunged in darkness, be prepared to put your seats wherever the sun is – after all, nobody likes to eat in gloom.

Your floor area should be proportional to your garden and determined by the number of people you expect to use it. A good pointer can be to bring your kitchen table and chairs outside and see how much room would be needed to settle furniture, while allowing enough space for good circulation. Trying to strike a balance in size is key. Acres of paving or decking will end up looking like a car park, and somewhere too small will just look cluttered and potentially twee.

Options for successful hard-standing materials are limited. Contemporary designers sometimes try to reinvent the wheel by using materials such as metal grille,

which is unsuitable for bare feet or stilettos. So stone, concrete, or decking (where suitable) are the best options. More informal areas, like sunken gardens, can work with turf floors if the amount of people traffic is limited. Good drainage is essential for any surface you choose.

Whatever size of garden you have, even if it is a balcony or roof garden, it is possible to make an outdoor dining space. You may not be able to squeeze in a long trestle table or a bank of storage seats, but even the tiniest garden can accommodate a few cushions on the floor. All you need to add is some shade overhead and provide the company – get that right and your meal will be a resounding success.

Furniture and furnishings

Hip boutique hotels and holidays are changing people's perceptions of furnishing entertainment areas in gardens. Tables, chairs and even outdoor couches are becoming conversation pieces. Outdoor furniture is about making statements and can create inherent drama. Obviously there is a desire that these pieces be comfortable and hard-wearing, but increasingly they are becoming scene stealers. Around a beautiful infinity swimming pool or on a chic terrace, the combination of style and relaxation carries through. Overly dramatic pieces, chairs with built-in canopies, four-poster-bed-style loungers, all create the feeling of fun and drama, an invitation to a place where you want to see or be seen, a place that becomes a lifestyle choice.

A place to sit

The tastiest meal can be a complete let-down if you have to eat it sitting on uncomfortable ancient chairs at a tatty table that has seen better days. If you are planning on throwing big dinner parties, then buy the biggest table you can afford or reasonably fit into your garden. There is nothing nicer than guests seated at a long, rectangular table. Reminiscent of Mediterranean weddings, they make it easier for the host to keep an eye on the number of portions required and whether anyone needs second helpings – and it makes clearing plates or dispensing drinks infinitely easier. Round tables, however, are more intimate and well suited to smaller gardens where there is a limited amount of space.

Wood is the best surface for a table. Not only does it have a tactile texture, but it does not get too hot in the sun and can be scrubbed down easily. Pick timber that does not warp or rot and that comes from a sustainable source. Now that some hardwoods are being harvested to the point of extinction, the Royal Horticultural Society in the UK has spearheaded a campaign to encourage gardeners to become ethical shoppers.

Before buying furniture, check with the retailer that it has been made from wood from a recognized scheme. These include the Forestry Stewardship Council (FSC), Programme for the Endorsement of Forest Certification (PEFC), Sustainable Forest Initiative (SFI), Canadian Standards Authority (CSA), Malaysian Timber Certification Council (MTCC) and Tropical Forest Trust (TFT).

Teak and balau are commonly used to make garden furniture but beware: not all of it is from sustainable sources. Avoid altogether furniture made from iroko. This wood is imported from Africa and is very popular, but none of it comes from a sustainable source and you will be contributing to the destruction of the rainforests. Cheaper but less durable than most hardwoods is pine,

◄ Although a canopy provides protection from the sun and light showers, permanent outdoor tables must be made of robust, weatherproof materials that will not warp or rot.

► Traditional furniture would look out of place in a striking contemporary garden, but these glass-topped tables and architectural chairs fall seamlessly into place against a backdrop of vivid orange walls and clumps of black bamboo in shiny, steel containers.

while oak looks good, but will crack and warp over time. Cedar is another good option.

Apart from wood, cast aluminium, plastic and steel are used to make tables and chairs, while tabletops may be constructed from glass, granite or mosaic tiles. There is a staggering range of styles to choose from, but simple bistro-type furniture is a foolproof option in smaller gardens, while in a more formal garden ornate steel latticework may look wonderful. Chairs, as far as possible, should be stackable or fold for storage so that matching spares can be held in reserve – it is amazing how outdoor parties start to grow when children want to bring their friends along.

Check before you buy whether the furniture can be left outdoors over winter, and if it can, consider water- and UV-proof covers to keep them in good condition. When they are unveiled again in the spring, most materials can be revived with a quick scrub, but some wooden furniture may need recoating with preservative.

In tiny gardens, a set of tables and chairs may eat up too much space so seating that doubles up as storage comes into its own. Benches built around the edge of the patio could have a hinged lid concealing space to stash tools or cushions. If you want mobile seating, look for chic metal storage-seats with fibreglass lids.

Soft furnishings

Making your guests feel comfortable and relaxed will mean that the meal will live long in their memories. Place cushions on chairs and bench seats so that sitting at a table for hours is a pleasant experience rather than an ordeal. Cushions need to be brought inside after use, except those covered with waterproof materials, but these tend to be rather unexciting. The best way to dress up your furniture is to choose a style or pattern that works well with the colour scheme or theme of your garden. For instance, a fuchsia pink cushion with gold thread would look great in a Moorish-style patio garden, or a chic, grey/green would suit a minimalist green-and-white scheme.

Blankets are essential for impromptu picnics on the lawn. There are lots to choose from, but if you are planning to be out late in the evening, it is a good idea to pick one with a waterproof backing to ensure you and the rug do not become damp. And a ready supply of cosy blankets is invaluable when there's a chill in the air.

◄ Dressing the table can help to create the perfect mood for an outdoor meal. Here, the owner has arranged a silver candelabra and a group of small plants in pots to make a simple, but effective display.

▲ A four-poster day bed is a fun place to enjoy an intimate meal and the antithesis of a formal seating area. The relaxed mood is completed by letting the grass grow long and training climbers over the supports.

COEN GARDEN
BELGIUM

DESIGNER
KRISTOF SWINNEN

Living Alfresco

This low-slung garden for a modernist house benefits from having an inherent feeling of openness. It is in a rural landscape in continental Europe but is somehow reminiscent of the flat, open plains of Texas. Simple fencing allows views of the landscape beyond, which, while not particularly dramatic, is serene and very green; it is not blocked.

The garden designer has decided to create an oasis that fits in and complements, rather than one that conflicts or contrasts with its surroundings. All in all, there is a feeling of acceptance and compliance – you don't feel challenged in any way. The garden is uncomplicated, uncluttered and, although very much contrived, fits into the natural landscape.

The garden is overtly formal, with strong lines of symmetry, which may be slightly austere for some people. Two pools have been created – one for swimming and one beyond that is purely ornamental. Both do a magnificent job of reflecting light and mirroring clouds rolling through the sky. They are also surrounded by a gentle carpet of lawn but accessed via a boardwalk of decking. Most of the paving is natural stone. Clipped trees are used to frame views and create walkways to a wood and glass pavilion.

The layout of the garden invites you in. It is not particularly large and yet it provides everything you need if you want to jump in a pool, have a meal outdoors or just relax and watch the sun setting. Low topiary is used to

▲ The geometric shape of the simple table that sits at the heart of the space is echoed by the vast containers filled with grasses and the sharp angles created by the raised beds, paths and hedges.

◄ A raised hedge of pleached hornbeams, which are kept tightly clipped, leads the eye to the house and creates a division in the garden without blocking the light or disrupting the view across the space.

▶ The clean lines of the modernist house are reflected in the simplicity of the garden design and the careful selection of paving and edging materials. These are similar to those used in the construction of the exterior of the house and help to bring a sense of unity to the space.

COEN GARDEN
BELGIUM

DESIGNER
KRISTOF SWINNEN

▲ Tucked away among dense verdant foliage, an outdoor shower is a practical way to cool down on a sunny day or to wash after a dip in the pool. Plants that thrive in damp conditions make the perfect, natural shower curtain.

▶ With its geometric shape, this swimming pool also functions as a formal canal. Its clean lines are continued by the smaller, square-shape pond behind. The flow of the water feature leads the eye across the boundary of the garden to the rural landscape beyond.

◀ This planting scheme, consisting largely of shades of green, gives the garden a lush feel, which perfectly complements the central swimming pool. Most plants are kept tightly clipped, which gives the garden a strong backbone, even in winter when the deciduous shrubs drop their leaves to reveal their structural silhouettes.

▶ Recessed lights built into the ceiling of the wooden garden house allow it to be used for meals long after darkness falls, drenching the space in a warm, glowing light that is ideal for intimate dinner parties.

form soft patterns, and ornamental grasses billow in the wind. The low hedges help to compartmentalize areas without blocking light and so contribute to the feeling of freedom. Cubed fibreglass planters, some transparent, some bright red, also define spaces. The red planters are further enhanced by the fiery tones of *Imperata cylindrica* 'Red Baron'.

A very simple but elegant wooden pavilion is set at one side. From here, the view across the garden is quite formal: there is a cruciform design built up with lawns, cut stone raised terraces, hedges and grasses, all joining together to create a simple but theatrical picture.

In the evening, the architectural pavilion becomes an elegant dining space. Its massively wide glass doors swing open, framing views and welcoming diners. At night, individual features such as the pavilion, water and trees are illuminated.

An outdoor shower surrounded by lush foliage creates a sense of fun, and hammocks sway between trees – another reminder that this garden is all about people enjoying themselves. The woolly foliage of the trees in the distance adds to the relaxed feel, while offering glimpses of the field beyond. This is a green garden where nothing shouts at you. Its gentleness is its genius.

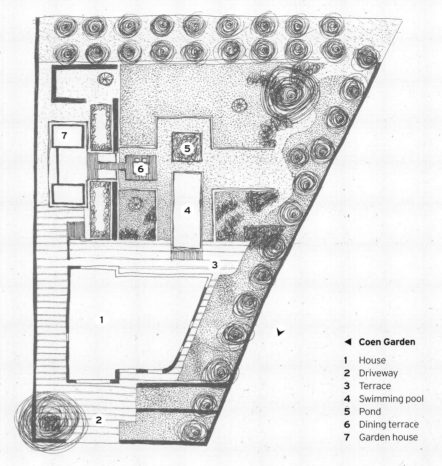

◄ **Coen Garden**

1 House
2 Driveway
3 Terrace
4 Swimming pool
5 Pond
6 Dining terrace
7 Garden house

▼ This modern-looking log pile fire heats up an otherwise cold and metallic eating area – a wonderful setting for a grand dinner party with impact.

▶ Set at a distance from the seating, these hot, blasting flames are placed primarily for drama in a bold contemporary stone piazza. A bright orange glow extends over the focal area.

Heat and Light

When the temperature dips in the evening there is no need to cut short a great meal and head indoors. There are many ways of keeping the cold at bay to extend the season of your outdoor dining room, from making a simple fire to using the latest radiant heaters. You could even pass each guest a blanket to keep their knees and shoulders warm, which is a sensible option when you consider the negative environmental effects caused by the burning of any fuel. Also, remember that trying to create general heat for a group of people can be a futile effort, unless you have a huge bonfire!

Whatever you decide to do, always have your guests' best interests at heart – for the meal to be successful, you do not want people sitting around the table shivering.

▥ Chimineas and outdoor fireplaces

The Mexicans use chimineas for baking bread, but this traditional oven has found popularity in many gardens, where they have become a magnet for guests on cooler evenings who gather around to enjoy the otherworldly glow of the fire. Chimineas run on charcoal or logs and some have grills for cooking on. They are made from a variety of materials, including cast iron and aluminium, but the authentic Mexican material is clay. However, terracotta chimineas can be brittle and are heavy to move, so if mobility is important, go for cast aluminium – it is significantly lighter than other materials. Most chimineas have either very ornate or rustic looks and may not sit comfortably in a contemporary garden, but in the right location they make an eye-catching focal point and provide bags of heat to make the most of cooler evenings.

Outdoor fireplaces are a common sight in American gardens, where the idea of alfresco dining and outdoor living took hold long ago. Often located on the edge of the patio, against a wall or in a corner, their flickering flames and comforting warmth make the perfect place for gatherings at dusk and, although they can be used throughout the year, they really are perfect when the nights draw in during autumn.

Rustic brick or stone fireplaces are ideal in a rural location, while a clean, geometric design is more suitable in a modern town garden. If you have a Mediterranean-style space, then you could make the fireplace stand out by coating it with blue-, green- or terracotta-coloured render. In the south west of the US and especially California, distinctive beehive-shaped fireplaces called kivas are popular. These have been inspired by the traditional cooking oven of the Pueblo Indians and are often rendered white.

◀ A small fire set into the wall is a strong focal point in this cosy outdoor garden room. Complete with a green grass carpet, table and chairs, the fire glows like a television in a living room.

▶ A fantastically fiery focal point brings warmth and reflection to this attractive entertainment area. The curved shapes and oversized coals create an informal and relaxed place for friends and family.

Fireplaces can be bought in kit form, giving you the satisfaction of putting the chunks of masonry and flue together. Another option is to go for a portable, steel fireplace, but the most successful and talked-about garden features are always custom-built. The best fireplace will have storage underneath for wood, ledges above the fire for a grill and a mantelpiece for putting down drinks.

Patio heaters

Many restaurants and bars with outdoor terraces for dining use quartz, infrared heating. Whether wall-mounted or set on a pedestal, these heaters provide warmth at the touch of a button and are ideal for patios, decks, balconies and even inside some garden buildings. Unlike gas-powered patio heaters, which heat the surrounding air, this system uses radiant heat and targets the people within the set range. A typical heater will keep guests warm within a distance of 16sq m (172sq ft). Although fairly nondescript, they earn their keep by keeping you warm in a very efficient way.

Somewhat noisier but with bags of style are gas patio heaters. Made from steel or aluminium, they are often mushroom-shaped on an extended 'stalk'. An average gas heater will warm an area of around 25sq m (270sq ft), but as the heat is indiscriminate, they are relatively inefficient. Look for models with a tilting reflector that will direct the heat, but remember that these heaters are environmentally unfriendly and the heat they provide may not be worth it. They are stylish additions to many gardens but come at a cost.

Fire pits

A pile of logs burning in the middle of a fire pit is a mesmerizing sight and has the power to take you back instantly to childhood camping holidays, when pleasant evenings were spent around a campfire, toasting marshmallows. But the first consideration is that fire, just like water, can be dangerous. This type of feature is appropriate only for grown-up enjoyment. Children love to play with matches, so they should not be encouraged to create campfires, and in certain environments where climatic conditions make the surroundings prone to ignition by stray sparks, such features should not be considered at all.

Where appropriate, have some fun. A fire pit is a small fire that is often sunk into the ground. Traditionally, it will be constructed from natural materials – stone boulders, for instance, set in a circular or oval shape. Like any good fireplace, ventilation is needed to get a flame

going, so allow some space around the fire, which will also give easier access for cleaning. The fire should not be encouraged to become too large. Adult supervision is necessary, with particular care taken over siting and shelter from prevailing winds.

If you have a small garden or few DIY skills, the good news is that you can simply buy a fire pit and put it anywhere, including on the lawn, without leaving behind a patch of burnt grass. Made from cast iron or stainless steel, there are many that are well made, robust and stylish, but there is an equal number that should be avoided at all costs. Go for a model that has an ash drawer underneath to make cleaning up easy, and make sure that it is fitted with a spark guard, as logs are unpredictable and it is likely to be near flammable materials such as cushions or rugs. There are gas versions available, but what is the point? The whole idea is to enjoy fire at its primitive best.

▲ The impact of this beautifully constructed canopy is further increased by illuminating the trees with pure white light and deepening the sunken garden with a warm orange glow.

▶ There are three layers to the illumination of this garden: a warm glow from the ground plants, strong uplighting that defines the verticals in the planters, and hot spots from the candles on the table that place your focus on the dining area.

▏▏▏ Lighting

To extend the use of a garden for alfresco eating into the evening think carefully about lighting. For special occasions, paper Japanese lanterns can be hung from trees, candles floated in water, flaming oil torches used to illuminate beds and pathways, and oversized flickering Moroccan lanterns to imbue a sense of drama. The trick with garden lighting is two-fold; it is a balance between the practical and the magical.

You need to be able to navigate your way through a dark garden: after a few glasses of wine, your senses may not be as sharp, and trip hazards such as uneven stepping stones or the garden pond need to be clearly indicated. But you are not flood-lighting a football stadium – you will just need low-level lighting along the main access routes, which is easily achieved with simple white spotlights.

The cooking area should be well lit so you can avoid burning food or yourself. A simple way of doing this is to use clip-on lights. These have rotational heads that will provide direct lighting to food-preparation or kitchen-style areas.

In your gathering area, candles and tea-lights on tables and in lanterns hung from trees will carve out an intimate and warm gathering glow, even in larger gardens. Candles and storm lanterns give a good quality of light, bright enough to eat by, but if you are worried, increase the number of candles.

For other reasons, such as creating a certain mood, you may wish to uplight or create dramas from features such as architectural shapes or tree stems. Subtle low-level lighting, carefully placed, can make a feature of a sculpture or a specimen plant. Get the lighting right and the mood will be perfect.

◄ A fantastically staged platform for drinking with friends. The lighting under the heavy marble benches makes them look as if they are hovering, while the focal uplighting beneath the wall screen makes you look up in anticipation that a film is about to start.

▲ The simple spot lights that have been placed within the lush green planting of this jungle-like paradise create a sense of intrigue. They deepen the planting and invite you to find out what lies beyond.

▼ High hedges and taller trees create essential shade for this chic lounging area. The soft furniture and cushions imply a relaxed and almost sleepy feel.

▶ A mature wisteria forms a living arbour over a simple outdoor bench and table setting, creating an uncluttered and tranquil scene. The shady spot for dining is cooled even further by the view over the still swimming pool.

◀ The bohemian feel projected by the well-used outdoor furniture and informal place settings indicates a warm climate. The overhanging tree provides the necessary dense shade.

▶ A permanent wooden canopy makes this a very usable outdoor space. The surrounding trees add to the coolness and provide rustling sounds and atmosphere. Tropical plants in pots also contribute to the effect.

▶▶ The chic contemporary feel created by this curved shelter in steel and wood is completed with two single classic 1950s loungers. The shelter provides shade as well as a feeling of protection from the elements.

Shade and Shelter

Shade is a must for any outdoor seating area. Eating in intense sunshine can be very uncomfortable and it ruins the food – salads start to wilt and butter melts. Depending on the garden, shade can simply be provided by trees, a parasol or concertina awning. A fabric canopy attached to a wall will lend a contemporary look, and if the dining area is further away from the house, it can be stretched between specially made metal supports. Structures like this are designed to be left in place for much of the year and are generally water-resistant. For simple picnics, try tethering a decorative piece of material between some trees or even fence posts. Alternatively, for a Mediterranean feel, create your dining area under a pergola and train a grapevine across the top. Then, in late summer, you can select one of the bunches of juicy grapes dangling overhead for dessert.

Even in a garden with fairly limited space, garden buildings are a must for all-year-round appreciation and entertainment. The delight of creating some architecture in your own garden is to create a destination that is one step away from the realities of your home life: a destination that can be simple or elaborate but, ultimately, it is a covered outdoor room where you can sit and enjoy verdant surroundings in the company of other people. Such a construction often acts as a focal point from the home, and gives a sense of destination to your plot. You can simply convert a cheap but water-tight garden shed, or if you feel the need to be more creative, you could build your own Japanese tea house or even a miniature mediaeval castle (but make sure that you check planning restrictions first).

Inside you do not need much: it can be as simple or elaborate as you like. Some furniture, chairs and tables, would simply allow adults to behave as if in a grown-up Wendy house. But you can let your imagination run away with you, or follow a theme: Enid Blyton's Famous Five, for example, or a James-Bond-type playboy lair complete with bar, sunken hot tub and relaxing sofa, including the obligatory wide screen television.

Entertainment systems

The luxury goods and gadgets market is an area of technology that is expanding for both manufacturers and retailers. As ground-breaking models are introduced ever

faster, and traditional styles of television and music players become obsolete, it should come as no surprise that entertainment systems are moving into the garden. But we must be aware of our social obligations. If not used with consideration for the wider community, technology may enhance the living experience of the user but have a detrimental effect on others – noise and light pollution can be a menace. Speakers throughout the garden, amplification docks for mp3 players and piped music are all beginning to have a role, and while they encourage the use of outdoor space, they must be used sensitively.

The possibilities for enjoyment are only just starting to be realized. The great excitement of the American drive-in movie of the 1950s can be brought much closer to home through images beamed from a projector hooked up to a television, laptop, games console or DVD player. The excitement of doing this through a night sky is wonderful, whether you have an elaborate automatic retractable screen, just a white sheet or even a white wall to project on to. Gathering people together, having a barbecue and experiencing an old movie in the garden makes a very special occasion. Recent years have seen the arrival of television that is suitable for outdoor enjoyment – they are used mostly by pubs where smoking is not allowed inside. But what works indoors – a flat screen hung like a picture on a wall – does not necessarily capture the imagination outside and can seem a little incongruous.

Lighting in the garden can transform a space into a completely different, magical world after nightfall. Equally, the magic of light through projection or plasma screens reinvents everything. It works just as well in an English cottage-style garden as in an up-to-the-minute sub-tropical-style contemporary outdoor room because the garden simply becomes a dark backdrop for the display. Be careful, however: always provide good access and lighting, and keep such entertainment away from water.

▦ Hot tubs

In various parts of the world, hot springs have traditionally led to an enjoyment of outdoor bathing. In parts of Japan, there are whole centres for such activities. In the west, tubs of bubbling warm water in the garden have become an accessory for the chattering classes, offering an opportunity to unwind and relax in sociable, outdoor surroundings. Hot tubs have something of a racy image, however, inviting the neighbours around to disrobe and enjoy themselves. And, aesthetically, they do not add much to the garden, veering from desperately ugly plastic whirlpool baths to chic cedar tubs. Hygiene and maintenance are paramount, as is safety where children are around.

▲ The white stone and large white wall screen create a cold stark space for social gatherings. The platform appears to float over the water, cooling the area still further and making it more appropriate as a public space than as somewhere for family and close friends.

▼ The warmth and welcome projected from this retreat urge you to enter. The hot tub is set among soft furniture and cushions that are waiting for you to put your feet up and relax. The surrounding bamboo and rush screens add to this desert island haven.

◄ A series of fantastically shaped windows draws the eye into a space where the ultimate party is taking place. The layers compel you to find out what lies in each room, but the reward lies in the heart of the building.

▼ There is a warm atmosphere on this sleek decked area. The row of well-proportioned pots is back-lit, illuminating the scene. All the pots contain the same plant species, which keeps the design tight. This is a slick space, and further views across the garden reinforce the feeling.

▶ This beautifully constructed staircase is illuminated by a deep yellow light, giving it direction and style. The up-lit white bark and elegant leaves of silver birch trees soften the space and compete for focus.

Planting

A party garden is a place for fun, for letting yourself go and for enjoying the company of your family and friends. The space can be fantastic in all its forms, be it a sunken area in the middle of a back garden, a courtyard of weathered stone, a small balcony or purely a patio under a garden arbour. Plants can be used in the same way that furniture, paints and floor tiles are in an interior, to create exactly the mood that you want for your personal space.

Atmosphere can be influenced by the choice and shape of the plants and by how you decide to maintain them. A tightly clipped box shrub, for example, creates a definite sense of control and moves towards a formal or minimal style. Similarly, positioning the plants symmetrically will provide a sense of formality and using a limited colour palette and restraint in the number of species will give a tidier and more elegant effect.

Plant combinations are a fantastic way of adding drama in both colour and structure. By juxtaposing plants with maximum contrasts, you can add real excitement and enliven the garden. Certain plant shapes draw you in so that you have to touch them, feel them and smell them. Plant the upright green stems of *Allium sphaerocephalon* among the beautifully fragrant mounds of *Santolina pinnata* with its tiny yellow pinhead flowers; or *Iris japonica* 'Variegata' within a bed of *Trifolium repens* 'Purpurascens', for amazing contrast in colour, form and texture that will wake up and arouse the senses of any social gathering. People will talk about it!

Planting can also evoke other feelings or associations. The foliage of *Rodgersia podophylla* or the enormous leaves of *Gunnera manicata*, for example, can imply the presence of water, whereas a banana plant can transport you instantly to the tropics.

Perfume is expected in the garden and delights the senses. Borders can be filled with aromatic herbs that release their essential oils as the sun beats down. Lavender,

▲ Walls are fantastic backdrops for plants, and the shadows they cast add depth and excitement. The warm-coloured paint contrasts well with the cooler silver planting in the foreground.

◀ *Dicksonia antarctica* is a wonderful ornamental that can single-handedly transport you to a hot humid place. Views through the screen enhance this and encourage you to slow down and enjoy your surroundings.

sage and rosemary all have terrific spicy scents, and your guests will not be able to resist brushing their hands over the leaves. Alternatively, try filling some containers with summer-flowering lilies or pelargoniums, perfect for a Mediterranean look.

With clever planting, you can include flowers that will give your evening meals a lift. Many plants have flowers that are at their most intense at night to attract moths and other nocturnal creatures. By covering vertical surfaces around dining areas with scented climbing plants, the flowers will be close to head-height and the warm evening air will carry their scent. *Jasminum officinale*, evening primrose and honeysuckle all have knockout scents, which hang heavy in the air on a still, warm night. If you can track it down, the annual climber *Ipomoea alba* is worth training up a trellis or around your dining space – also known as moonflower, it has saucer-sized white blooms and a hefty fragrance.

Inside Outside

This garden is a true extension of the house. In fact, in some ways it seems to mimic the physical layout of a typical interior. It is a garden suitable for a beautiful climate where people have a desire to spend a lot of time outdoors. Inspired by the great weather and entertaining friends, the design allows for choice in outdoor living. Through layout, compartmentalization, proportion and the physical framing of areas, it encourages the owner to entertain out of doors on either an intimate or a lavish scale. Even the food preparation takes place outdoors, so ultimately the chef is never separated from his guests. Indeed, the evening would start when visitors sit on tall stools at the worktop and watch the chef in action while drinking cocktails. A whole kitchen has been built, including barbecue, refrigerator, cooker and sink, as well as acres of worktop. Accent colours, in this case the soft greys used on bookcases inside the house, are picked up in the exterior paint and indeed the paving.

Glass doors on both the house and the separate studio pavilion slide to create great gaps in the wall so people flow from inside to outside as if boundaries did not exist. Paths and patios merge into one. Simple concrete pavers, used liberally, are the defining hard landscaping material and accommodate large blocks of decking and planting, which soften the architecture.

In other areas, 'rooms' are defined by a change in paving type. A large rectangular decked area supports a table with ten chairs, all framed by a modernist pergola,

▲ The fabulous polished stone of this patio area allows a seamless transition from the small house to the outside, with the simple seating and horizontal wooden fence complementing the style of the house perfectly.

◄ This part of the building concentrates on shades of brown, which is reflected strongly in the choice of patio stone and outdoor furniture. The result is a more formal space, and the dense deep evergreen planting adds to this, although the cream arbour does bring a certain lightness.

ENTERTAINING

DICKENS STREET
CALIFORNIA, US

CASE STUDY #6 CONTINUED

DESIGNER
RUSS CLETA

which in time will be softened by a fast-advancing column of climbing plants. So, eventually, the pergola will not be simply a structural accent – it will work practically to provide some shade and to give a feeling of enclosure, under which diners will enjoy their freshly prepared meals. Elsewhere, as the evening draws in, a fire bowl becomes the focus as guests gather on low wooden cubed benches softened by slimline upholstered cushions.

In most areas, there is a definite feeling of separation from the surrounding greenery, as if the garden, with all its rectilinear shapes and shiny surfaces, floats above the subtropical foliage. A more intimate raised patio immediately outside another set of glazed doors allows for a small number of people to gather and sit on built-in sofas while contemplating the luxuriant growth around them.

A different gathering point for groups of guests, as well as a strong sculptural focal point, is a large bowl of gently rippling cool water at the furthest point from the cooking area. Its sound is refreshing and it may even contribute some air-conditioning on a hot summer's day. It echoes the shape of the fire bowl and thereby contributes to the strong feeling of coherence in this ultra-sophisticated garden.

▼ An open and casual feeling is created by soft furnishings and a simple coal fire. Limited but well-chosen planting gives the patio a strong finish.

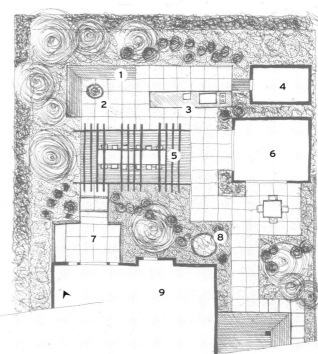

▲ The polished stone leads past the kitchen to a chic dining area with bar and relaxation zone. The space is well decorated with pots and surrounded by lush planting, completing the atmosphere.

▶ **Dickens Street, California**

1 Wooden bench
2 Fire bowl
3 Barbecue/Kitchen area
4 Wine cellar
5 Dining terrace
6 Home Office/Studio
7 Elevated patio
8 Water feature
9 House

▲ Established and mainly evergreen planting ensures that this decked patio area is well decorated all year round.

◀ A fantastically luxurious outdoor kitchen area is set on the same polished stone and uses the same wood featured in the patio. It is extremely important to keep the number of different materials used to a minimum to draw in all the design elements.

▶ Simplicity, good proportions and well-chosen furniture create an effortlessly tranquil scene.

► The pure white marble platforms create bold and dramatic levels on this beautiful roof terrace. The bright orange coal fires heat the space and give it a Greek mythological feeling of power.

► Wild flowers are the epitome of summer. In this garden, a carpet of yellow and white wild flowers jostle each other in the breeze beneath the boughs of broad-leaved trees. The grassy path allows you to walk among them so you can appreciate their scent and enjoy the buzzing of pollinating bees.

Natural

If your idea of a wildlife garden is nothing more than a tangle of brambles, weeds and overgrown shrubs masking the banks of a muddy sump, prepare yourself for a surprise. With proper planning and care, a garden designed for nature can be a beautiful place to relax in, and a haven for all sorts of wild creatures. To be attractive to a variety of birds, insects, mammals and other wildlife however, it is essential to establish a harmonious balance of plants and features, which is sometimes more difficult than it seems. Wherever possible, use trees and shrubs that provide a bounty of berries, fruit or nuts that will help to sustain wildlife. Pick varieties that you know will attract certain species where you live; it may not be realistic to expect red squirrels, but you could increase the number of wild bird species that visit. And when choosing flowers, aim to include some that are loved by pollinating creatures, such as bees, butterflies and even flying beetles. Insects may not be glamorous, but they are the most important creatures in a garden, and do the most to help gardeners. Birds, insects and mammals can be enticed into your garden by providing habitats for sheltering, nesting and hibernation, and by making sure there are places for them to drink.

Gardens for Nature

The best wildlife gardens are those that are inspired by the natural surroundings. If you live at the foot of a mountain, close to a forest or moor, by a river or lake, or at the seashore, take elements from what you can see and incorporate them into your own space. For instance, if there is woodland on your doorstep with a thriving population of wild *Rhododendron ponticum*, it is a fair bet that your soil will also be acid and you could plant rhododendrons in your garden, although you would be well advised to choose less thuggish varieties.

The local environment can also influence features within your space. With a garden by the sea, you might collect pieces of driftwood or other treasures that are washed up and use them as sculpture. Locally quarried stone, such as slate or limestone, should also be used in your own garden to make paths, walls or other features, sourcing the materials from a reputable supplier rather than taking anything away from the countryside.

The way a garden is managed can determine how successfully it will be as a haven for wildlife. A garden designed for nature is never going to resemble the clinical interior of an operating theatre and, in order for it to work, you need to accept that there will be a degree of untidiness. This may be difficult if you are accustomed to the clean lines of a minimalist garden, but by leaving the odd patch of long grass, a stray weed or by arranging a

▶ For a natural perennial planting of sun-loving species to have the greatest possible impact, you need to plant in layers, with the larger varieties at the back of the display. By not scrimping on numbers and planting in large, dramatic swathes, you will create an unforgettable spectacle.

pile of logs as a shelter for beetles and spiders, a garden lacking in life could swiftly become a nature reserve.

Wherever possible use sustainable materials. For instance, garden furniture and timber for decks or buildings should be certified to show that it comes from a well-managed forest and, if at all possible, use wood that has been cut down locally to reduce the number of air miles used. Elsewhere, devise ways to recycle as much as possible. Capture rainwater with a simple water butt or by installing a sophisticated rainwater harvesting system. You could also make your own compost by rigging up some bins for grass clippings, old newspapers, vegetable peelings and plant prunings. If you have enough trees,

try creating your own leaf mould. In a small garden you will never be able to make enough compost to be totally self-sufficient, but if you have a large space, you may never have to buy soil conditioner again.

Although it is not essential to become an organic gardener, it is a good idea to use chemicals only as a last resort. The problem with chemicals is that they are largely non-specific and will probably cause a detrimental effect further along the chain. However, there are times when your resolve may weaken and no one could blame you for using a herbicide on a particularly pernicious weed, or for dispatching aphids with a quick squirt of a pesticide if they are on the verge of destroying a cherished plant.

Woodland Gardens

Woodland gardens can be magical places, especially in autumn when russet- and golden-coloured leaves float lazily to the ground, allowing shafts of light to break through summer's dense canopy. The crunchy carpets of dry leaves become ever thicker, and both adults and children will stomp through them with delight.

A garden full of trees is an ideal place to support a thriving population of birds, insects and mammals, and it is a mistake to believe that gardening with degrees of shade and damp is a challenge. Such gardens are ideal places to grow a rich selection of bulbs, perennials, ferns and shrubs loved by plant connoisseurs, such as the dog-toothed violet, which is found naturally in Californian woodland, and hellebores, which are coveted for their delicate petal markings.

When creating a garden in woodland, or planting one from scratch, it is important that it looks unplanned, as if the plants have made the decision to grow there themselves. Avoid regimented rows or formal beds altogether, and give plants plenty of space in which to grow – sometimes there is nothing nicer than seeing a plant growing unhindered with nothing around it except bare earth or a layer of bark mulch.

Although a woodland garden should look as much like a natural wood as possible, you will be able to introduce features to make it more rewarding, such as carefully positioned paths. When walking through a forest or wood, it is fun to go 'off piste', but in the garden you will need to avoid trampling on any emerging shoots. More importantly, a path can be used to inject drama into your space by designing it to lead to a breathtaking view. You can achieve this by cutting a serpentine path to lead mysteriously through the dappled gloom provided by trees until it nears its end where light is allowed to flood in. For added drama, the path should terminate at the best view you have, whether it is the highest point with views out to sea or a simple, tranquil space. For paths to blend in seamlessly, or steps if you have a garden on a slope, avoid laying hard materials in formal patterns. In a natural environment, the path should feel like an inviting corridor through the trees and not be a major garden feature – a simple path of chipped bark is ideal.

◄ A lush planting of shade-loving plants, rich in texture, flanks a path of stone paving slabs. As it wends its way, disappearing into the undergrowth beyond, the path suggests that a mysterious journey is about to start.

▼ The unexpected formality of this shady spot is achieved through the repetition of planting and the symmetry of the curved, brick-edged borders, which are all clearly visible beneath the trunks of the trees.

▲ Pink scabious, which sits on long wiry stems above the dense heads of yellow euphorbias, rub shoulders with other perennials to make a colourful display in a light woodland corner. Different types of foliage create a verdant tapestry of textures.

◄ Texture, form and colour should be just as carefully considered in a woodland setting as in the rest of the garden. Here, standing out against a green backdrop, yellow poppies and white anemones make a particularly pleasing contrast in both colour and shape.

► A long tunnel created by trees in a sylvan setting makes a bewitching pathway that appeals to adults and children alike. Left temptingly open, the old iron gates lead to a sunlit glade, which is in marked contrast to the shadowy passage.

Planting

A woodland garden is not just a collection of trees; it is a multi-layered planting scheme, where the trees provide shade for shrubs, perennials, ferns and bulbs. An essential part of the planning process is to determine the characteristics of your soil. Use a pH kit to test whether it is acid or alkaline, and assess how well it drains.

If you are starting from scratch, the first step is to plant some trees. There are no hard-and-fast rules about what you should grow, and it is best if you go for varieties you like. It might be a collection of different types of birch, conifers for year-round greenery, or a mixture of deciduous and evergreen trees so you can enjoy spring blossom, berries, autumn colour and structure. Deciduous, broad-leaved trees not only create a natural progression of seasonal interest, but make a valuable contribution to alleviating the global problem of carbon emissions.

Trees can be bought at various stages of development, from inexpensive year-old saplings to mature specimens that will stretch even the largest budget. With so much choice, the answer is to buy what you can afford, but try to include some larger specimens or it could be many years until your woodland starts to take shape.

Trees provide the ideal conditions for creating an understorey of shrubs. As long as they have the right soil and enough moisture, many plants will flourish in light shade, including hydrangeas, dogwoods – which are invaluable for their bright winter stem colour – and azaleas, a large plant family with a stunning spring floral display in breathtaking, zingy colours.

At ground level you can really express yourself. Woodland is perfect for many perennials loved by the

cognoscenti, including erythroniums, some geraniums, hellebores and hostas. These can be grown with many ferns that will provide a verdant feel to your scheme. Plant bulbs throughout: snowdrops and crocuses to welcome in spring and then sheets of native bluebells, which no British woodland should be without.

Apart from making the woodland a visual feast, think about how you can delight the other senses. The golden yellow flowers of *Rhododendron luteum* are so aromatic that you often smell the plant a long time before you set eyes on it. Another delightful fragrance that suffuses the air of a still woodland is that of the Katsura tree, or *Cercidiphyllum japonicum*. The tree originates from Japan and is pretty enough, but it is at its best in autumn when the fallen leaves emit a heady burnt sugar scent that smells just like candyfloss.

Although a large space is necessary to make a woodland garden with real impact, it is possible to evoke the feeling of one in a tiny area. Many town gardens are large enough to accommodate a small group of slender trees, such as birch. By raising their canopies and thinning the branches, the trees are kept within bounds and make dappled shade where a variety of plants can be grown.

A woodland garden should look natural, but without some interference from you, weeds, such as brambles, will quickly establish and reclaim the space. To keep on top of them, remove any invading plants on sight and mulch to prevent weed seeds germinating. Allow some plants to self-seed, but manage the numbers to prevent them from spreading too much and smothering other treasures in the garden.

▲ Most trees have leaves, flowers or fruit held high above the ground, but lower down there may be little of interest. The naked, buff-coloured stems of these saplings have been given a lift by the planting of semi-shade-loving euphorbias with their clouds of acid-yellow flowers, turning a dull scene into an electric one.

▶ Woodland gardens do not have to be devoid of colour - by picking the right varieties, it is possible to fill the space with many different flowering plants. Deep shade suits only a few flowers but, here, the dappled shade created under the branches of an old gnarled tree is suitable for bulbs, perennials and even flowering shrubs.

◀ Old stumps and even rocks with a lovely old patina make perfect planting pockets for shade-loving perennials, such as variegated hostas. These can be combined with glossy-leaved hart's tongue ferns and other ferns with more feathery fronds to create a lush and textural display.

▲ The sturdy branches of an ancient tree open like the palm of a giant hand to support a tree-top home. Built on three separate levels, this is a magical hideaway.

▶ A newly installed fence would look completely out of place in this setting, but by using twisted pieces of driftwood found nearby, the designer has built a rustic boundary that is in complete harmony with the landscape. It is also completely sustainable.

Garden buildings

The strong branches of mature trees make perfect supports for tree houses. Find a tree with open limbs and either lash pieces of timber together with rope to create a simple high-rise resting spot or commission a specialist company to design a tree house for you. If you do not have a suitable tree or your woodland is newly planted, a freestanding tree house can be supported on chunky timber uprights, with a couple of new trees planted alongside to give a leafy effect.

Larger woodlands provide the opportunity to erect a building in a clearing. If you want to create a romantic, fairytale scene, there are some wonderful examples you can buy, complete with thatched roofs and gothic windows. More practical would be a log cabin – equipped with a table, chairs, a cooking device and even bunk beds, it could become the perfect retreat from everyday life (as long as you leave your mobile phone behind).

The interplay between shadow and light that exists in a woodland garden makes it the perfect place for a mysterious grotto. Built simply with breeze-blocks then rendered, grottoes are usually adorned with pebbles or decorative shells laid out in patterns. For a contemporary grotto, make an elliptical shape from metal formwork coated with wire mesh, then hire a specialist contractor to spray it with liquid concrete. You can then paint it any colour that grabs your fancy.

Art in the garden

Woodland gardens are great places to display works of art. A collection of sculpture or objets d'art can be placed under foliage, next to a stream or hung from the branches of trees to make walking around the garden an exciting and stimulating experience. This works particularly well at the garden of Little Sparta in Scotland, where Ian Hamilton-Finlay's bronze busts of classical figures and

▲ A winding path through a wild woodland garden opens up to reveal a grassy glade, its gloom brilliantly illuminated by a resin and gold-leaf head of the god Apollo. This scene perfectly illustrates how sculptures can be placed in the most unlikely places to provide an element of mystery and surprise.

◄ Gnarled pieces of driftwood are full of character and make wonderful natural sculptures, whether used as a solitary totem or bound tightly together to create a secret garden room.

► Similar lengths of logs arranged together like a dry stone wall make a multi-purpose structure. This log wall is both boundary and bench, while the gaps between the logs provide many habitats for wildlife.

words carved into stone are hidden in the dense undergrowth. Elsewhere, designers like Ivan Hicks or artist Siegfried Speckhardt and his plantswoman wife Ri have taken random, everyday objects and turned them into surreal works of art that have an affinity with their natural surroundings. At the Speckhardt's garden in Germany, bicycle wheels have been turned into a structural support for climbing plants.

Found objects, such as stones, pebbles and fallen down tree branches, can be used to make artworks that are completely natural. Stones can be arranged neatly to form a cairn shape, or flat pebbles can be stacked neatly on top of each other in ascending size. Artist Andy Goldsworthy has made this type of sculpture his life's work – it is often ephemeral, becoming more interesting as the materials age naturally and their physical properties alter, whether it is wood that eventually rots, or ice and snow that simply melt.

Wildlife habitats

Although areas of woodland are naturally attractive to wildlife, it is important to boost populations in a garden setting by giving them a helping hand, especially as many natural habitats are under threat. Nesting boxes, in every shape and size, make a suitable home for all kinds of birds and mammals. It is important to fix boxes with the correct aspect and at the recommended height. For instance, owls prefer to nest at a particular angle, and some bats like boxes to be exactly 3m (10ft) off the ground. These shy mammals also need an untreated wooden box, as they are extremely sensitive to preservatives.

Elsewhere, you can provide plenty of nooks and crannies for beetles, ladybirds and other small creatures by arranging piles of logs, placed randomly or put together as a living artwork. These quickly become home to an amazing variety of wildlife and should be allowed to rot down naturally with very little disturbance.

Flora For Fauna

When, in 1987, Pamela and Peter Lewis inherited 1.5 hectares (4 acres) of unpromising rough farming land, they had a dream to turn it into beautiful garden. Sticky Wicket is testament to their vision. While some wildlife gardens are a tangle of plants left to grow naturally, this is a successful marriage between a natural and ornamental garden – it looks spectacular, but also provides shelter and food for many beneficial creatures.

The garden, set in the heart of rural Dorset in the southwest of England, is perfectly in tune with its surroundings. However, it is not untidy or unstructured, like so many wildlife gardens, but thoughtfully laid out with a strong backbone that keeps the exuberant planting scheme within bounds. Rather than treat the plot as a single space, Pamela has sculpted it into a series of adjoining rooms. Her skill at combining plants and colours is unsurpassed. Each area is completely different, providing inspiration and surprises for the visitors who flock to her gate when she opens the garden during summer.

Where it surrounds the Lewis's bungalow, the garden is traditional and looks similar to those you find attached to rural homes up and down the country. One area – called the Frog Garden – is home to a small pond and boggy area that is a magnet to wildlife. In winter, the colourful stems of dogwoods come into their own, especially when the red, yellow and green stems are back-lit by the sun.

This leads to the Bird Garden, which is alive with the fluttering of wings throughout the year. Feeders of all shapes and sizes are strung from branches or the timbers of a pergola, while the grassy space is enclosed by a tapestry of shrubs, many of which provide berries for birds to feast on during the colder months. Stripped of their leaves in winter, some shrubs reveal little woven willow nesting pockets, which have been stowed among their branches.

While the garden rooms near the house are popular with wildlife, they seem rather restrained when compared with the rest of the garden. For instance, further away from the house is a large meadow that feels completely

▼ Neutral colours create a rather restrained display that is in contrast to the exuberance found elsewhere. Foxgloves and lupins in soft shades mix with white-flowered perennials and shrubs noted for their autumn foliage, to give this space long-lasting interest.

◄ With feathery seed heads caught on a breeze, a sea of squirrel tail grass almost glows and makes a memorable sight in late summer. Despite being a wild grass with a rather lax habit, planted en masse they help to support each other. Interest is provided below by carpets of flowering thyme.

natural, but has, in fact, been planted with thousands of native flowers and grasses. A serpentine path has been cut through it, and on a hot summer's day it is an idyllic spot to rest – children also love to run along it.

The garden's *pièce de résistance* is the Round Garden. Here, Pamela has made concentric beds around a central circle, which are navigated by gravel paths. In summer, this space is alive with the sound of bees and the flitting of butterflies as they descend upon the nectar-rich plants, which include many herbs. Pink, lavender, violet, magenta and crimson tones dominate in this striking planting scheme. Among the key plants are the pom-pom heads of allium, and in midsummer the beds are a haze of pink, thanks to squirrel tail grass, *Hordeum jubatum*, its gently flushed, silky seed heads swaying gently in the breeze.

Throughout the garden, wildlife habitats are displayed unashamedly and are valuable for their sculptural form. A circular ring of logs will rot down slowly and provide shelter for beetles, while the amusingly named 'habitat seat' is a bench made from coppiced ash that has been peppered with holes to make hiding places for insects.

Despite being completely man-made, the garden never feels contrived, and it blends effortlessly into its natural environment. Through the careful selection of natural materials, as well as native and ornamental plants, the designer, with her great eye for colour, has created a unique garden that is the perfect inspiration for anyone wishing to attract wildlife.

▲ Like a giant bicycle wheel, the Round Garden has five spoke-like paths leading to its centre. In midsummer, the structure disappears under a blaze of flowering shrubs and perennials, such as geraniums, knautia and evening primrose, which knit together with masses of grasses.

▼ In this detail from the Round Garden, the bright red heads of *Allium sphaerocephalum* stand proudly above a tapestry of pastel-toned perennials and foliage plants. A large number of these bulbs have been planted to help unify the space visually and also to make a dramatic statement.

◄ Over 30 meadow species have been planted in an idyllic meadow alive with wildlife flitting from flower to flower. Orchids, ragged robin and birdsfoot trefoil thrive to create a floral carpet that is easily explored by following the serpentine path cut through it.

▲ A pond can became an important oasis for wildlife if carefully planned. Incorporate shallow edges or rocks for creatures to perch on or drink from, and plant with a rich selection of leafy and flowering perennials that will provide food and shelter.

▼ Shrubs and trees make a closely knit boundary, ideal for supporting birds. The natural planting in the foreground encourages foraging insects and mammals. The largely green display is broken occasionally by blood-red imperata grass and angel's fishing rod.

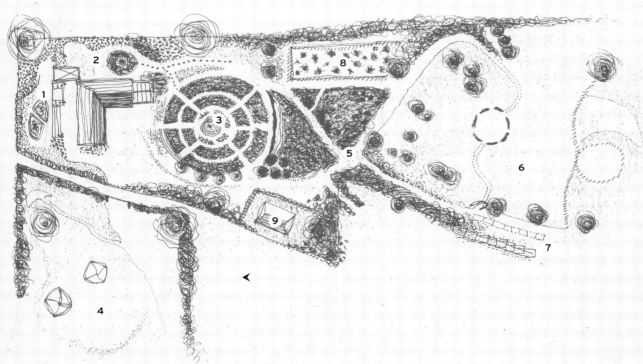

◄ **Sticky Wicket**

1 Frog Garden
2 Bird Garden
3 Round Garden
4 Davey Meadow
5 White Garden
6 New Hay Meadow
7 Vegetable Garden
8 Hen Run
9 The Barn

Meadows and Lawns

Running through a field with grasses and wild flowers towering above is a memory from childhood shared by many who grew up in the countryside. Whether the field had a predominance of poppies, wild orchids or cow parsley, this wild and natural planting scheme would have had a thriving population of wildlife, including dormice, shrews, insects, possibly even lizards and snakes. Today, transforming a part of the garden into a meadow has become popular, and the meadow's American cousin, the prairie, has inspired a completely new style of planting.

▓ Making a meadow

Perhaps surprisingly, a meadow is best created in a garden with a strong structural backbone. Allow it to flow unhindered across an expanse of garden, but define the area and contain it within hedges or walls or by using paths. Some boundaries, like a yew hedge, make the perfect backdrop, allowing subtle flower colours to stand out.

Most meadows will do best in a sunny spot – a requirement of many grasses is that they need plenty of light to thrive – but they will still do well in the dappled shade provided by trees, making sites such as orchards ideal. Garden soil is often too fertile for making a meadow; under normal conditions, strong-growing grasses would quickly crowd out the wild flowers. It is best to neglect the soil for a year or so before planting, and on no account apply any fertilizer.

Devise a planting scheme choosing from native plants that will thrive in your soil. It could be based on one type of flower, or on the combined colours of several grown together. Whether you like pastel shades or hot colours, break up the harmony of the display by planting bulbs in contrasting colours to provide seasonal highlights. Alternatively, there are many seed companies that sell mixes of grasses and wild flowers, which can be simply scattered onto bare soil. These are often custom-made

for a specific purpose, which could include attracting butterflies, providing a long season of interest or peaking in spring. A typical mix may be composed of around 30 different grasses and flowers.

Unlike a natural meadow, a garden meadow needs to be cared for, and it is not an ideal choice if you are short of time. Apart from the initial work, the display needs cutting down once a year, which keeps the fine, desirable grasses healthy and prevents coarse, weed grasses from invading and getting a foothold. This is usually carried out between midsummer and late autumn, and it is hard work because the plants will be tall and strong.

▨ Prairie planting

Taking its inspiration from the Great Plains that once covered 20 per cent of North America, prairie planting is the American equivalent of a meadow garden. It consists of ornamental grasses, such as stipa, pennisetum and miscanthus, which are planted in bold swathes and broken up by patches of colour from perennials, such as echinacea, rudbeckia, helianthemum and *Verbena bonariensis*. This style of planting is a real delight to the senses; the grasses make a wonderful swishing sound in the wind, and you cannot help but brush your hands through the silky flower heads of the grasses. Although the perennial flowers used in prairie planting are not native to the UK, they are loved by our indigenous wildlife. The buzz of activity from bees, hoverflies and butterflies on a summer's day is truly extraordinary.

In recent years, prairie planting has become increasingly popular in the UK. This is partly because it is fairly low maintenance, compared to looking after traditional herbaceous borders. There is hardly any staking required, and rather than chopping back plants in early autumn, the grasses and spent flowerheads are left for their bold, skeletal shapes, which provide so much interest

▲ A natural meadow basking in the golden light of late summer is the epitome of the rural idyll. Landscapes like this provide the inspiration for man-made meadows in a garden location.

▲ A cultivated lawn makes a soft and durable surface to walk on, but a natural look has been achieved here by allowing a rectangular patch of grass, enclosed on three sides by a hedge, to reach full height alongside wild flowers.

▶ Trees grown closely together are a striking sight, but it is possible to boost the interest at ground level by sowing meadow flowers and allowing wild grasses to gain a foothold. The neatly maintained hedges bordering the meadow will also provide shelter for many creatures over the winter.

◀ A doorway cut through a formal hedge that encloses this space, beckons the visitor to follow a simple stepping stone path. The verdant meadow is entered after passing through an equally informal part of the garden, but where the emphasis is on cultivated plants.

over winter, especially when dusted with frost. Prairie plantings are at their most effective when covering large areas, but do not let a lack of space put you off. If you have an urban garden and can spare a border only a few metres long, you can successfully create a condensed version.

Apart from adorning gardens in the UK and Europe, in an ironic twist, prairie planting is being promoted in the US, where natural prairies now cover roughly as little as one per cent of the area that they did originally. Conservationists believe that interest from gardeners will bolster attempts to stop the further decline of these irreplaceable natural environments.

Wild flower lawns

While it will not have the biodiversity of a meadow, a traditional lawn can still be turned into a feature that is teeming with life. To convert a verdant blanket into a wild flower lawn, simply stop fertilizing, raise the cutting height on your lawnmower and plant ready-grown wild flower plugs in small, natural-looking groups. Alternatively, buy rolls of turf that have been grown with wild flower seeds and a mixture of native and non-native grasses. It can be laid like traditional turf on levelled but poor soil.

Let the grass grow

Neatly clipped ornamental lawns make a great surface for ball games, but they have absolutely no value as a habitat for wildlife. However, taking inspiration from the uncultivated strips left by many farmers around their fields, it is possible to boost a lawn's potential as a home for a teeming mass of wildlife. Let the grass grow in unhindered bands along the edge of your lawn or allow it to prosper among trees in an orchard, where it will be used by butterflies, lacewings and foraging beetles, and become a place for ladybirds to overwinter. While the flowerheads of some grasses are pretty, you can improve the display in areas of long grass by planting spring bulbs and wild flowers. Either spread seed or buy ready-grown plugs, which will root and quickly grow away.

◀ By leaving clearly defined areas of lawn to grow naturally, the designer has added an informal structure to the garden, which disappears when the long grass is cut later in the year. This square patch of unmown lawn also changes the dynamics of the garden, providing the visitor with a choice of routes to reach the gates of the walled garden.

Water Gardens

Without water, the number of wild visitors to your garden will be limited. Frogs, toads, newts, dragonflies and damselflies are found in great numbers on or under water, while many birds and mammals like to drink from the edges of ponds, pools and streams.

Natural-looking water gardens are the most conducive to wildlife, and it is a good idea to study as many examples of ponds as you can – in the wild, in gardens and in books – to make sure that you create one that will look attractive in the garden as well as offering all the benefits that you require. Plants that grow in natural bogs do best in waterlogged soil, while there is a rich combination of plants that prefer to be in the water, from deep water aquatics to those with leaves that float on the surface and many more that root at the water's edge.

If you are starting from scratch, make your water feature as large as possible – once planted, they often appear to shrink, and sometimes the water's surface in a smallish pond is barely visible through the greenery. Make your plant choice from a mixture of mainly native plants to attract wildlife, and add flowers from other countries to make the space more appealing. A naturalistic planting scheme will provide a wild look in keeping with rural gardens. However, in a small, urban space, there is a small margin for error between creating a wildlife haven and making a smelly, messy corner that looks neglected and unwelcoming to any creature.

Natural swimming ponds

With climate change predictions, our summers will become warmer, and taking a dip in crystal clear water to cool off will become ever more desirable. But is a bright blue swimming pool that relies on a cocktail of chemicals really what you want? A natural swimming pond – a hybrid of a pond and a swimming pool – looks like a pond, is perfect for growing all the native and ornamental aquatic plants found in traditional ponds, but has the added benefit of clean water that you can swim in. The water is kept clean by plants growing around the edges of the pond that are chosen specially to help to purify it, while a small, submerged pump keeps the water moving. A skimming device can also be added to remove dead leaves and other surface debris.

Although relatively new to this country, swimming ponds have been popular in Europe for a long time and are a feature of many gardens in Germany and Italy. They are perfect in a large, rural garden, where they can be designed to look like a natural pool and may also enjoy a beautiful vista. But even in a town garden, swimming ponds as small as 7 x 5m (23 x 16ft) can make ideal plunge pools for escaping the heat of the city.

◄ You do not have to forsake good design when creating a natural-looking wildlife pond. Here, damp-loving plants, such as yellow irises, have been mixed with foliage plants to create a dense display that boasts texture and structure. A cleverly placed urn brings extra interest to the scene.

▼ Combining the function of a swimming pool with the aesthetics of a pond, a swimming pond is a place for humans to exercise and have fun, and wildlife to drink or take shelter. Unlike a swimming pool, it relies on natural methods, not harmful chemicals, to keep the water clean.

Bog gardens

There may be a tendency to curse areas of the garden that are naturally waterlogged but, rather than admit defeat, you can easily transform a quagmire into a beautiful bog garden. There are many plants that will thrive with their roots in damp soil, including native plants, such as marsh marigolds, purple loosestrife, flag irises and snakeshead fritillaries. These can be mixed with ornamentals, such as astilbes, candelabra primroses and arum lilies. If you have the space, you could even plant a group of huge-leaved *Gunnera manicata*. By removing some of the lower stems, you could make space for a path that would be magical to walk through when the sun is shining and light flickers through the leaves above.

Bog gardens tend to be built from scratch, although it is possible to convert an existing pond. Usually, they are positioned close to a pond, a natural neighbour, to extend the variety of moisture-loving plants that can be grown. Always position the bog garden slightly lower than the pond to prevent nutrients from the soil running into the water, which would encourage surface-covering weeds or algae to grow. It will be necessary to install raised paths or stepping stones if you need to cross the bog garden, as well as allowing access for maintenance.

Pools/ponds and lakes

A well-designed wildlife pond can be a shimmering oasis full of beautiful flowers and foliage, and a magnet to all kinds of creatures, including water boatmen, dragonflies,

◄ Although this looks like a natural pool, the submerged wooden jetty and buildings, reflected in the still waters, reveal that it is a man-made swimming pond.

▼ Rods of living willow have been bent and tied together to create an informal, natural archway to this shallow pool. Grass edges are easier on the eye than stone, and blend easily into their surroundings.

▲ Lengths of timber can easily be supported on stocky stilts to make a raised path that winds its way across a large pond. This structure is the perfect platform for seeing the many pond plants at close quarters and observing the wildlife in and around the pool.

◄ Grey weathered stepping stones, raised on supports to sit just above the surface of the water, make an interesting path across a pond, especially if the stones are offset from each other in an interesting pattern.

► Simple wooden bridges are quick and easy to construct, and are a classic feature in a rural water garden, allowing you to cross a small stream or venture onto an island. Birds and dragonflies love to perch on the railings.

bottle (*Nuphar lutea*) and marginals, which provide most of the colour. Try water canna (*Canna* 'Erebus'), golden Japanese rush (*Acorus gramineus* 'Ogon'), Bowles' golden grass (*Carex elata* 'Aurea') and arum lily (*Zantedeschia aethiopica* 'Crowborough').

Paths and bridges

Unless you do not mind getting your feet wet, it is necessary to make wet areas navigable by constructing sound hard surfaces to walk on. Not only will this help to keep your feet dry, but it will enable you to walk among the plants and flowers of the water garden and see any visiting wildlife at close range. Install decking boardwalks around lakes or large ponds, and add jetties – perfect as a viewing platform, if you fancy a spot of fishing or just want to sit and dip your toes in the water. Raised decking paths are also an excellent way to cross a bog garden – if the garden is large, devise a network of paths to cross the wet land, which will open up different views and give you plenty of hard ground to work from when planting new specimens or maintaining plants.

Natural or man-made streams can be married with the garden, rather than just being a watery barrier, by making them passable. You can achieve this very simply with stepping stones. For a natural look, go for large flat stones that have plenty of space for the largest feet, or for a contemporary look, try cubes of stone, such as granite. Slabs of stone can also look good when raised on plinths in water. This particularly suits formal water gardens, found in chic city spaces that are in close proximity to the house. Here, the colour, shape or texture of the stone reflects similar materials used indoors.

If using pieces of stone, avoid anything too highly polished or with a very smooth surface because getting across the stream will become a risky business, rather than a delight. For wider streams, try a stone or wooden bridge, or even a jungle-style rope bridge, which makes crossing water lots of fun for children.

frogs and toads. They are ideal for all but tiny gardens, and although they blend most comfortably into a rural garden due to their wild look, many fine examples have been built in urban locations. The only rule of thumb is to make your wildlife pond look as if nature had intended it to be there. To achieve this, position the pond where two-thirds of it will receive full sunlight. This will ensure that plants quickly romp away, providing seeds, nectar and places to hide for insects, birds and mammals. In addition, make sure that the pond liner is totally concealed

When designing the pond, go for an irregular shape, and plan it with shallow, sloping sides that will attract birds and hedgehogs to drink. Always make it bigger than you think you will need, because when plants begin to grow, it will appear much smaller. To make a pond that is buzzing with life, stock it mainly with native plants that are loved by indigenous wildlife, but add a few exotic plants for extra flower colour. Plants worth trying include: submerged oxygenators, such as water buttercup (*Ranunculus aquatilis*) and water violet (*Hottonia palustris*); floating plants, like water lilies and water hawthorn (*Aponogeton distachyos*); deep water aquatics, such as brandy

Flower Gardens

During the warm months of summer, nothing is more pleasant than reclining on a comfortable chair and sipping a cool drink. For you, all of the hard work put into planting and maintaining a garden culminates in a few glorious months when your garden will be at its best. But, while you can take the weight off your feet, elsewhere there should be a buzz of activity – bees, hoverflies, hornets, butterflies, hummingbird hawkmoths and many flying beetles should be visiting the flowers at a frenetic pace.

If your garden is not host to such hustle and bustle, then it may be time to think carefully about your planting schemes and add some plants that are rich in nectar. Native plants are always going to be the most popular with local wildlife but, visually, most of them lack the punch of many of our well-loved garden plants that have been specifically bred to produce bigger, better or more colourful flowers.

The flowers of native plants are often small and subtle, with their foliage lacking in vigour – in the wild, the leaves are often hidden by grass or other plants. Rather than slavishly planting beds and borders with these shy and retiring plants, it is a good idea to grow them with ornamental perennials, small trees and shrubs to add impact, colour and structure throughout the year.

It is also possible to achieve a natural look by using only ornamental forms of native plants. These are better behaved than their wild cousins, offer more decorative value and are also popular with wildlife. For instance, rather than growing wild geraniums, which can often make rather scrappy plants, grow something more robust, but with similar flowers such as *Geranium* 'Johnson's Blue'. Elsewhere, try an attractive variety of *Buddleia davidii*, a plant that has become naturalized in many parts of the UK, and instead of planting *Clematis vitalba*, the scrambling climber seen in hedgerows, use a well-behaved, small-flowered ornamental variety.

As with any border, design it with a colour scheme in mind, and use plants to give interest from spring into winter, when the seed heads of many flowers will provide skeletal interest over the cold months ahead. Since most native wild flowers have subtle colours, a pastel scheme using harmonious colours in either pinks and purples or yellows and whites would work well.

◀ This tonal scheme of complementary shades of red, white and pink makes a pretty and harmonious country border. The large, open flowers, spikes, buds and sprays of blooms have been placed together skilfully in a layered display.

▶ Weathered pieces of driftwood, full of character, have been bolted together loosely to make a fence in a seaside garden, although it barely contains the mix of broom, sea kale and valerian, which are ideal plants for a windswept, coastal position.

◄ Part of a large lawn has been left unmown to create an oasis for wildlife. The dense undergrowth makes the perfect hunting ground for many insects and mammals. In addition, pollinating insects will flit between the flowers, while the wiry stems of the grasses will be used by beneficial insects to overwinter.

▼ Bushy perennials with a profusion of long stems that grow closely together, such as this white-flowered *Gaura lindheimeri*, will soon attract the attention of spiders. Their webs, woven among the slender stems, will trap less beneficial insects, such as flies.

Wildlife habitats/hibernation boxes

Flick through the pages of a wildlife gardening brochure and you will find an amazing number of nesting boxes for insects, as well as the more predictable bird boxes and boxes for mammals, like hedgehogs. The brochure will probably also include bee houses, ladybird houses, lacewing chambers, mason bee nests and butterfly houses. Insect boxes come in many shapes and sizes, from simple tubes to open-fronted frames crammed with pieces of garden cane, which provide a place for insects to hibernate. In the spring, many of these insects will emerge with a healthy appetite for your aphids and other garden pests.

Unless you want to fill your garden with all manner of bug boxes, which would be great for wildlife but may not look that attractive, go for a box that has a selection of different-sized nooks and crannies, which should provide homes for a range of insects. Among the best boxes are those filled with plant stems, such as buddleia, cow parsley, teasel and elder. Lots of creatures will nest in here, including solitary bees. These boxes are much better for the environment because they can be filled with material gathered in your own garden.

Mount boxes on a tree, wall or the outside of a shed. Some creatures are particularly fussy about the location of their box: ladybirds, for instance, like a north-facing position so they are not woken up too early in the spring when there are very few aphids to eat.

Quick flowers

If you want to fill your garden with quick colour and attract bees, butterflies and other pollinating insects at the same time, then try growing some hardy annuals – the ultimate in no-fuss plants. Sunflowers, mallow, cosmidium and nasturtium are all easy to grow and can be sown directly on well-prepared soil, where they will flower just a few months later. To thrive, all they need is a sunny spot. Hardy annuals can be used to fill gaps in a border or between shrubs, or to create huge swathes of colour that simply buzz with life. There are many different varieties, and the flowers are good to combine, mixing colours or even leaf

texture. Among the best flowers are bright orange Californian poppies, which contrast well with powder-blue love-in-a-mist or complement the narrow blades and dainty seed head of quaking grass, *Briza maxima*.

Many perennials grow just as easily from seed, but have a more permanent place in the garden, while some self-seed so freely you will never be without them. *Erigeron karvinskianus*, with its tiny white-fading-to-pink daisies, for example, is essential in a natural garden, and will seed itself freely in gaps in paving and stone walls. Thyme seeds can also be sown in the cracks to add extra colour and fragrance, and to attract insects with its nectar.

Green roofs

We tend to think of making gardens in the soil at the back and front of our houses, but in recent years landscape designers have found that many flowering plants will thrive when grown on the roof of houses or garden buildings, such as sheds, dog kennels, bird tables and chicken coops.

Green roofs are being installed in ever-increasing numbers in the UK, and modern architects, concerned about the environment, are adding them to new buildings as eco-friendly alternatives to traditional roofing materials. They have been popular in Germany, Sweden and the US for many years, and since 2000, over 30 million square metres (11½ square miles) of green roof have been laid.

To be suitable, roofs need to be fitted with a frame and be able to take the weight of plants and the substrate they grow in. If you are planning on installing a green roof on your home, it is essential to employ a structural engineer to check its weight-bearing load. Specialist companies will advise on the complete installation process.

Many plants can be used to make a green roof. Typically, it will consist of different varieties of sedum, which are highly resistant to drought, provide year-round colour, need very little attention and have flowers that are attractive to butterflies. Native wild flower varieties can be sown among the sedums. To increase the roof's attractiveness to wildlife, add small stones or even pieces of bark stripped from old logs to make habitats for insects.

▶ **Clockwise from top left:** the gaps provided by upturned roofing tiles from a reclamation yard will soon be used as a shelter by garden wildlife; provide plenty of pollinating plants to attract bees and hoverflies; fill a wooden frame with pieces of bamboo to make a simple bug box; a green roof makes an attractive surface on many garden structures; mount bug boxes out of direct sun to make sure that they are used regularly by insects; cone flowers are striking plants for a prairie-style border and are loved by butterflies; create boundaries in the garden by recycling old stems, rather than buying new timber; a combination of different-sized nooks and crannies will appeal to a wide range of creatures; disguise or provide some shelter for insect boxes to prevent predators from eating garden allies.

NATURAL

NIJMEGEN
THE NETHERLANDS

CASE STUDY #8

DESIGNERS
WIM KANBIER

In Tune With Nature

A wildlife garden needs careful planning or the result can be disastrous. When gardening in tune with nature and using native plants that are less restrained than their ornamental cousins, you may be tempted to ignore basic design principles. Look at some wildlife gardens and you will find all sorts of random plant groupings growing cheek by jowl; this makes no difference to the wild creatures, but is not particularly pleasing to the human eye.

Here, at the Oase garden, near the town of Nijmegen in the Netherlands, the designers have established a wildlife sanctuary that looks good and attracts huge numbers of insects, birds, mammals and pond-loving creatures. Appropriately, it is also home to Stichting Oase (Oasis Foundation), the leading wildlife gardening group in the Netherlands.

The garden has been constructed on a roughly linear site in the heart of the countryside and is enclosed on all sides by mature deciduous trees. A series of waterways runs down the length of the garden, starting as a narrow canal before widening to a stream that can be crossed at various points by simple wooden bridges. The stream ends at a large, tranquil pool edged by reeds and wild flowers.

On the far bank of the pond sits a garden building that is perfectly at ease with its environment. This small white pavilion, designed in the shape of a leaf, was built to be a meditative space, while housing regular art and educational exhibitions. The designers created the structure using sustainable building techniques: the exterior walls are built from a mixture of earth and straw, covered with a breathable lime finish; the frame is unseasoned timber; and inside, earth blocks have been used to form partitions. The building is topped by a living, green roof that provides shelter and food for numerous insects, as well as birds looking for a tasty snack.

Various different paths wind around the garden, providing exciting routes for visitors and making the garden an interesting place to explore. Some paths cut through the low-growing meadow that is alive with the

◄ New bricks take many years to look weathered, but these reclaimed ones, used to make a dry stone wall and flight of steps, have a wonderful patina. The gaps between the bricks will become home to a number of beneficial creatures and also support a variety of self-seeded plants.

▼ The edges of a meandering stream wash gently up against a watery meadow, which is populated by many wild flowers and grasses. Although these areas need a helping hand at the start, by planting small plants or sowing seeds, wild species will naturally take hold after time.

▲ An unusual sloping green roof in the shape of a leaf sits on top of a white garden building, which has been made out of environmentally friendly materials. The structure looks magical in this natural setting dominated by water features, such as this large pond planted with native species.

◄ Simple bistro furniture is perfectly in keeping with this low-key garden. Placed on a quiet patio, it is perfect for relaxing while observing the wildlife visiting the pond. Extra seating made from old tiles and reclaimed paving slabs has been built into the wall.

▲ Plants have been allowed to self-seed freely around the garden, which gives the space an informal, unplanned feel. Although the designers have encouraged a relaxed display, plants will still need removing from time to time to prevent strong, fast-growing varieties from dominating.

▶ In this wildlife garden, bridges are simple and rustic, ensuring they marry perfectly with the naturalistic planting scheme, rather than becoming a dominant feature that jars with the surroundings. Eventually, this bridge, which spans a shallow section of the stream, will be completely enveloped by the growth of water-loving plants.

sight and sound of bees and butterflies in the summer, while others immerse the visitor among taller-growing natives, such as *Tragopogon porrifolius*, or purple salsify, which has pinky-blue flowers and edible roots. The colours in the garden are never harsh, but soft and pretty, from a limited palette of white, pink, blue and yellow. Among the plants used to great effect are the damp-loving spotted orchid (*Dactylorhiza maculate*), meadow cranesbill (*Geranium pratense*) and yellow verbascum (*Verbascum thapsus*), whose spikes of yellow are like huge exclamation marks among low-level planting.

The garden is a blueprint for sustainability and is run on environmental and organic principles. Chemicals are never used to control pests, diseases or weeds, and reclaimed materials have been used to create many of the garden features. For example, stacks of roofing tiles form a textured edging to a bed, while an assortment of old bricks, tiles and slabs has been arranged to make a distinctive curved wall. Not only does this add a sense of structure to the natural space, but every nook and cranny provides shelter or a place to hibernate for ladybirds, lacewings, spiders and other beneficial creatures.

This is a wonderful example of a garden where the hand of man has almost matched nature at creating something beautiful – it is a garden to enjoy at leisure, where the frenetic pace of modern life can be left behind.

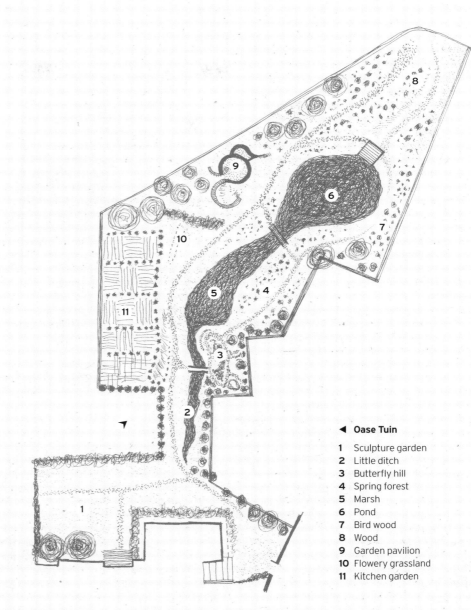

◄ **Oase Tuin**

1 Sculpture garden
2 Little ditch
3 Butterfly hill
4 Spring forest
5 Marsh
6 Pond
7 Bird wood
8 Wood
9 Garden pavilion
10 Flowery grassland
11 Kitchen garden

► Due to the narrow width of this path, the dense planting at ground level and on top of the sloping brick retaining walls dwarfs those who walk along the passageway and adds a touch of mystery.

◄ Nothing is more exciting than discovering a secret area or room when walking around a garden. Here, a well-planted path, full of towering native plants, gives way to reveal a paved seating area on the banks of a stream.

► Perched like a nest in the boughs of a majestic tree, this wooden house is a sturdy and safe tree-top hideaway. Shed of its leaves, the deciduous tree reveals its secret, but when the buds burst and clothe the branches in emerald green leaves, the foliage forms a cloak to conceal its inhabitants.

Family

||||| Sharing your garden with children does not mean you have to abandon every ambition to have a well-planned, beautiful space. But you may just have to make compromises – on the way the garden looks, what you grow and the kind of features you include. Although this would fill some gardeners with horror, it is not necessarily painful. Look at it as a short-term fix: once the children have flown the nest, the garden will be yours again. To benefit children, a garden needs to be a stimulating place, an arena where they can discover the joys of gardening and nurture a love of wildlife. These simple interests will, with luck, stay with them throughout their lives. There should also be places to play, such as sandpits and tree houses, dens for adventures and a little patch of soil where they can grow plants from seed. Safety is a major issue with family gardens, and the advice is usually to fill in ponds, to make sure there are no hard, sharp edges where children can hurt themselves and to avoid planting anything with poisonous leaves, berries, flowers, roots or bulbs. You must do as you see fit, taking precautions to make the garden a safer place, but more often than not, common sense and a watchful eye will suffice.

▼ Simple plastic hoops set in a spiral arrangement create a colourful magical tunnel that excites and invites play.

Family Gardens

Most, but not all, gardens are family gardens; if they are not now, they probably would have been at some time. The garden is in a constant state of evolution. That can be over a day-and-night cycle or an annual cycle, but also over generations. Our notion of the family garden really centres on one thing: children and youngsters. A number of images flood through our minds when you say these words: girls in summer dresses on tricycles, boys playing football, sandpits, swings and slides, and sunflowers. Idyllic summer memories are what our subconscious conjures up. And the great thing about these memories is that they are true. There is a growing awareness of how gardens can be many different things to many different people, and for children a garden is primarily a haven. This is one of the reasons that socially aware architects in Eastern Europe during the 1920s and 1930s were eager to move

families out of tenements and flats into healthy spaces that could be enjoyed by young and old alike.

When you consider creating a family garden, there are many wishes and desires to take into account. Although sometimes these can seem to conflict, with good planning it is possible to create a garden that is relevant to every member of the household, whatever their age, and also a garden that evolves with the family.

For parents and guardians, there is a new imperative when planning and designing gardens that will be used by children. An emphasis must be placed on environmental concerns so that the garden becomes a teaching aid and, indeed, a life aid. Home is the first port of call when it comes to education, and the garden is an invaluable classroom. This should not imply stern lectures or austerity but, instead, focus on being creative and having

◀ These beautifully formed thick bamboo canes create a fantastic grid in which children can run around and play. A different play area that is easy to construct and fabulous if set in the garden amongst living bamboos.

◀ When gathered together, a jumble of traffic, advertising and for sale signs becomes a fascinating contemporary hideaway. Haphazard by nature, this patchwork-quilt collage intrigues and invigorates.

▶ These huge red bouncy balls are a fun focal point in a garden for children. The strong solid red spheres contrast well with the single colour palette of green trees and shrubs.

fun. By showing youngsters the abundance of produce that can be garnered from even the smallest of plots, by demonstrating how to reuse and recycle by developing compost heaps and placing equal emphasis on growing from seeds and cuttings and on using recycled materials, young minds will be expanded and open to a new way of green living.

There is also an extra ingredient when it comes to creating a garden to entice children. It is something that can be hard to define but you know it when you see it – a sense of magic. Children love exploring and playing make-believe. Encouraging children to play, keeping them away from computer games and allowing them to explore on their own or with their friends is a gift for life. Planning a garden that contains surprises, surreal elements and temporary features, a garden that can sometimes be silly,

adventurous or even bonkers, creates the association of fun and adventure being outside. This can be as simple as an Easter egg hunt, when the garden is transformed into an enchanted place.

What do children like? Drama and colour, and they love excitement. What do they dislike? Things they have to be careful of, places they are not allowed to go. What are they fascinated by? Seeds growing into food, pumpkins, watercress on blotting paper, beans going up bamboo canes, popping peas in pods, a tortoise crawling slowly up and down its domain, frogs and frogspawn. They love helping Granddad with the vegetable plot and plants they can play with – bits of bamboo they can break off and use as canes to battle their way through subtropical jungles. They like drama – plants that grow up and up and up, alliums that they can chart from bulbs in the spring to exploding firework flowers. They love trees to climb and mounds to roll on. They love technology – bright twinkly lights from fibre optics or fairy lights. They love stepping stones and gushes of water. Children like adventure. They love the idea of pitching a tent in the garden, having sleepovers with friends, wigwams made on a summer's day through criss-cross poles draped with bed sheets. They love making tree houses and playing in Wendy houses. They love forts and sandpits – anything that is different, anything that seems to be their territory that keeps adults out. They like pirate ships, their own world of make-believe. As they grow up, they like space to run around, for football, for games of tennis, areas for space hoppers, paths for tricycles and bicycles, ramps that work – space for energy.

And how does all of this fit into a stylish outdoor garden? By design. You do not just plan sophisticated decks and outdoor dining rooms with subdued elegant lighting. You plan and build in features for children from the very start. You accept the fact that youngsters need a lawn for football games, and maybe you suspend your high-maintenance plans. You allow for daisies and dandelions. Let the garden live a little. Encourage creepy crawlies, build hedgehog hotels, set nesting boxes. With thought and planning you can make features and dens that will age gracefully with the garden, and when your children are grown up, they will point out to their children where they used to play in grandparents' garden. Allow an array of gaudy invaders such as gnomes, fairies, Edward Scissorhands topiary – everything that celebrates young lives in a society where so much encourages kids to grow up too fast. Your garden is your children's gateway to nature and in it they will learn skills and crafts that will stay with them for the rest of their lives.

Hard landscaping

One of the first factors you will want to consider when designing the family garden is the hard landscaping. Surfaces are important aesthetically as well as practically, but if you set out what you need from a practical viewpoint first, you will be looking at the right materials as you create the visual impact you prefer.

If your children are very young, their little feet cannot take too much of a challenge. Gravel can be difficult to walk on and, unless it is a very forgiving pea shingle, will hurt them when they fall over. Brick or stone surfaces are easier to walk or cycle on, but be wary of how slippery stone can be in wet weather. Remember, too, that brick and stone are hard to fall on. Decking, on the other hand, is softer to walk on, and fall on, and provided it is properly treated, will not get too slippery in winter.

Other surfaces available now are resin-bonded stone and rubber matting, often seen in playgrounds. These surfaces are great for pathways, too, and can be used to create a sense of fun, using different colours. Aside from hard paths, you may want to plan in some pathways made of bark mulch. These can go through planted areas to give a wild look. Imagine what it must feel like from a child's eye-view to walk through a border with shrubs, ferns and tree ferns.

The structure of your garden should also be based on the age of your children. If they are under five years old, you will want their play area and tricycle track near the house and preferably visible from at least the kitchen window. If you want to have a patio area for adults that is

▲ The designer of this garden has incorporated a small football field into a very organized plot, allowing for strong controlled statements as well as play.

◀ In a garden created with indestructible materials, children can enjoy their space hoppers without undue restraint.

◄ In an urban garden, a hideaway has been created for a tiny daughter with a princess fixation. This treehouse without the tree is just two steps from the garden and comes complete with its own stylish deck.

used after the children go to bed, or even while they play, try using different surfaces for the 'bike track' and the adults area. You will be surprised at how well they will stick to it – children love clear boundaries!

As they grow older, children will want more mystery attached to garden play and, at this stage, you may be glad to see them disappear into the depths of the garden for an hour. This is when you can move their area further down the garden. They will want structures and hideaways, but in terms of your original hard landscaping, it may be helpful to have thought about a smaller patio area where they can use old garden furniture for their picnics, or work on their seed-sowing projects, or just make mud pies.

A good family garden has to be well thought out in advance, so look at the chapter on planning, research all the surfaces available and try to think ahead. You will be glad you invested time in these things at the beginning.

Built structures

Another factor to think about is garden structures, the purpose they will serve and who will use them. If you decide that you would like a garden room to sit in on rainy days or to use as a painting studio, be aware that it will become filled with toys and children very quickly if you do not provide a structure for your children, too. In fact, you can provide all sorts of structures for children quite easily and cheaply in the garden; the more basic and rough and ready, the better – their imaginations will go crazy.

When buying a wooden playhouse for younger children, it is a good idea to take them with you to help choose one. They will love it for the sense of adventure, but watch them going in and out. Can they open the door by themselves? Are there steps that may need a rail? Most important, if you close the door, can they open it themselves from the inside? Although very young children will need supervision, if they can play in it themselves without help, they will love it (and you will not be jumping up to open a door every ten seconds!).

With older children, a tree house will go down a treat. People often have visions of their children plummeting to the ground from a great height when you mention a tree house, or they think that they do not have a large

▲ An intriguing contemporary garden room with both Georgian and industrial echoes acts as an inviting focus for children as it hovers over a gentle slope.

◄ This Wendy house with a thatched-style roof and built-in window boxes is the perfect getaway for little children to play house.

enough tree. A hut or tree house on a platform raised only 1.5m (5ft) above the ground can be made to feel as though it is in the sky. Add some mystery by hiding the base with shrubs, and if you do not have a tree – plant one! It can grow with your kids.

Other structures that children adore are tunnels, wigwams and little rooms or hideaways made of living plants. If you plan to make these structures each summer, you could create a little hazel coppice area for yourself in the garden, and you will be able to cut your own hazel rods. Imaginative structures that you have built yourself are always the most popular with children, and they can usually be left in place for a few years. Another versatile plant for playful building is willow, which roots very easily so you can create living structures that are simply trimmed each year. Perhaps you can create a tunnel that the children have to walk or crawl through to get to their own part of the garden, or even to a secret garden that is surrounded by a living screen.

Wigwams are easy to construct, too. If you have ever made a structure for beans or sweet peas, you can use the same principles here. Just get four or five bamboo poles, each about 2.5m (8ft) long, and space them evenly in a circle. Sink them into the ground about 30cm (12in) down if you can manage it and tie the top. Then you can cover it with a sheet, or if you want to leave it out in all weathers, use an old tent. Above all, use your imagination – your children do!

▲ A tepee nicely corralled in a garden and beautifully positioned in a rural location sets a quirky tone. The simple but dramatic shape invites discovery and becomes a gathering point. The scene is completed with a hammock.

◄ An extremely creative children's hideaway constructed with branches, twigs and vines that nestles comfortably within established shrubs and trees. A cosy area like a huge birds nest that cannot fail to inspire the most fabulous outdoor adventures.

► This raised platform comes complete with a straw hat. Its whole form seems to echo that of the surrounding landscape. It demands attention.

Family Activities

Building these garden structures is not just creating work for you. On the contrary, assembling them is an activity in which all the family can get involved. No doubt, at some point you will find yourself eating your lunch in a wigwam, too. It is important to have fun parts of the garden that you will enjoy as much as the children.

One addition seen more and more often in modern gardens is a trampoline. They are great fun and great exercise. It is possible to get them with a netting cage surround for safety, but children should always be supervised, as accident statistics are alarming. If you plan to have a trampoline in the garden, the design stage is, once again, a good time to think about the wider implications. Decide where you would like it to be. There are families who do nothing but move their enormous trampoline around all summer to mow underneath it and let the grass get a bit of light. Why not decide where you want it to live, and have that area surfaced with rubberized playground matting, for which you can get shock-absorbing bases. They come in green, too! Another aspect to consider is winter storage: will the trampoline remain outside or does it come apart so that it can be stored indoors? Will it blow over in strong winds? Find this out before you buy so that you can plan the garden and possible storage accordingly.

Another project that the children would certainly enjoy is planning and planting a maze of sweetcorn, sunflowers or a mixture of both. They can mark out the footprint of the maze they want on the ground, plant it up with you, and then watch as the plants grow and the maze takes shape.

Sandpits can provide great activity for younger children and, again, will need to be planned close to the house. A good cover is necessary to keep animals out. Get the children their own mini garden tools so they can learn to dig with a trowel and rake the sand. Your budding gardener will be all ready to do some gardening chores when they are old enough.

Paddling pools are enormous fun in summer and do not use a great deal of water but, again, constant supervision of your children is essential. If you empty the pool carefully, you can reuse the water on plants. The water is perfectly safe, provided that it has not been treated with chemicals, as it would be if it were a more permanent swimming pool.

Swings and other play equipment can also be great fun in the garden. If you do not have the space for a full standard set of play equipment, work with what you have. Sometimes the most modern play equipment cannot measure up to a simple wooden swing or, better still, an old tyre, hanging from the branch of a tree.

▲ A woven rope bridge linking platforms is suspended through a group of trees. Designed for fun, this obstacle course doesn't make for an easy journey but it certainly creates lots of laughter.

◄ Often it's the simple things that intrigue the most, and children love playing with sand.

▼ A small garden with integrated play things, including a swing, square lawn area and an outdoor dining room, is designed for family use.

◄ This garden of mystery and colour makes brave use of materials not normally found outdoors, and is pure delight for children. A place of fun and learning, this is a psychedelic fairytale brought to life.

▼ An idyllic Edwardian potting shed finished with the perfect tone of green, thatched roof and window box. The most traditional country planting of hollyhocks, foxgloves and roses complete the scene.

Water features

Water features in the garden can range from a dipping pond to a half-barrel for goldfish, or a bubbling fountain from which the water disappears. Just as adults are fascinated by the sound of running water, kids love to touch it. They like to get closer to it, feel it, play with it and get wet!

Safety is very important, and water features should always be sited where you can see them from the house. If you have young children, a covered reservoir of water with a pump can be used to create a water fountain or spray that disappears. You can really play around with this concept, even create a waterfall, and as long as there is not an open pool or pond into which children can fall, it will be perfectly safe.

As the family gets older, you can create a goldfish pond in a half-barrel, or if you have the space, create a lined garden pond in which all sorts of wildlife can thrive. Looking at fish and frogs in the pond, and watching the cycle of life from frogspawn to tadpoles to frogs is another exciting way for children to learn about nature. Again, at the planning stage think about where you would like to position the pond, weighing up the pros and cons of various locations. Placing it directly under a deciduous tree, for example, will create a lot of leaf-clearing work for you in the autumn. Even if your children are too young at the design stage, decide where you would like the pond to be, and perhaps plant up a pond-shaped bed until you are ready to install it.

Appropriate planting

The planting in your garden is the aspect of your design that you may find the trickiest, depending on your gardening experience. Look at how well nature does without us. If you give it a try, you will be surprised at how well you get on with planting. Ask your children what they would like in the garden. They might want a jungle, or a long grass meadow to play hide-and-seek in. They might want magical hidden areas or a forest. With plants it is possible to create all sorts of fun areas in the garden.

Try growing large-leaved, exotic-looking plants, such as bananas, hostas, fatsias, tithonias and hollyhocks. They give a giant jungle feeling, especially if you plant up a wide enough bed or border and put a little skinny path through the middle. To accentuate the giant scale of the plants you can be really clever and, before planting, create the line of your path by mounding the earth slightly higher on either side.

The magic forest is great fun, too. If you have the space to do so, plant one or two garden trees, say a birch and a cherry. Plant them far enough apart to give ample room for them to grow. Next, plant tree ferns underneath and between them, and plant the 'forest floor' with other ferns such as the maidenhair fern (children love them because they are so delicate) and the shuttlecock fern for drama. How about planting a contorted hazel at the edge of the forest for its twisted, creepy branches? You can fill up with some hostas and some tough plants like variegated ivy and comfrey.

Grow plants to catch children's attention, as well as delighting their senses, such as *Stachys lanata* (lamb's ears), which is soft and fuzzy, and heliotrope, which smells very sweet. Encourage them to smell flowers to discover if they are scented. Above all, encourage them to grow their own. Some flowers are foolproof for children to grow. The classic is the sunflower. It always amazes children when they see a huge 1.8m- (6ft-) tall sunflower in August, and recall the little seed they started in a yogurt pot at Easter!

If you wish to create a specific area for children, a living willow fence can be a wonderful boundary for defining the space. It makes the area feel more like a wild, hidden garden and is a softer barrier when it greens up. If you have a football area, this is a good screen to have alongside, as the willow withies are much cheaper to replace than a whole shrub that is continually beaten by a football.

There are some plants that are best avoided, such as laburnum, which is beautiful in early summer but has very poisonous seeds. Also, foxgloves and daturas are deadly if eaten, and even the best-behaved children sometimes put things in their mouth.

The plants in your garden can really make the difference and create fun and mystery, while teaching your children an appreciation of nature. Take them to the garden centre and see what catches their eye. Visit the garden often with them and let them pick flowers to put on the kitchen windowsill. Give your children a garden that delights them, and they will remind you of some of the magic in nature that you may have forgotten.

▼ A large dining table inside a tepee is suspended above a low-level seating area by four strong chains. When the meal is finished, the table can be lowered into the gap to extend the decking floor. It sits flush with the surface thanks to some stout stilts.

Home from Home

When fashion designers Wayne and Gerardine Hemingway moved into their country retreat in West Sussex, their plan for the 1.2-hectare (3-acre) garden was to turn it into a stimulating playground for children and adults. The couple, who are behind the Red or Dead clothing label, have perfectly realized their aim. The garden is crammed with adult-only spaces for entertaining and relaxing, while there are lots of exciting structures and places for adventure to entertain their four children.

The designers have let their imaginations run wild in their private space, which has resulted in some ingenious garden buildings. Perhaps the cleverest is a large tepee, a multifunctional structure used by the whole family. It is a den, a place to sleep and a sheltered, intimate outdoor dining room. During the day it can be used as an office, a wonderful place to concentrate and work creatively.

Made from reclaimed telegraph poles and clad with the same hardwearing waterproof fabric used to make sails, the tepee is built over two floors. Climb up the ladder and there are beds for the children, while below is a table suspended on robust wires. Cushions scattered around the table make this a relaxing place to enjoy a meal, and afterwards the plates can be cleared away and the table

lowered into the gap beneath. Once it sits flush with the floor, a mattress can then be placed over the top to increase the outdoor sleeping space.

Elsewhere, a play area has been overtly targeted at children. Massive poles have been used to create an elevated jungle walk, which is concealed by climbing plants and makes a brilliant place for playing hide-and-seek. The path leads to a large platform above a sizeable sandpit. The space above is accessed from a ladder, while a swing hangs from the sturdy joists of the structure. As the children get older, the sandpit area will be reclaimed by the adults and turned into an area for potting up plants.

This is the perfect garden for outdoor living: there is a large swimming pool with an outdoor kitchen alongside. A long table provides enough seating for almost 20 guests, and parties continue long into the night, illuminated by retro-style arched lights.

Beside the barbecue is a line of outdoor kitchen units that provide plenty of storage space, as well as concealing a fridge and hi-fi. To create unity within the dining and kitchen area, the Hemingways have covered the work surfaces with brown Zodiaq, which is also used to pave the floor. The material, which is 93 per cent quartz crystal,

◄ Hidden behind a tapestry of climbing plants, this fun garden tepee is a space for both adults and children. The rampant nature of the planting that conceals the structure is in complete contrast to the neatly clipped low hedging and restrained planting within it.

▲ The tepee is designed to extend the use of the garden. The upstairs of this two-level structure has a pair of welcoming beds, where youngsters can sleep while the adults enjoy a leisurely meal.

▼ More often seen on the deck of cruise liners, this shuffleboard court reveals much about the owners' great sense of humour and shows that a garden does not only have to be a place to play traditional sports and games.

FAMILY

WEST SUSSEX
ENGLAND

CASE STUDY #9 CONTINUED

DESIGNER
WAYNE HEMINGWAY

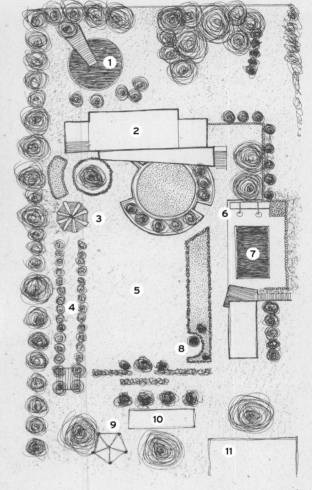

▲ The sword-like leaves of phormiums created a textured display alongside mahonia, with its spiky foliage, and tightly clipped shrubs. The dense planting scheme provides privacy for those using the brightly coloured hot tub.

▶ Even in an outdoor kitchen, storage is essential. Here, a line of kitchen units made from weatherproof materials provides plenty of space for cooking implements.

▼ To ensure privacy for the family and their guests, a wooden screen has been installed around the boundary. Trees and bamboos soften its hard lines, while helping to filter any harsh winds.

▲ **West Sussex**

1	Pond	**6**	Barbecue
2	House	**7**	Pool
3	Tepee	**8**	Hot Tub
4	Jungle Walk	**9**	Den
5	Lawn	**10**	Shed
		11	Tennis Court

is ideal in this much-used area, as it is extremely hard-wearing, non-porous and scratchproof.

Further down the garden is a shuffleboard court, built on the edge of the lawn, and a bright orange hot tub that is heated by a wood-burning stove. The emphasis is on making the most of the fresh air with plenty of simple, fun activities waiting to be enjoyed.

The planting in the garden gives an air of secrecy. The boundaries are blurred by bamboos and trees, which provide privacy and act as a windbreak. Climbers have been planted beneath vertical structures, such as the tepee and the posts that support the jungle walk, and provide a dense cloak of foliage.

Apart from perennials that give splashes of summer colour, the Hemingways have planted drifts of evergreen shrubs to give their garden form and texture. Bay trees, topiary and dwarf box hedging contrast well with the loose planting scheme and give a delicate sense of formality in an otherwise informal, lively family space.

◄ Wisteria winds its way up the chunky posts that hold a platform above the play area. Children love to play in dens like this, which are perfectly safe but hidden by a jungle-like display of foliage that gives them enough privacy to let their imaginations run wild.

◄ This huge family of elephants are beautifully formed in grass and bring massive drama and surprise to this space. They invite you to touch them and despite their size are elegant and graceful as are the living versions.

Lawns

In summer, there is nothing more sensual than walking barefoot across a lush lawn, but grass is not just grass, and it pays to think very carefully about how your lawn will be used and then choose suitable varieties.

For most family situations, a hard-wearing lawn containing a high proportion of dwarf perennial rye grass is ideal – not only does it look good, but it can also cope with being used as a football pitch or as a race track for bicycles. In most instances, the rye grass is mixed with other, finer grasses, such as slender creeping red fescue and brown top bent. You can either create the lawn from scratch by sowing seed or, if you want to go for instant impact, you can lay turf. For large projects, huge rolls of turf are available, which can cover up 20sq m (24sq yd) when unfurled.

Although a neatly manicured lawn will set off borders or other features, it will not inspire creative young minds. There are many ways, however, to make a verdant sward more exciting. Creating raised shapes or mounds is one way to give a horizontal plane of grass some oomph. It is

▼ Children will love racing along the closely mown path and up the grass mound to see who can reach the top first. Created by sowing grass on a mound of earth, this small hill provides an interesting focal point in a large swathe of lawn.

▶ Careful thought must be given to lawns in small town gardens, especially if the space is enclosed or gloomy. Ensure there is adequate storage for mowing machinery and use shade-tolerant grasses so the lawn retains its emerald colour.

► Walls and floors made of hardwood decking are strong, durable and easy to maintain, but they can be hard on the eye. To soften the look, the owner has provided an oasis of grass, which must be kept neatly clipped to retain the crisp, contemporary design.

◄ In a large garden, nothing inspires young minds more than a space of their own. Here, a sea of grass grows wild, and arranged among the jungle is a menagerie of topiary beasts.

▲ A rectangular stretch of lawn complements the clean lines of this garden. The space can be used by the whole family, and is ideal for picnics, large gatherings and also for ball sports, as long as tough strains of grass are used.

▼ To ensure a maze retains its appeal throughout the year, you will need to use evergreen hedging, such as yew, holly or cherry laurel. Deciduous species look good in summer, but once they have dropped their leaves, reaching the centre of the maze becomes a mere formality.

easy to make basic animal shapes, such as crocodiles, turtles or snakes out of topsoil, which, once compacted, can be laid with turf or sown with grass seed to create a unique play feature. To prevent the shape of the animal being lost under an unkempt coat of grass, make sure that you mow or clip it regularly.

Mazes are particularly exciting places for children, and there are several ways to transform your lawn into a labyrinth. In early autumn, plant spring-flowering bulbs in spirals or put a plan for a maze down on paper and replicate it in on the lawn. The easiest way to do this is to create your maze with a trickle of builders' sand and then lay out your bulbs over the top. Once you are happy with the design, the bulbs can be planted. Many bulbs will grow well in grass, including crocus and narcissus, but you should plant them densely otherwise the maze pattern will be indistinct.

Alternatively, if you have a meadow or do not mind allowing part of the lawn to grow a little longer, try cutting a maze with a lawnmower. In an area where the grass can grow several feet tall, allow your imagination to run wild and cut paths that will make a stimulating place for children to run and play hiding games.

While large lawns offer the greatest scope for creating an exciting place to play, there are ways of transforming even the tiniest corner of turf into a place for adventure. Allow patches to grow longer around trees or at the edges. In this way, you will not only provide a habitat for wildlife, but it will also give your children somewhere to create miniature imaginary worlds for their action figures, dolls or toy cars.

Planting

What do laburnum, sweet peas, lupins, foxgloves, yew and irises all have in common? Well, apart from being some of our most popular and well-loved garden plants, they are all poisonous. Some gardening books or experts will take an overly cautious approach and tell you to avoid altogether planting these, and hundreds more plants, in a family garden. However, then you would be missing out on some of the most fabulous plants you can grow. I am a great believer in educating children about plants and teaching them what they can or cannot pick. After all, if children do not come across these plants in their own garden, they will probably discover them in a friend's garden or even find them in the hedgerow.

If you do want to grow flowers, trees or shrubs that are poisonous but have a tendency to worry about your children, then you can always put the plants out of the way. For instance, perennials with poisonous parts could be grown further back in the border. Of course, it is

▲ Even the tiniest garden can be used to grow a range of ornamental and edible plants. Old wooden trays, which have been lined to prevent water leakages, make perfect containers for vegetables such as onions, which the children can pick when they have reached maturity.

▶ This rendered wall, which has been painted purple, makes an exciting backdrop for a vibrant display of perennials, such as multicoloured cannas. The exotic look of the garden has been assisted by the bug sculptures attached to the wall. These also help to break up the monotony of the vertical space.

common sense that you would not place poisonous plants in an area of the garden that you have specifically designed for children to play in.

Architectural plants, such as agaves, palms and cacti, are enjoying enormous popularity and are great for adding a dash of the exotic to the garden, but it pays to be careful about where you plant them. Some palms have rigid leaves covered with sharp barbs, while agaves have tough, sword-shaped leaves with a spiny tip – when these are grown in a pot on a much-used part of a deck or patio, or at the front of a bed, they can be particularly hazardous to toddlers, crawling babies and the ankles of anyone walking past. Put these plants where they can grow harmlessly and, please, avoid the horrible technique of harpooning a cork on the end of each spike!

Rather than having a planting plan that is completely set in stone, it is far better to be flexible and adapt what you grow, depending on the age of your children. When they are very young, include plants that they can touch, crush, stroke or brush their hands through. Include a mixture of grasses that have fluffy seed heads such as pennisetum and briza, herbs and shrubs with aromatic, textured or hairy leaves such as senecio, stachys and, especially, *Salvia argentea*, which has large leaves covered in a fine soft down.

As the children get older, the garden will almost certainly be used as a football pitch, so learn to relax and accept that some plants are not going to survive the rough and tumble. It is a good idea to plant some hardwearing shrubs around the playing area: euonymus, mahonia, cotoneaster and shrubby honeysuckle are all ideal and will quickly bounce back into shape if they are hit by a ball or trampled. They are not the most spectacular plants to grow in a garden, so consider them to be short-term tenants, providing you with colour and structure until the children move on to the next thing.

◀ Children can be inspired to garden from an early age by hiving off a patch of earth and putting it into their ownership. Give their patch identity by painting a storage shed bright colours and allow them to grow their favourite salads and vegetables in a series of small raised beds.

▲ While children are young and active, it makes sense to plant tough evergreens around the edges of a lawn because they are less likely to be damaged by balls or misplaced feet. More delicate plants, such as these colourful perennials, can be planted further away and at a higher level, out of harm's way.

◀ Youngsters will love having their own space in which to grow vegetables and flowers, whatever the end results, but ensure they feel ownership over their patch by painting features in primary colours and clearly marking them with their names.

▲ A small raised bed is all that is needed to grow a range of delicious crops, and it is the perfect tool for teaching children how to produce their own food. Small quantities of salads and many other types of crop can all be grown in this way, whether in a patio garden or other compact space, such as a balcony.

Get children growing

Many adults' earliest memory of gardening is tending a small patch of land as a child. This was often a corner of a vegetable bed or the end of a border, where, armed with a packet of seeds, trowel and a watering can, they could try raising plants for the first time. I was no different from many other children and had my own little patch when I was moved out of London to the countryside at the beginning of the Second World War. We were all encouraged to grow vegetables, which really helped me discover a passion for gardening.

With so many flowers and vegetables to choose from, it can be mind-boggling to decide what to let your children grow. To keep them interested, grow easy, fast-growing edible crops and flowers, and avoid anything that is slow to reach maturity – children will be fascinated by plants that change visibly from day to day.

There are many vegetables they could try. Radishes, carrots and cress are all easy and, after very little effort, your children will soon be picking their own produce to eat. Not only will this encourage them to garden, but they will develop a taste for fresh vegetables and learn about healthy eating. This is all-important today when there is so much concern about our children's diets and the amount of fast food that is eaten.

If they would like to grow flowers, choose annuals, which will grow fast and bloom within months of sowing. Pansies, marigolds, nasturtiums and poppies are all simple to grow and can be sown directly into prepared soil.

However, the flower that is most associated with children is the sunflower. They are one of our best-loved flowers and epitomize the long hot days of summer. It can be great fun to have a sunflower-growing competition, or why not make a sunflower screen? To do this, choose several varieties in different colours that grow to different heights, and sow in staggered rows, with dwarf types at the front and the tallest varieties at the back.

Although there is more scope for allowing children to grow plants in a medium-sized garden, they can discover their green fingers in the smallest garden, or even on a patio, terrace or balcony. Many plants can be grown in pots, including herbs, strawberries and mini-vegetables such as baby sweetcorn, golf-ball-sized aubergines, radishes and finger-sized carrots, and a collection of brightly coloured annuals in pots will be a cheerful addition to any garden, regardless of the gardener's age.

Tool and equipment

Years ago, children's gardening equipment was hard to find, and most youngsters helping in the garden would have been lucky to have a spade or fork adapted from an adult's tool by a dexterous grandfather. Today, however, it can be hard to choose what to buy from the bewildering range of miniature kits offered in supermarkets, garden emporiums, mail order catalogues and garden centres. The quality is variable, and you generally get what you pay for, but most leading brands offer a children's range. It is possible to buy spades, boots, forks, brooms, watering

◀ Nothing will give a child more pleasure than picking sweet peas on a hot, summer's day, after raising the plant themselves from seed. This fast and easy-to-grow climber is ideal for training up an ornamental archway, which could be placed at the entrance to the child's own patch of garden.

▼ Narrow window boxes, attached to a wall or placed on a sturdy sill, are ideal for growing robust herbs, such as coriander and rosemary. For the herbs to thrive, ensure they are planted in moisture-retentive but well-drained compost.

cans, rakes, wheelbarrows and anything else a budding gardener might need. For really young children, choose tools with plastic heads. These come in lots of bright colours that are guaranteed to grab their attention. As they get older, move on to small replicas of adult tools, which are specially designed to be light and compact. Again, quality varies, but good tools with stainless steel heads and ash handles will last a long time.

Children should be encouraged to use their tools properly and to look after them as well. Nothing too obsessive like rubbing linseed oil into a wooden handle, which is guaranteed to put them off gardening, but simple care, such as cleaning soil off the head of a spade. Their ownership of the tools can be increased by giving them a special place to store them, whether it is the corner of a shed, garage or even a play house.

Protective gear is a good idea for green-fingered children. Aprons will prevent clothes from getting dirty, while Wellington boots, available in lots of bright colours, patterns and designs such as zebra stripes, spots or retro daisies, will keep feet dry. Gloves may encourage a squeamish child (or parent), but most will relish the thought of playing with earth, water, snails and worms.

Apart from tools, there are many gadgets that are aimed at nurturing a child's fascination in the garden. This includes bug viewers – clear plastic containers with removable lids that contain a magnifying device. These are ideal for children to learn about wildlife and, ultimately, to treat the creatures with respect.

Planting and Play

A successful family garden is a happy marriage between the needs of the adults and those of the children. The designer must provide an area for relaxing and entertaining but, if the space is to be well used and much-loved, there should also be visual stimulation to inspire the imagination of youngsters.

In this small, awkward plot in the affluent Pacific Heights area of San Francisco, California, the designer's brief was to connect a steeply sloping garden to the looming, four-storey house and make it a safe place for the client's four children to play.

When designer Andrea Cochran first saw the plot, it was completely lacking in structure, and no thought had ever been given to its design or planting. There was a small level area at the back of the house and another sliver of flat land at the bottom of the garden. Between them was a steep and slippery slope that left about one-third of the garden unused. The garden was overlooked on three sides and was plunged into deep shade for much of the year.

To make most of the sloping site navigable, the designer has created a series of zigzag grass paths leading from a large deck that is accessed from the ground floor of the house. Strips of Corten steel have been used as retaining walls for the grass path and for building the sides and risers of a flight of stairs that run down the right-hand side of the garden – after a few years, this material weathers wonderfully to leave a distinctive rusty finish.

▼ A simple slide makes a fast way to get to the bottom of this steeply sloping garden. To stop the garden from looking like a municipal playground, the designer has concealed this piece of play equipment under a tunnel of woven willow.

▲ Paths add structure to a garden, while at the same time providing a useful way of getting from A to B. Here, a path that zigzags from side to side, to make light work of walking from the top to the bottom of the space, has also become a prominent, geometric design feature.

◄ Plant choice is important for a garden that receives very little sunlight. Most plants that thrive in these conditions are picked for their foliage, which can lead to a textured display that is lacking any significant colour. In this garden angular beds of striking bacopa light up the deeply shaded space.

The design of the path has left four triangular beds that have been planted with bacopa, a tough, spreading annual that will quickly form a carpet over the soil. Both *Bacopa* 'Snowstorm', which has white flowers, and yellow-leaved *Bacopa* 'Gold 'n Pearls' are ideal in shade, and their light, bright blooms help to lift the gloom of this dark space. Although requiring little maintenance once planted, they will have to be replaced every year.

Privacy is a key issue for the owners. Willow panels help to screen the deck, while at the bottom of the garden a living barrier of *Salix caprea* 'Kilmarnock' has been planted, with root barrier fabric installed to prevent this aggressive willow from getting out of hand. Existing trees, such as a plum, magnolia and rhododendron, have been kept, and many clematis and climbing roses have been planted along the fences on both sides.

Apart from enjoying running up and down the grass paths, the client's children have fun whizzing down a slide that runs down the left-hand side of the garden and is hidden from view by a woven willow tunnel. Elsewhere, an air of magic is brought into the space with two huge woven willow balls that can be rolled around the garden, while a whimsical grass armchair makes the perfect place to rest after a busy day playing. The humorous theme is continued on the upper deck where a wheatgrass table is flanked by a pair of sleek, tapered wooden stools.

Looking down from the windows of the house, the garden's strong geometric lines are obvious but, once at ground level, the cleverness of the three-dimensional design is revealed. The ascending and descending path and the sloping beds of bacopa turn this into a space that is exciting for children and adults alike.

▲ A grass armchair rises organically out of the lawn at the bottom of the garden and makes a novel place to rest after playing with outsize willow balls. Creating shapes like this is easy to do by forming soil into mounds and sowing grass seed over the structure.

▶ There are many clever ways to brighten up a gloomy space, including using light-coloured paint to cover garden structures. Here, reclaimed wooden boundary fences have been painted in a neutral shade, which is complemented by the light tone of the gravel. In a small space, light-coloured walls will also make a garden appear larger than it actually is.

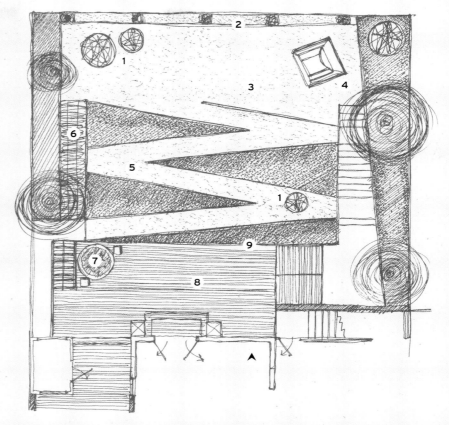

▲ Pacific Heights

1	Movable willow balls	5	Lawn ramp with steel edge
2	Living willow fence	6	Willow tunnel slide
3	Lawn	7	Wheatgrass table
4	Lawn chair	8	Deck
		9	Willow fence

◀ A pair of hand-carved wooden stools has been arranged around a grass-topped dining table. Although this is not really a practical solution to outdoor entertaining, it does inject a light-hearted, humorous element to the space.

▼ Corten steel, valued for its rusty appearance that is achieved through being exposed to the weather, adds a sleek look to the garden. It is widely used here, which helps to draw the whole scheme together.

► A trampoline built to sit flush with a neatly manicured lawn makes an unobtrusive piece of play equipment for all the family. It also complements the clean lines of this architectural garden, rather than jarring with its sleek design.

▶ A swathe of squash leaves in the foreground contrasts with dark-leaved cabbages and flowers in a striking display, showing how vegetables can be used to great ornamental effect. The eye is drawn upwards to the specimen trees and to a seated alcove, the perfect place to relax among such abundance.

Productive

Supermarkets have their place, but nothing compares to picking your own vegetables or fruit, fresh from the garden. Plump raspberries tugged gently from the cane, succulent bunches of grapes cut from the vine, and potatoes unearthed specially for dinner, taste so much better than anything you can buy. Apart from a superior flavour, growing your own produce means you know exactly what has gone into it, eliminating fears over whether it has been doused with pesticides or man-made fertilizers. Growing your own crops in a productive garden also helps to ease concerns over sustainability – plants grown in your own back garden have to travel only a short distance from plot to plate, rather than being flown thousands of miles to the supermarket or shipped across an ocean to reach your table. For many, the first encounter with a productive garden is a small plot of land, usually tucked out of sight at the back of the garden, where father or grandfather spent Sunday afternoons raising serried ranks of cabbages, Brussels sprouts and potatoes. Although gardens like these still exist, with a divide between ornamental and edible plants, for many the joy of growing vegetables is to have them where they can be seen. Today, a productive garden is more inspirational and rather than being hidden away, crops have moved into the forefront. Attractive vegetables are mixed in with ornamental plants in beds and borders, some are grown in pots on patio gardens, while fruit trees, such as apples and pears, can have their branches trained to become an edible screen or barrier.

Kitchen Gardens

If you have a large garden and the time, it is possible to grow enough crops to become largely self-sufficient, but even if your space is restricted, you can still grow enough edible plants for several meals. For instance, a collection of crops in pots can be arranged on a balcony, and if you live in a flat, a window box holds enough compost to grow three or four herbs and vegetables.

A well-designed kitchen garden, full of carefully selected varieties of fruit, vegetables and herbs, is a wonderful sight. In its splendour during late summer, beds are crammed with delicacies just waiting to picked and transformed into a wonderful meal. For some, it is difficult to wait that long and hard to resist snapping off a few pods of peas or pulling up some baby carrots, quickly wiping off the soil and crunching on them. Their fresh, earthy taste is lost when they are pulled and stored.

Edible crops have been grown in gardens through the ages. For instance, the Persians in the seventh century mixed fruit trees, such as pomegranates, with flowering plants. In Britain, from the seventeenth to the nineteenth century, owners of stately homes created enclosed kitchen gardens, which were often built a fair distance away from the house and ornamental gardens. In those days, when there was a strong division between the classes, the separation of the gardens was to prevent the working classes, toiling among the vegetables, from being seen by the upper-class members of the household.

Many of these productive gardens were contained within high walls. These served two purposes. Not only did they screen the flurry of activity within the walled garden, but they also provided shelter from strong winds and helped to retain heat. They were also the perfect vertical support for many tender fruits, such as peaches. These were grown under lean-to glasshouses, and the walls were often double thickness, with the space between heated by a boiler.

Fortunately, we are no longer embarrassed by growing fruit and vegetables, and kitchen gardens are now very much in vogue. There has been an increasing trend for us to understand the connection between plant and plate, and nowhere is this more evident than in the chef's garden found at some restaurants. For instance, at De Kas in Amsterdam, a former glasshouse nursery has been turned into a celebrated restaurant, and the vegetables used in the kitchen grow in beds that are never more than a few feet from the diners' tables.

▲ There are many different types of container suitable for growing vegetables, but there is no need to restrict yourself to those designed solely for the purpose. Try recycling old buckets, oil drums and many other objects that can be bought cheaply or unearthed in second-hand shops or reclamation yards.

◄ Paths give a kitchen garden structure and enable you to work and harvest plants in comfort. They also allow you to divide up a large area into a number of geometric beds, where you can grow manageable numbers of plants, avoiding any gluts of produce.

◄ Although beds and borders planted with shrubs provide year-long interest, the effect gained from planting vegetables is striking but short-lived. Here, a large sweep of onions combines with spikes of lavender before the leaves collapse, indicating that they are ready to be harvested.

▶ Raised beds are the ideal solution if the soil is poor, waterlogged or even non-existent, such as in a roof garden. In a contemporary space, large steel containers perched on sturdy legs are an alternative to traditional beds. The look can be extended by using steel mesh to support climbing vegetables.

▼ There are no hard-and-fast rules about the dimensions of a raised bed, but for a deep-rooting crop, such as asparagus, you need to ensure there is enough depth for the roots to grow unhindered, resulting in lots of delicious spears to harvest.

▥ Structure

To get the most out of a kitchen garden it needs to be planned well, so it is both practical and pleasing to the eye. If you are starting from scratch, you need to decide how you will contain the garden – wind is the greatest enemy of a number of plants that you may want to grow, so you will need to provide some form of protection.

If you live in a rural location and have lots of space and a large budget, building a traditional wall around the kitchen garden would be perfect. Use weathered-looking reclaimed bricks so that it blends in with your surroundings and does not stand out like a sore thumb. Less costly but equally effective is to encircle your kitchen garden with a hedge. Yew will provide excellent shelter and responds well to being tightly clipped. However, do not expect instant results – it can take five or more years for your hedge to become established.

In towns and cities, surrounding buildings will give your plot protection, so tall hedges or walls are unnecessary. If you wish to screen your kitchen garden, consider erecting trellis screens or surrounding the area with pleached limes for a contemporary look. To get the most produce out of the space, you could create a screen by planting a hedge of trained fruit trees – apples and pears can be grown as espaliers with their branches trained horizontally along a series of parallel wires.

Although you could grow vegetables in long, wide beds, it is better to divide the space up into bite-sized chunks. This will make the garden easy to maintain and allow you to rotate crops in order to prevent soil-borne pests and diseases from getting a foothold. Perhaps the easiest way of splitting the garden is to make a series of raised beds. In large gardens, you could use timber, new railway sleepers (which do not contain any noxious

◄ Lengths of wood from young trees are extremely supple and can easily be woven together to form low edging to define a bed planted with a combination of fruit, vegetables and ornamental plants. To prevent the edging from falling apart, it needs to be attached to short stakes along its length.

▼ Even the tiniest garden can become home to a thriving range of edible plants. On this sun-kissed, hardwood-decked patio, a corner has been elevated and turned into a contemporary-looking raised bed featuring a range of culinary and scented-leaved herbs, such as lavender.

preservatives), short brick walls or lengths of log. In smaller gardens, try using large galvanized steel or Indian sandstone planters.

Growing crops in raised beds has several advantages. Rather than toil with the soil, which could be heavy clay and difficult to cultivate, you can provide your own mix of compost, which will help ensure your plants will thrive. Beds are also the ideal solution if your ground is naturally boggy or you live in an area with heavy rainfall, as the beds can have plenty of drainage material incorporated to ensure that they do not become waterlogged. Watering is also more effective and efficient because you can be sure that whatever you add to the bed goes straight to the roots, rather than running off across the bed or being soaked up by other plants. If you suffer from a bad back or cannot bend properly, raised beds also ensure you can look after vegetables at a comfortable level.

When designing raised beds, make sure that you can reach the middle of them easily from both sides. This will make picking, weeding and cultivating easy. Beds do not have to be the same length and you may wish to dedicate longer ones to an individual crop, such as asparagus.

It is best to make a scale plan of your kitchen garden on paper before starting to construct it. The essential thing is to leave enough space between beds for paths. These are crucial for the garden to be useful, and they must be wide enough for a wheelbarrow to be pushed along them without snagging plants or bashing it against raised beds. Grass is a popular surface in rural gardens, but a hard surface means you can use the garden all year round without the wheelbarrow tyres making a mess of the ground. Bricks and paving slabs are ideal but, for a simple surface, try gravel. Do not make it too deep, though, or the wheels of heavy barrows will form huge ruts.

▼ For a bountiful kitchen garden, you will need to equip it with a number of growing structures to enable you to grow the maximum amount of healthy plants. Once seedlings have germinated, you can move them into small pots and then place them in a cold frame for hardening off.

▶ Tiered staging, offering generous amounts of space for pots and trays at several levels, will help ensure you make the most efficient use of your greenhouse. Use staging for growing and displaying lightweight pots, and stand tall plants or those in heavier containers on the floor.

▶ Space in the centre of the greenhouse can often become redundant, but a simple trestle table running down its length is a cheap and effective way of providing lots of room for raising plants. Once the plants have been moved into the garden, the table can be easily folded down and stowed away.

◀ Birds and flying pests, such as moths, will descend upon crops, especially cabbages, and eat the leaves, reducing them to skeletal forms. To prevent this, keep a number of cloches in a storage area and bring them out to protect plants until they are well established. Cloches can be clad with polythene, glass or wire mesh, which allows you to see the plants underneath.

Raising plants

Starting seedlings off on the windowsill works well if you have a small garden and only a few pots to fill, but for a kitchen garden you will need something more substantial. A greenhouse is an essential bit of kit and, once you have one, you will wonder how you ever managed to survive without it. Choosing the right model is not easy, as there are many on the market, from inexpensive, utilitarian aluminium-framed structures to Western red cedar models that can cost about 20 times more. Although pricier, top-of-the-range greenhouses look attractive and can be a wonderful feature within the kitchen garden.

Apart from picking a greenhouse that is within your budget, base your choice on its specifications. They come in many shapes and sizes, and yours must fit into your garden while preserving plenty of outdoor growing space. Most are freestanding, but if you have a sunny wall, it may be worth considering a lean-to greenhouse that will not eat up too much of the garden.

To be really useful, a greenhouse needs to have vents in the roof and a louvred vent on the side – you can specify the addition of automatic vents to the suppliers of expensive greenhouses, or you can fit one yourself by buying an automatic vent kit from a garden centre. Make sure the ridge is high enough for you to work comfortably, and install a heater and light so you can still potter about as dusk falls. More important than anything else is to ensure you have adequate greenhouse staging. Made from metal or wood, it should consist of a waist-height top surface, usually with shelves beneath. There needs to be enough space for tender plants to be left in the greenhouse all year round, and plenty of room for trays of seedlings, and for growing on your young plants in pots.

An alternative to the greenhouse is the polythene tunnel. These are functional structures – you certainly would not choose one for its looks – but basic models are the fraction of the cost of a good greenhouse. They are also simple to erect: metal hoops are sunk into the ground and a plastic skin stretched over the frame. There are many sizes to choose from and with varying levels of sophistication. For instance, you can choose to add

◄ Many greenhouses are utilitarian, providing a functional place to raise plants before moving them to the garden. But there are many models, constructed beautifully, that are ideal in a well-designed garden, offering aesthetic appeal as well as a practical place to grow plants.

overhead irrigation systems or louvred vents in the side to allow plenty of air around the plants, and you can even pick from a selection of covering materials. To make the most of the space, choose a polythene tunnel with flat sides so you can have staging inside.

Apart from a greenhouse, it is also worth thinking about installing a fruit cage. This is a large metal- or wood-framed structure that can be erected over a bed planted with fruit and then covered with netting – this keeps the birds out but still allows plenty of light and air to get to the plants. In a rural location, a timber fruit cage would look ideal, but the most popular models are those made from black, powder-coated galvanized steel – some are square, while others have a raised roof and fancy finials. Aluminium fruit cages are cheaper than those made of wood or galvanized steel, and their sleek look would suit a contemporary kitchen garden.

There are lots of other specialist growing aids that can be used in the kitchen garden. Cold frames are low structures that act as a halfway house for plants grown in the glasshouse, allowing them to get used to outdoor temperatures before going into their final planting position in the soil. Shaped like a rectangular box, they have solid sides and a clear lid (usually solid polypropylene or polycarbonate) that can be removed or opened for access, allowing the plants an open-air environment for some of the time. They are available in a wide range of materials, including aluminium, galvanized metal and many types of wood – as with all wooden garden structures, check that the timber comes from a sustainable source. Cold frames can be bought ready-made or as a flat pack that needs nailing together. Alternatively, you can easily build a loose structure from reclaimed bricks with a pair of recycled cold frame lights fitted on top – you can sometimes find these among the wares of vintage gardening tool suppliers.

Other protective devices for plants include terracotta rhubarb and seakale forcers, which look like long clay pots with a lid on. They can be put over plants to force

▲ Standing in a serried row, these traditional Victorian glass cloches with cast-iron frames are a practical but elegant addition to the kitchen garden. They are ideal for protecting seedlings or tender plants, and their lids can be removed in more clement weather.

▼ Collections of old gardening tools, such as scythes, shovels and hoes, can be bought cheaply from gardening auctions and salvage yards. When displayed on a brick wall or the outside of a shed, their metal blades will weather wonderfully to leave a rusty finish.

◄ Many items can be recycled in the garden, including broken terracotta pots. Keep the pieces in a large container and use them as crocks to place over the drainage holes of large pots. This will prevent compost falling through the holes and provide efficient drainage.

▶ To make the most of a garden shed, make sure there are plenty of hooks, pegs, shelves or racks where tools can be stowed away after use. This will allow you to move freely around the shed and you can easily find a tool when you need it.

◄ A potting bench is an essential bit of kit that will be used regularly throughout the year – as a surface for sowing and pricking out seeds, and potting up plants. Plan its position carefully and ensure that it is at a good working height. Provide shelves and storage so that all tools, composts and pots are within easy reach. The underside of a bench is useful for storing pots.

► A water butt can easily be attached to the downpipe of a garden building and is a great way to ensure you always have a supply of water, even during a drought. There are many purpose-built butts on the market or you can recycle old barrels or other large containers. To keep the water clean and algae-free, fit the butt with a lid.

them to make tender shoots earlier in the growing season and, although functional, they still look fabulous and can be left as decorative objects in the garden when not in use. Vintage forcers can be bought from suppliers of antique horticultural tools or you can buy them newly cast. Cloches are useful to protect individual plants: traditional Victorian glass bell cloches look stylish and elegant, while bamboo cloches add a quirky touch and would be ideal used in a kitchen garden where the emphasis is on growing unusual or oriental vegetables.

Kitting it out

The ultimate kitchen garden should be self-contained with everything close to hand so you do not have to traipse to other parts of the garden to fetch tools or bags of compost. A storage area is essential, whether it is a shed or brick-built building, which can be constructed alongside a wall. Apart from being able to stow away pots, compost, spades, forks, trowels and seeds, the building should be equipped with a potting bench to allow you to pot up, prick out or propagate plants. It is also a useful shelter when the weather is poor.

An outdoor water source is essential both for plants growing in the ground and for any that need nurturing in the greenhouse. Ideally, this will be an outdoor tap, but also fit a water butt to channel rainwater from the gutters of sheds, greenhouses or other garden buildings.

Whatever the size of your kitchen garden, build some compost bins. If the garden is particularly large, it may be worth having two or three bins. Use them to collect leaves, peelings and plants after the vegetables have been harvested – once the material has rotted down well, it can be used to condition the soil or to mulch around plants. There are lots of types to buy, from black plastic bins shaped like giant bell jars to wooden bins disguised to look like beehives. But why be an undercover compost maker? Compost is the key to gardening organically, and an open bin constructed from old wooden pallets provides much more space than any manufactured bin.

What to grow?

What should you grow in a kitchen garden? Well, it may sound like an obvious answer, but the best thing is to raise plants that you like to eat and not those that are likely to go to waste. There is very little point spending time, effort and money on raising cauliflowers if you or nobody else can bear the taste of them.

Perhaps the greatest joy of having a kitchen garden is trying out new varieties or gourmet fruit and vegetables that you either cannot find in the supermarket or are expensive to buy. Among those worth finding space for are borlotti beans, Tuscan black kale and globe artichokes, and fruit such as strawberries, summer- and autumn-fruiting raspberries and maybe a heritage variety of apple.

There are many seed companies that cater for kitchen gardeners, and their catalogues have a bewildering selection to choose from. It is easy to get carried away and order much more than you will grow or be able to eat. It pays to be selective, and the ideal way of doing this is to make a plan showing all your beds, then order the right number of varieties. Do not sow the whole packet (unless you have a huge family), but just what you think you will need, then add a few more to allow for a few failures or seeds that do not germinate.

Apart from edible crops, the kitchen garden is the ideal place to grow flowers. Traditionally, a selection of blooms was grown in a kitchen garden to decorate the rooms of the owner's stately home – there is no reason why you cannot use this idea today. It may be worthwhile dedicating a bed to a cutting garden, raising annuals and perennial flowers that can be cut in generous bunches.

When planning what to grow, there are two important considerations. You must ensure that there is always something to pick (and avoid gluts), and it is vital that you work out how much time you have to maintain the kitchen garden. This is not low-maintenance gardening, and plants will require a lot of upkeep. The list of jobs goes on and on, from sowing the seed to pricking out, and from growing the plants on in pots to planting out. Plants will then need watering and keeping weed-free, and a watchful eye is essential to ensure pests and diseases do not spoil any of your hard work. Being able to harvest the plants comes a long way down the line. If you do have the time, then it is possible to become entirely self-sufficient – at Barton Court (see pages 196–203), we grow pretty much everything for the table from spring until the autumn. Only after this time do we venture to the supermarket, but we still have bags of potatoes and onions stored away.

◀ A large kitchen garden means that as well as being able to produce a great range of edible crops, you can also grow flowers, such as lupins, which are so spectacular in early summer, when the large spikes of blooms emerge. Flowers like these are ideal for cutting and displaying indoors.

▶ Deciding what to grow in a kitchen garden is never easy because there are hundreds of varieties to choose from, so go for vegetables and fruits that you like or that will suit your size and style of garden. Clockwise from top left: onions are an easy crop to start with; grow artichokes at the back of a sunny bed; kohlrabi is an unusual vegetable, grown for its swollen stem; raise enough seedlings to ensure you have plenty of crops to harvest and put into store; currants are a delicacy but will need to be protected in a fruit cage to prevent birds from eating all of the jewel-like berries; white and red cabbages are easy to grow but they take a long time to reach maturity, as well as taking up a lot of space.

Home Grown

Barton Court was built in 1772, then substantially altered in 1882. One previous owner, Admiral Lord Dundas, was the promoter of the Kennett and Avon Canal, which runs with the Kennet river between the house and the village of Kintbury. The land on which the house is built is said to have belonged at one time to my father's family, whose large house, West Woodhay, is just the other side of Kintbury – a nice idea but I don't know if it's really true.

The river is a magnet for me. The Environmental Agency has recently made it narrower and deeper so that it flows faster. I had doubts at first about the changes, but the work has been done beautifully, with river plants dug into the water's edge, and a little rill constructed in front of the house where the water rushes by.

When I bought the house and garden (about 20 acres/ 8 hectares) in 1970, it was all deeply derelict, the roof had fallen in, and dry and wet rot ravaged the place. The garden was in a similar state of disrepair. The only reason

▲ Gravel paths are used throughout the walled kitchen garden, making an inexpensive, hard-wearing but attractive surface. To ensure a gravel path remains low-maintenance, spread compacted stone or hoggin over it to prevent humps and hollows forming.

▼ Viewed from above, the structure of the kitchen garden is clearly evident. Fruit cages run down the sides, while the rest of the garden has been separated by two central axes that divide up the space and allow the creation of distinct usable beds.

◄ Dwarf box hedging has been used to contain beds and borders in the kitchen garden. Slow-growing, dense and the perfect foil for ornamental vegetables, box responds well to clipping, leaving a crisp, clean outline that maintains its shape over a long period of time.

▲ Vertical interest is brought to the kitchen garden by rows of garden canes, used as supports for climbing beans. By early summer, the canes are covered in leaves, followed by flowers and later the beans themselves.

▼ Vulnerable seedlings are covered with wire mesh to prevent rabbits, birds and other pests eating them.

PRODUCTIVE

BARTON COURT
BERKSHIRE, UK

CASE STUDY #11 CONTINUED

DESIGNER
TERENCE CONRAN

▲ Taller-growing vegetable crops often need some form of support to prevent them from collapsing under the weight of produce or being flattened by the wind or a heavy downpour. A simple technique is to restrain plants with lengths of heavy-duty twine wound around a framework of garden canes.

▼ Sowing seeds in short rows, rather than long, serried ones, helps to prevent gluts and makes it easier to reach plants when harvesting. To ensure a steady supply of frequently picked plants, such as lettuce, sow rows every few weeks.

◀ Rhubarb is a highly decorative plant that looks equally good mixed with ornamentals, where it provides an architectural shape, or when it is grown with other vegetables. Terracotta forcing pots placed over the crowns of plants block out the light to produce early blanched shoots.

▼ A traditional style lean-to greenhouse is the perfect place to start many seedlings off at the beginning of the year and can be used throughout the growing season to raise many tender crops that need protection from strong winds or cold temperatures.

I was able to afford to buy it was that it was seen as a lost cause by people who came to view it. In fact, it was this that appealed to me, as I could almost begin again and do as I wanted, rather than be dictated to by planners.

The garden had been quite grand at one time, with one of the best walled vegetable gardens and walled orchards, which I was determined to restore. The walls were still very beautiful, but cracks and fissures had to be repaired, and the vegetable garden's forest of Christmas trees and head-high thistles had to be rooted out.

The walled garden is now my real pride and joy. Jon Chidsey, my amazingly enthusiastic and energetic gardener, produces a cornucopia of every vegetable you can dream of. Given my passion for food and my wife's talent in the kitchen, this is a daily pleasure. We produce enough during the spring and summer months to be able to send bi-weekly consignments to my restaurants in London – not only vegetables but soft fruit and huge quantities of herbs, as well as apples, plums and pears in the autumn. We grow 12 different varieties of potato and a large selection of tomatoes, plenty of artichokes and peppers, aubergines and chillies, but never enough asparagus. My best moment is when the first peas, broad beans and haricots fines are ready.

We have rather gravelly soil, so we make a large quantity of leaf mould that gets dug in during February, along with manure from local farmers. Luckily, we can water the garden, as we pump our own from an artesian well.

◀ Over winter, a row of cold frames are bursting at the seams with plants that need protecting from frost or harsh weather. On warm days, the glass lids can be raised to ensure adequate ventilation and help prevent fungal diseases.

▶ Early in the year, the leafless stems of a grapevine hold very little promise but, with lots of water and feeding, the vine will crop prolifically by midsummer. Both green and black dessert varieties are worth growing, but some will need the protection of a greenhouse to do well.

▶ In a rustic greenhouse, a plastic or galvanized steel water butt would look totally out of place. However, an old barrel has timeless appeal and blends perfectly with its surroundings, turning into a garden feature, rather than something purely functional.

The whole of the south and east sides of the house are covered with a beautiful display of white and blue wisteria every year. One year the frost got them in April and the whole thing looked like a huge display of faded underwear. So now I put an army of gas cylinders around the house and light the burners if there is a frost warning. It works – no more faded underwear.

Years ago I saw a picture of a famous choreographer from The Royal Opera House standing in his topiary garden. It looked like a wonderful abstract sculpture gallery, with Henry Moores and Barbara Hepworths, together with a few Paolozzis and Picassos, arranged behind him. I thought, 'I'd like one of those,' so I planted lots of small box bushes and yew trees. Twenty years and many hundreds of hours of clipping later, I now have my sculpture gallery. It was planted on some rather poor ground to the west of the house.

One sad thing is our trees, which were planted at the same time as the house was built, and are now coming to the end of their natural lives. We also had the dreaded

▼ Veteran fruit trees with wide, spreading canopies are a majestic sight in the orchard and provide ample fruit to eat immediately as well as store. Trees like this are not only valuable for their productive qualities, but also for the shade they cast, becoming a restful place to spend time on a hot summer's day.

▲ Imposing red brick walls surround the kitchen garden, defining its status among the rest of the garden. Apart from providing shelter from the wind, walls can be used for training fruit trees, helping to make the most of the available space.

▼ A simple frame made from lengths of wood joined together and wire mesh is ideal for protecting young vegetable crops early in the year. As plants establish, the frame can be easily lifted and moved along the row to safeguard more vulnerable plants.

◄ In the shadow of a tall brick wall, a block of Tuscan black kale, or cavalo nero, with its upright and highly textured leaves, combines with other dark-leaved vegetables to create a dramatic display of edible produce that is also highly ornamental.

PRODUCTIVE

CASE STUDY #11 CONTINUED

BARTON COURT
BERKSHIRE, UK

DESIGNER
TERENCE CONRAN

▶ With a large kitchen garden, it is possible to grow enough crops to become almost completely self-sufficient. Courgettes are produced prolifically throughout the summer but, despite the huge numbers, none goes to waste.

▶ Tools stored and displayed on a simple rack system are easy to find, preventing wasted minutes hunting for an elusive trowel or half-moon edger. This storage system also allows you to make the most of the floor space, and tools do not become a safety hazard.

▼ Terracotta pots can be used for raising seedlings as well as for growing vegetables. After years of being displayed outside, these pots have developed an attractive weathered white patina.

▲ On a hot summer's day, lavender comes into its own. The spikes of flowers attract bees, butterflies and other beneficial wildlife, while the essential oils released by the grey leaves create an evocative scent that permeates the entire kitchen garden.

◀ The large bulbous heads of artichokes, with their thick, fleshy scales that slowly open, bring a touch of the Mediterranean to an English garden. Artichokes are greatly prized for their architectural shape, which is best displayed at the back of a border.

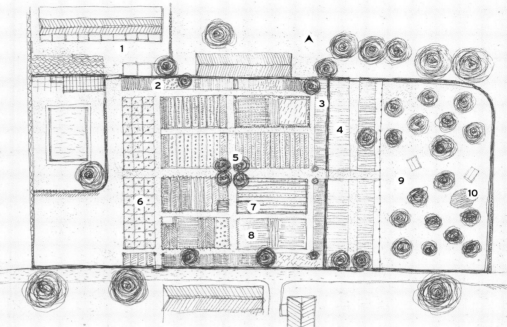

▶ **Barton Court**

1 Greenhouses & coldframes
2 Cut flowers
3 Vegetable beds
4 Perennial herbs
5 London Plane tree canopy
6 Soft fruit cages
7 Pond
8 Vegetable beds
9 Orchard
10 Pond for geese

Dutch elm disease, which polished off a nice little copse. Perhaps the saddest thing was when an enormous cypress tree on the lawn in front of the house was blown over during one of the great winds in the Eighties. However, I have been a keen planter of broad-leaved trees and have now planted more beeches, oaks and limes than have been blown down or have died. It is one of the greatest pleasures for a gardener to plant trees and see them grow at an extraordinary pace. One of my best is a medlar in the front garden, which has grown into a strange oriental shape and pours itself over the wall; pretty flowers in the spring and delicious fruit in late autumn. I have now planted another one on the other side to balance it.

We grow lots of cutting flowers among the vegetables, and roses with the rows of herbs. Flowers for the house are one of the great pleasures of a garden.

We have carpets of snowdrops in January and February in the woods, followed by narcissi and then bluebells. I like lichen, wild flowers in the fields, hollyhocks and different varieties of clematis, box bushes, wisteria, of course, oak trees, all sorts of herbs, parrot tulips, paper white narcissi, white roses, cowslips, asparagus, sweet peas and, the most beautiful flowers of all, fritillaries. I love butterflies in the garden, so buddleia and cabbages are important; both are handsome in their very different ways.

Potagers, Orchards and Nutteries

Potagers

While we may of think of vegetables, herbs and fruit as some of the ingredients for a great meal, they can also be attractive plants in their own right. Many are blessed with showy leaves or flamboyant flowers, and can even out-perform ornamental plants when it comes to good looks. The French realized this long ago and are masters of the potager – a garden where edible plants are combined with flowers and shrubs – and examples can be seen in gardens large and small, in rural settings or in the heart of towns. Most notable are Le Potager du Roi at Versailles and, more famously still, the jardin potager at Villandry; both have inspired and influenced vegetable gardens around the world.

Traditionally, potagers have been designed with a very strong structure. The space is divided up with a series of identical square or rectangular beds that have enough space between them for pushing a wheelbarrow through. In some gardens, tightly clipped dwarf box or lavender is used, but for a more contemporary look try making raised beds using chunky lengths of hardwood.

The formality of the layout is blurred when the beds have been planted up, and the flowers, herbs, vegetables and fruit should be encouraged to spill over the sides and be allowed to knit together. In some garden situations, such unruly behaviour would not be tolerated, but in a potager it is a positive bonus.

Create cohesion in your potager by thinking carefully about the plants you use. A colour scheme is the perfect answer, and remember that some plants come in many tones (for instance, there is large- and small-leaved basil in shades of purple, dark and light green). Mix together plants for their flowers and foliage, and ensure that you make the most of vertical space by adding wigwams or ornamental obelisks for runner beans, gourds, sweet peas, morning glory and other climbers. In most potagers, the bed is designed with a tall plant or structure at the centre and with planting arranged in the rest of the bed, so that the height graduates down towards the front.

By choosing your plants and edging material carefully, it is possible to create a potager that will suit your garden. Even some traditional vegetable gardens are being given a revamp; at Castle Howard, Yorkshire, the original walled garden is being filled with a mixture of flowers and edible plants – a sign that the formal vegetable garden is no match for the exuberance of the ornamental kitchen garden.

Orchards and nutteries

Wandering lazily around an orchard on a hot, sunny day in late summer is a bit like being a child in a sweet shop. Red, black and green plums hang within tempting reach,

while glowing red, acid cherries dangle like blowsy earrings on compact trees. Glossy, swollen black mulberries look irresistible, and jewel-like miniature apples in yellow, red and pink smother the branches of crab apple trees. It is a wonderful sight, and there is little you can do to prevent yourself from sampling the delicious goods on offer.

Deciding what to grow can be difficult because there are so many different types of fruit to try, and then you will still face a choice between the different cultivars – sometimes in their hundreds. For instance, a good nursery may stock over 100 different types of apple, from unusual and wonderful heritage varieties to brand new ones – for example, breeders have recently introduced apples that are low in sugar and claimed to be perfect for diabetics.

As these are long-term plants that will produce a crop for many years, there is little point in taking a risk on growing a fruit that you have never eaten before or do not know how to prepare in the kitchen. For instance, the medlar makes an attractive tree and has delicious fruits that taste of caramel. But before these can be eaten they need to be bletted, or allowed to rot, something that most of us are unlikely to do these days when instant gratification is the norm.

Base your choice on what you and your family like to eat. Among safe bets for most people are plums, apples, pears and cherries – fruit that can be picked and enjoyed immediately or, in the case of apples and pears, stored for eating later in the year. First, before making any decisions, work out how much space you have to grow them in. In

▲ Standard red roses are planted in a row above neat beds of vegetables. The colour red is repeated throughout this potager, which draws the whole scheme together. Beds are laid out in a geometric pattern and edged with low box hedging, providing year-round structure.

◄ A sylvan pathway opens onto an orchard, planted with a variety of fruit trees. Neatly maintained grass paths contrast with the wild grass that has been allowed to flourish under the trees.

▶ By following a few simple rules, such as making the most of the vertical space and using ornamental plants to edge the beds, it is possible to create an attractive and productive garden in the most utilitarian of spaces, such as an allotment.

order to flourish, fruit trees need plenty of space to grow without touching the branches of neighbouring trees – often they will need spacing about 3–3.7m (10–12ft) apart.

If you have a tiny garden, it is possible to make a mini-orchard by growing trees that have been bred for their compact habit. This includes the Minarette, an upright fruit tree that holds its fruit close to the stem. Apples, pears, cherries, plums, gages, damsons and crab apples are all available on these trees, which can also be grown in containers. Alternatively, if you have space for only one fruit, try a family tree – a tree that is made up of more than one variety of a specific type of fruit. The nurserymen achieve this by grafting different varieties onto one rootstock, and it is possible to buy a pear family tree consisting of 'Conference', 'Doyenné du Comice' and 'Williams' Bon Chrétien', or the apples 'Lord Lambourne', 'Egremont Russet' and 'Gala'.

Another solution for growing fruit in a small garden is to train plants along a fence or wall. Apples and pears are ideal to be trained as cordons or espaliers, while plums, cherries, greengages, damsons and apricots can be fan-trained. Not only will you be rewarded with delectable fruit, but the plants will provide all-year interest, starting with blossom in the spring. You do not need a wall to train the fruit on – they can be grown on parallel wires strung between sturdy upright posts. This makes it possible to use the plants as a screen or an edible boundary to divide your garden into rooms.

A nuttery is similar to an orchard, but with the obvious focus on nut-bearing plants. Examples can be seen in some of the UK's finest gardens, including Sissinghurst in Kent, Levens Hall in Cumbria and Hardwick Hall in Derbyshire. Although these collections of plants have been a feature of gardens for centuries, there is no reason why you should not create a nuttery today, especially if you enjoy their produce. This is exactly what leading garden designer Arabella Lennox-Boyd has done at her own garden at Gresgarth Hall, Lancashire. Among plants worth considering are cobnuts, sweet chestnuts, almonds, filberts and walnuts.

▥ Productive container gardens

Many people today have tiny gardens, whether on a patio, balcony or roof terrace. Although small, these compact spaces are perfect for raising many edible crops.

To inspire gardeners who are strapped for space, Terence Conran created a Chef's Garden at the Chelsea Flower Show in 1999. His idea was to design a rooftop garden owned by a chef, where the plants were within easy reach of the kitchen and could be swiftly turned into a delicious meal. Vegetables were grown in large, galvanized steel containers and the plot enclosed by white canvas sails, which provided shade for the exposed space and protected the crops from strong winds.

▲ The heat of a baking-hot day in midsummer is tempered by the leafy branches of fruit trees in the orchard, which open like parasols and make a cool, shady refuge from the sun.

▼ Metal troughs bring a contemporary elegance to a garden and are perfect for growing many different crops, such as tumbling varieties of tomato. Arrange several containers in a grid pattern on a patio or roof garden to create an attractive, above-ground productive garden.

◄ Although the natural habit of fruit trees is to make a bushy shrub or tree, their branches can be trained into various shapes, such as fans, espaliers and step-overs, to produce neat and attractive edible boundaries in a kitchen garden.

▼ A ribbed drum, planted with a mix of chard and carrots, adds a touch of industrial chic to this garden. Recycling old containers is a great way to make an unusual feature and also an environmentally friendly alternative to buying new pots.

▲ This compact corner of a garden is bursting with produce, showing how even the smallest of spaces can become productive. Tomatoes are supported by trellis, while growing beneath them are aubergine plants, with their distinctive and ornamental dark purple fruit. Even some of the flowers are edible, such as marigolds and nasturtiums.

Growing plants in large troughs is the ideal solution for many small spaces, as several different plants can be placed in the same container. Galvanized metal looks very contemporary, but for something more formal, go for terrazzo, granite, concrete or sandstone. Fill the troughs with a selection of attractive plants, such as cherry tomatoes, aubergines, chilli peppers and multi-coloured chard. These containers are invariably very heavy, especially when planted and watered, so make sure you know what weight your balcony or roof terrace can support.

Even if you live in a flat, there should still be room to grow crops. Mount a window box near the kitchen window and fill it with herbs, short-rooted carrots or radishes. It is even possible to make your own pesto from a few plants of basil growing on a sunny, indoor windowsill.

Back on terra firma, many fruit plants make good specimens for containers, and will add plenty of interest to your garden. An old olive tree with its fantastic gnarled trunk would instantly add a touch of the Mediterranean to a garden, as would oranges, lemons, limes and pomegranates. These look great grown in the largest terracotta pots you can afford, and they will do well in a warm, sheltered spot, although they do need protecting in cooler climates over winter.

Herb gardens

Walking into a herb garden on a warm day should delight all of your senses. The aroma will be heavenly because the sun brings out the essential oils of many plants, such as rosemary and lavender, and the display should be alive with bees, butterflies and hoverflies as they flit from flower to flower. Get closer to the herbs and you will have an irresistible urge to touch, caress, rub or taste your plants.

Herbs can be grown in gaps among other vegetables or even in traditional borders, but it is more useful to grow those you like to use in the kitchen in the same place – it will make your life so much easier if you can gather all those needed for a meal at the same time.

The different colours, shapes, sizes and textures of herbs make them perfect plants for creating attractive displays. An exciting way of growing them is in the gaps created by a formal parterre of dwarf box. At the herb

◄ Vegetable and herb beds should always be created within close proximity to the kitchen, so the ingredients are used in the freshest state possible. Here, the chef only has to step out through the glass doors to be able to pick courgettes, beans and a tapestry of herbs.

▼ A sunny but unexciting wall can be given a lift with a neatly spaced row of potted herbs, clipped as low domes to complement one another. Compact-growing plants, such as sage, parsley and thyme, will thrive in large terracotta pots filled with free-draining compost.

garden of Kinoith, County Cork, Ireland, a parterre has been created that features over 70 types of herb, including lemon balm, bronze fennel, parsley, chives and purple sage. These have been planted to create striking combinations of colour, and towering above the lower growing plants are cardoons, globe artichokes and runner beans growing on ornamental iron poles.

Herbs can also lend themselves to modern gardens, and they look good planted in geometric-style beds cut into crisp paving. Even though it has been created at an historic garden, the herb garden at Wave Hill in the northwest Bronx is a particularly eye-catching example. Rectangular gaps in a paved area are filled with herbs at this 11-hectare (28-acre) New York garden on the banks of the Hudson River.

At the Thyme Garden Herb Company at Alsea, Oregon, a traditional herb wheel has been created with each spoke of the large circular bed planted with a variety of thyme. In total it features over 60 varieties, arranged for their colour, texture and foliage, proving that even a single type of herb can make an attractive display.

PRODUCTIVE

FOURNIER ST
LONDON, UK

CASE STUDY #12

DESIGNER
PAUL GAZERWITZ

Chimney Pots and Carrot Tops

Living high above a city does not mean abandoning ideas of having a beautiful garden but, unlike creating a garden at ground level, a roof garden has a number of challenges that need to be overcome. Apart from making sure that the roof is strong enough to support a garden, the design will be dictated by the ease of access to the roof, which, in turn, will determine the size and type of plants and landscaping materials used.

This tiny garden measuring 6 x 7m (20 x 23ft) is built on top of an eighteenth-century building with fine views of the white stone spire of Christ Church in Spitalfields, East London. Landscaping materials were hoisted up to the roof by a pulley but, fortunately, plants were spared this treatment. They were brought to the roof via an internal flight of stairs, which was possible only because the clients own the whole building.

Although a structural engineer confirmed that the roof would support a garden, the designer kept everything as light as possible. Drainage consists of a 100-mm (4in) layer of lightweight expanded clay pellets, and rather than have heavy topsoil in raised beds, he used a mixture of perlite and multipurpose compost.

▲ Trellis panels and a mixture of low- and taller-growing vegetables in front of a traditional garden bench have turned this corner of a roof garden into a private space. The air of seclusion has been assisted by filling the planters running along the wall behind the bench with lavender.

▶ Every inch of space has been utilized, including the gap between the low box hedging in the seating area and the deck, which overflows with delicious wild strawberries. This rampant plant also helps to soften the hard edges of the timber.

◄ A border of low-maintenance chamomile lawn edges an expanse of reclaimed timber, which has been used to create a deck. As well as being sustainable, recycled wood gives the space a lived-in, weathered look.

PRODUCTIVE

FOURNIER ST
LONDON, UK

CASE STUDY #12 CONTINUED

DESIGNER
PAUL GAZERWITZ

▲ Although this garden possesses many contemporary qualities, the overall look is rustic. Old watering cans, lanterns and other rusty items found in a junk shop have been combined with cottage garden flowers to create a rural idyll in the heart of the city.

▼ A garden must have seating if the space is to be used to the full. However, if the garden is small, it does need particularly careful consideration. Here, a bench sits snugly against a wall, while the compact bistro furniture can be easily stowed away when not in use.

▲ It pays to make the most of a fine view. Here, the simple set of garden furniture has been placed to take full advantage of the handsome church tower. The design of the tower has also influenced that of the garden, with the vertical lengths of timber used on the storage cupboards echoing the lines of the church.

▶ Lengths of coppiced wood have been loosely tied together to create a rustic wigwam that is perfect for supporting climbing beans. Structures such as these enable the gardener to make the most of the vertical space and provide interest above eye level.

▼ Wild strawberries are the perfect edible plants for squeezing into a small nook or cranny, and they will thrive in a sunny or partly shaded spot. As well as providing masses of juicy fruits, they smell wonderful, filling the garden with a fruity perfume.

The clients briefed the designer to transform their urban rooftop into a cottage garden. To create a rustic atmosphere, reclaimed timber was used for the deck and to clad the large storage cupboards, housed cleverly under the eaves. Apart from providing space for a barbecue and tools, the eaves give plenty of protection from the wind.

This has helped to create a unique microclimate, which is perfect for growing a colourful mixture of cottage garden flowers, vegetables and herbs. Many of the plants thrive in a small, rectangular space at one end of the roof garden. Here, a mass of herbs, such as purple sage, chives and basil, knits together in two beds edged by low box hedging and strawberries, which spill their succulent fruit onto the deck. Height is provided by bronze fennel and scarlet-flowered runner beans that wind their way up a wigwam of rustic sticks. At the back of the edible garden is a raised trough planted with lavender – a wooden garden bench beneath it makes a wonderful place to sit, especially in summer when the essential oils of the herbs are released in the heat of the sun.

Although these plants require regular watering and need picking often to keep them bushy and healthy, other plants have been chosen for their ease of maintenance: a chamomile lawn is a scented alternative to turf and is perfect for busy lives, as it never needs to be cut. But when you have a weekend to yourself, it makes a wonderful green blanket to stretch out on.

The use of simple French garden furniture and junk shop finds, such as a galvanized watering can, a water jug and an old-fashioned oil lamp, contribute to the relaxed, unpretentious atmosphere of the space.

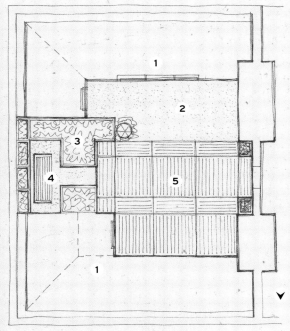

▲ Fournier St, London E1

1 Storage
2 Chamomile lawn
3 Planting
4 Seating area
5 Timber deck

► A group of ancient fruit trees, with gnarled stems supported by a stout trunk, still flourishes in a traditional orchard. Although they were planted decades ago, fruit trees like this will remain productive for a lifetime. Annual pruning helps to maintain their shape.

▶ Two chairs set in the shade of a tree in a garden clearing invite rest. The temporary nature of their placement adds to the informal arrangement and implies that the owners of the garden move regularly throughout the site.

Relax/Work

Many people strive to create the perfect idyll in their gardens. In our minds, a garden is often the ultimate Utopia, free perhaps from materials things and a romantic place of everlasting beauty. So, just for a moment, let us imagine, suspend our realities and conjure up this idyll. It is beautiful, of course, and overflowing with colour and scent, with an abundance of trees and shrubs, flowering plants, fruit and vegetables, water gushing and maybe some ornate statuary as a focal point. And our ideal is to be lazing around in such a place. There is, however, another factor, a reality: work. If we step off our cloud, we realize that a garden needs work, often hard manual labour, to create and maintain it. In Victorian or Edwardian times, wealth in the middle and upper classes meant that many gardeners were employed and had a base within the garden, such as a potting shed or bothy. These people were certainly using the garden as a place to work, but the notion of work and gardens in the 21st century often means something different. The new idea of a garden as a place of work does not imply the creation or maintenance of the garden itself. Now the garden has become a location where we might carry out our paid occupation (on non-gardening activities); the garden can be our workplace. It signifies that the garden owner, often in the new smaller garden, works from home but from a structure detached from the house, often at the end of a beautifully cultivated plot.

The Garden Workplace

There is a lot of sense in working from home but there are also a few potential pitfalls. On the positive side, if your profession is not dependent on you being based in a central hub, new technology such as hi-speed internet connections means that you can live in a place of your choice, often many miles away from the office. You can be more productive by having fewer interruptions, decide on your own working hours and, by remaining in situ, you will often have a much-reduced impact on the environment by not clogging up public transport or emitting petrol or diesel fumes into the atmosphere. You will probably also be less stressed. On the minus side, you do have to be well disciplined and you have to create an appropriate environment for your work. You may also have a feeling of isolation being away from colleagues.

Creating a suitable environment

Building a place to work in your garden is not a new idea. Around the world, garden sheds have been the home of many traditional crafts, such as clockmaking, which Swiss farmers turned their skills to during the winter months. Garden sheds have also been the hideaway for many an inventor: Trevor Baylis, for example, who created the first wind-up radio. The important thing is that the building serves its purpose, and thinking how it works within the garden as a whole is an opportunity to make the most of its aesthetic value.

Primarily you need shelter. You need to plan to create something that is solid and warm and waterproof, which means an enclosed structure. But this is not enough – it needs to fit with the general layout and structure of the garden. It can be turned to the garden's advantage by being used as an architectural backdrop. If you decide to steer clear of the bland, wooden garden shed, you have the opportunity to create an eye-catching focal point. In fact, there is as much scope as if you were creating a pavilion for enjoying the late sun or for holding dinner parties. Although its main purpose is for work, this does not have to be its sole function. So, from the outset, keep in mind the possibility of having a multi-purpose structure. Something as simple as adding a porch or veranda to the front could create a relaxing seating area for after work, giving the building an inclusive and welcoming look rather than creating a mental keep-out sign.

By reflecting your tastes in architecture, be it a rustic country-cottage-type structure or your version of a billowing, titanium-clad Frank Gehry opus, you can create a focal point or, quite simply, end the garden in a very definite way. The creation of such a structure can be viewed as an opportunity. But it would be easy to get carried away: you should always keep in mind a budget. A simply constructed garden shed could be ideal or you can buy one of the elaborate off-the-shelf concoctions advertised in the glossy magazines and Sunday supplements. These buildings often do not need planning permission because they are regarded as temporary and can be built in kit form or be lifted over the house by crane in no time at all. Alternatively, it may be that you engage the services of an architect to design an individual masterpiece or have some fun yourself. Make sure you have all the services you will need, such as electricity, phone lines, perhaps even plumbing, but never attempt these on your own. Get qualified people in, for safety and peace of mind.

▼ An outdoor desk takes the idea of the garden as a workplace to its ultimate conclusion. Quirky in its simplicity, it remains primed for use as soon as a sign of good weather allows an escape from indoors.

◄ A pathway sheared through a lazy meadow creates relaxed access to outdoor workshops. Simple and utilitarian, these work spaces look completely at home in the garden.

◄ The ultimate box office. Wood and glass, combined with a green roof, has created a workplace with sharp lines and an enviable simplicity.

▼ In a small city courtyard, this glass and steel cube is in deep contrast to its pretty garden surroundings. Large panes of glass shed the maximum amount of light for the artist working within.

▥ Fitting in with the garden

If your place of work is not going to be camouflaged and hidden, or tucked round a corner to create a deliberate surprise, the rest of the garden will probably lead up to it. Although many decisions depend on the overall style – formal or informal, for example – it must be practical. You must make sure there is good access day and night, with adequate pathways, no unnecessary obstacles such as ponds with fiddly bridges, and good lighting. Think of the potential pitfalls of running to answer the office phone – if it is too awkward, you will end up working at the kitchen table. Your place of work must be easy to get to, but it must also be secure. With more and more thefts from garden sheds, the safe storage of work and related material is paramount.

Consider the architectural style of your garden workplace carefully. You do not want a conflict, and your piece of architecture should not dominate its surroundings. Remember that, although it is an office, you are working within a garden environment, which means that it must fit in with the garden, or maybe contrast with it in a non-overbearing way. Unfortunately, our domestic architecture is often a bit of a let down; we tend to live in houses with few individual or redeeming features. So creating a home office is a real opportunity to have some fun and create something individual that reflects the type of person you are. Looking at it from the house could be the redeeming factor of your property: something uniquely inspiring.

◄ Rustic harmony is achieved by both the soft architectural design of the chalet-style building and the simplicity of the surrounding landscape. Placed among a grove of silver birch trees, the structure appears anchored to its spot.

▼ A harmonious picture is achieved by viewing this garden pavilion through a succession of colours. Its entrance is framed by two lollipop bays, while the powder-blue and white paintwork provides a real lightness of touch.

Your view down towards this structure from the house is important but so is your view looking out from your desk. You will have the advantage of working in a green environment, so make the most of it – pay more attention to the details in your garden that you otherwise might overlook. You could decide that your view should be a symphony of tree ferns of different sizes, the doors or windows framed by wonderful fronds, which would also soften the view when looking back at the structure. Or it could be that your traditional building could host some beautiful old roses, such as *Rosa* 'Madame Isaac Pereire' whose fragrant boughs of flowers would act as external drapes. Working in the garden will give an enhanced feeling of joy throughout the seasons and make you much

more aware of nature and wildlife – nesting birds or even hives of bees could vie with the computer screen for your attention. You will be lulled into a gentle and holistic lifestyle, which is particularly beneficial if you have a stressful job, and it enhances creativity in those with artistic jobs such as potters and painters.

Materials

The choice of the dominant material for your structure may be determined by its style. Depending on the statement that you want to make, you should consider your materials very carefully. The whole range of personal tastes can be explored and, rather than relaxing into something standard and obvious, it may be a good time

◄ This building has been practically enveloped by the garden, with clever planting framing and softening the sturdy architecture. It appears almost as if the structure is emerging from a jungle.

▼ A contemporary structure, slightly elevated over the garden, approached by steps and with its own terrace, becomes a destination. This simple construction is ultimately inviting due to its open, full-length sliding window.

◀ This wonderfully aged boathouse positioned at the end of a garden provides an idyllic space to clear the mind of cluttered thoughts. Flowers, dappled shade and water lilies all help to inspire.

to consider what you love, if you do have strong preferences. The dominant material used in garden buildings is timber. But even this can be used in either a rustic or a contemporary way. Shiny metals, such as stainless steel or zinc, or glass blocks or the rusting effect achieved from certain steels are all alternatives often explored.

Positioning the office within the garden

One of the advantages of having your workplace in the garden is that your garden becomes a daily destination, not just somewhere to enjoy at weekends. And if you create an interesting journey, so much the better, as you will get a lot more out of the garden not only Monday to Friday, but for the entire week. The contemporary garden is generally smaller than its predecessors so, to make best use of the space, it is usually sited at the back of the property. If it is at the far end, it therefore becomes the final focal point. As most buildings of this type are fronted by glazed windows and doors, the play of light on these reflective surfaces adds a lightness of touch to the garden – it can be almost like having a vertical pond.

If you get it right, the garden office will become one of the rooms you spend most time in, so its aspect – how it is oriented – is of prime concern. In most cases, unless you are building a photographer's darkroom, good light conditions are essential. This may dictate that your building is at an angle to your house and the line of the garden. Another possibility to consider is having large french windows or doors that fold back onto themselves to create a wide opening. Not only will they let in the most light, but they will allow you to work as close to the garden as possible during good weather. This is certainly an opportunity to make the most of. Conversely, however, make sure that it will be cosy and inviting in winter – think about a stove or underfloor heating.

There may be a temptation, because of light saturation and the wonderful views of the garden, to create a building with a large proportion of glass in the walls, doors and roof. But be careful – this will be hot in summer, often unbearably, and cold in winter. Yes, you can have the feeling of being surrounded by nature, but at the cost of being uncomfortable. A good balance in your use of glass is to be advised.

A Peaceful Retreat

This is a very simple but clearly contemporary garden. It is a working garden designed to allow the owners to enjoy a small city space and take advantage of the trees in the borrowed landscape. All the age-old components of a garden are here – lawn, borders, seating, hard standing, sculpture and pavilion – but they are organized in a very clean way. The exceptionally lush planting provides the softness.

A wooden pavilion created on stilts – four green oak beams – ends the view of the garden. It is multipurpose, originally devised as an office in the garden but now often used as a spill-over bedroom for guests. Although small, it manages to contain a pull-out bed, shower, toilet and even limited cooking facilities. From a design point of view, its main purpose is to create a definite end to the green landscape. It also acts as an everyday destination, drawing the householder through the garden, whatever the weather, every day of the year, whether to check emails, do some sketching or change the bedlinen!

In front of this building is a simple wooden deck, which, with the way the garden faces, is drenched in sunshine. And before the deck, there is an ornamental pond crossed by a simple, straight wooden bridge. The main area of the garden is a rectangular lawn, surrounded by a simple wooden pathway made from the same wood as the deck. On both sides are borders: to the right, a flowering summer border full of lilies, solidago, sedum, perovskia, melianthus and verbascum, while on the opposite side, the scene is framed by birch trees and greenery: pittosporum, dicksonia, *Rheum palmatum* and iris create a subtle division that allows the pond and deck beyond to emerge as a surprise. The planting plan ensures a succession of colour, with the full-headed sedums promising a beautiful display of pink in early autumn. In the middle of the herbaceous planting is a lollipop bay tree. This is echoed elsewhere in the garden with trimmed ligustrum standards.

The sculptural feature of the garden is a hanging chair – a generous steel ball and chain – into which you throw armfuls of cushions and then swing in it gently, your feet grazing the soft grass beneath. The steel girder supporting the chair will soon be clothed in rampant honeysuckle.

◄ A profusion of cheerful daisies poke through gaps in the wooden decking, softening its appearance and contributing to the informal ambience.

▼ A hanging, metal, spherical chair, suspended from a steel beam, adds structure to a green oasis and suggests repose.

◄ A wooden pavilion built on stilts with an attached deck becomes the final destination in a suburban garden. A rectangular pond, almost the width of the garden, acts as a moat, with a narrow bridge defining the psychological move from garden to workplace.

RELAX/WORK

FURNESS ROAD
LONDON NW10

CASE STUDY #13 CONTINUED

DESIGNER
DIARMUID GAVIN

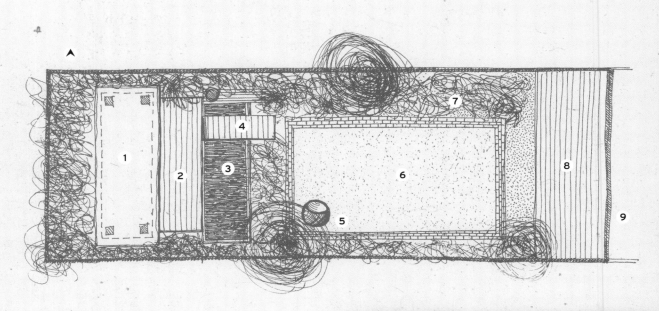

▲ **Furness Road, London**

1 Pavilion
2 Deck
3 Pond
4 Bridge
5 Hanging Seat
6 Lawn
7 Planted Border
8 Deck
9 House

◄ Lilies and achillea combine to add spots of colour in a garden that is predominantly green.

▲ A rectangular pond is finished to a very high standard with a stylish wooden deck. Deep green ferns thrive in the moisture and the pond provides the garden with a new planting opportunity in the semi-aquatic species.

The borrowed landscape includes trees from neighbouring gardens – a mature willow on one side, horse chestnut on the other and, behind, a smaller cherry tree. Despite the number of straight lines, the formal layout of the garden and the relatively large proportion of building, decking and paths, the whole picture is of a luxuriant green space, softened by lush, almost tropical, planting. As the built structures are all made from wood – a relatively warm material – the effect is soft and light.

Brightly coloured butterfly chairs adorn the deck and suggest relaxation, even when they are not being used. On the other side of the deck, a large glass and steel table is used for family dining. Behind the pavilion and hidden to all except the owner, there is a smaller shed filled with essential garden tools, as well as space for a water butt and compost heaps.

This urban plot makes the most of every square foot. It has a flexible extra room, and provides a sunny area for eating and lounging but, most importantly, it is a practical, lush green space that continually invites the owner to relax and forget the stress of city life.

◄ The rectangular lawn echoes the dominant shapes in this heavily planted urban idyll. The boundaries of the garden have been completely hidden by heavy planting, and willow and horse chestnut trees in the neighbouring properties frame the wooden structure.

▼ By the side of the pond, a *Dicksonia antarctica* planted in a tall clay plot benefits from the moist environment.

DIARMUID GAVIN & TERENCE CONRAN

Time to Relax

Contemporary life is busy and stressful. For many of us our homes are a refuge, and our gardens vital places to where we can escape. Traditionally, the perfect garden is a place of enjoyment. Our dream of a paradise garden is not one that focuses on the rigours of garden maintenance – mowing lawns, weeding and pruning. It is about taking in our green surroundings, wandering through floral spaces, lying on soft lawns and eating lunch in a beautiful outdoor setting surrounded by family and friends. Yet gardens are not only to be used. They should also provide a relaxing scene to be viewed from inside the dwelling – a picture or composition framed by a window.

▥ Paths

On a superficial level, the function of a path is to give us access to an area. On a deeper level, they are leading us, telling us where to go and creating or altering our mood along the way.

Japanese gardening embraces this fact, and it is fundamental to the philosophy that our journey in a garden should mirror our journey through life. Japanese gardens tend to mirror nature and create a grand view on a small scale. Similarly, their paths often represent aspects of nature, such as a dry riverbed, achieved with stepping stones carefully placed within gravel to create a restful route. This, like most Japanese garden features, works well within a modern or minimalist garden.

If you favour a stepping stone path in a more rustic setting, simply plant up all around and between the stone slabs. If you take the opportunity to plant with scented herbs, such as pennyroyal, chamomile and thyme, you will create a pathway that further delights the senses and lifts the spirits.

Mosaic paths can be very beautiful, but they are more difficult and time-consuming to create than they appear. Cobble mosaics fit particularly well in a garden setting, and the making of such a path can be viewed as an art project, which can be enormous fun and involve all the family. When it is finished, you can sit back with a well-earned drink and admire your work.

Gravel paths are easy on the eye with their soft colour and flowing texture, and there is a lack of geometric lines inherent in brick paths or paving. The distinctive noise caused by walking on gravel may evoke childhood memories, particularly of family visits to historic houses and gardens.

Bark chips make a more organic loose path, creating a woodland feel. If you wish to make a pathway though a large bed or an overgrown area of the garden, bark will fit in very well and give a relaxed informal feel. Ideally, paths should invite garden users to explore at their leisure.

▲ A keyhole-shaped patio made from crazy paving and dry stone walling, with a surrounding wall built from rubble, creates a very simple but beautiful relaxing space. The arrangement of the elegant furniture suggests time to stop, relax and to look beyond one's own boundaries.

▼ A contemporary workshop, cleverly adapted from a shipping container and set at an angle in a narrow garden, manages to become a stylish workplace. The glass panels built in at both ends serve to create a picture frame.

◄ A very simple, curved pathway made with broken slate leads the visitor on a meandering journey through a beautifully planted scene.

▲ The ingenious use of the wooden framework from an ethnic tented dwelling creates an intriguing open pavilion. Combined with wooden steps and simple and dramatic planting, it is an enticing vision.

▶ A tree house in the shape of a traditional garden shed, with circular portholes, has been developed around an existing tree. Dressed with rugs and cushions, it seems the perfect place for simple fun.

Built structures

The ultimate luxury in garden relaxation is to have a pavilion or summerhouse, which allows the garden user to enjoy a covered and shaded space, summer or winter, day or night. What could be better than an informal space free from all the associations of home; somewhere to escape to from the rigours of domestic life. Classical, contemporary, whimsical or exotic, a pavilion may be built in any architectural style, using a variety of materials. The whole structure often becomes the focal point of the garden and, even when not in use, can be illuminated to complete a relaxing picture.

A summerhouse is just one of many structures in which to relax in the garden. Tree houses, for example, are often perceived as the domain of children, but for an adult there is nothing more relaxing than lying on a platform in a tree, listening to and watching the leaves rustle in the wind. In the absence of large trees, a scaled-down version can be a simple wooden platform, raised 1.5–1.8m (5–6ft) above the ground. Clever planting underneath and around the platform can camouflage it to a degree. If you build one sturdy enough to take the weight of planters around the edges, these can be planted with tall bamboo, giving you relaxing sounds when the breeze blows through, and framing the sky as you lie on cushions while your cares melt away.

Conservatories can be very relaxing and are a bridge between the house and the garden. But if space is limited, it may become cluttered with cane furniture and bright plastic children's toys, and instead be a busy, almost stressful environment. Keep in mind that conservatories were originally for plants, and sitting in them among the foliage, drinking tea, was a treat. They are most relaxing when they are filled with lush, green plants – think of the Palm House at Kew Gardens. Of course, there should be space for people, but use some large terracotta pots to grow specimens that will thrive under glass if well watered and fed, such as *Monstera deliciosa*, the Swiss cheese plant. Try some hanging plants – the reliable spider plant can fill a lot of space, and some trailing sedums, such as *Sedum morganianum*, will give an exotic feel.

Pergolas and arches can be used to define a change in function between one area of the garden and another. They can suggest entry into a magical place, especially if clothed in a fabulous rambling rose or clematis that obscures the view beyond. Pergolas are great for creating a restful patio or seating space, too. Imagine a patio of large thick terracotta tiles beneath a wooden pergola draped in the pendulous purple flowers of *Wisteria sinensis*. The sunlight streaming through it makes shadowy shapes on a chunky wooden table on which there a few glasses of red wine. Do you feel relaxed?

▲ A Balinese-style structure appears to float over a water garden, complemented by shards of stone, dramatic aquatic planting and the golden slivers of koi carp. Water is the unifying factor of this harmonious scene, and the whole magic is contained in its reflective quality.

▶ A circular building with a low cone-shaped roof clad in cedar shingles makes for a gentle focal point and destination.

Outdoor fireplaces

For centuries, in many homes worldwide, the open fire as a source of heat has been a traditional means of drawing people together. Installing a fireplace outdoors, on a patio or a roof garden, creates a similar atmosphere, yet there is something even more evocative about sitting in front of an outdoor fire, whether a chiminea or a purpose-built fireplace, and being mesmerized by the flickering flames that, in turn, illuminate well-planted spaces or contemporary exterior surfaces.

Focal points

Meditation and contemplation in the garden are aided by providing the eye with something interesting or even soothing to focus on. If there is too much going on, the eye will have difficulty choosing where to rest, whereas a well-chosen focal point is a relief to both eye and mind.

Stone sculpture or an ornate urn spilling over with flowering trailing plants can provide a subject that is beautiful and not too fussy. It is important to choose items that you consider beautiful, as you are the one who will be relaxing the most in the garden. This can include pieces with a personal story or something humorous. You should choose something quite distinct to single out, otherwise the focus will be lost or possibly confused with other items in the garden.

Living sculpture such as topiary can provide interesting and often humorous focal points. Japanese-style topiary gives a restful feeling and you can easily get lost in thought while gazing at a cloud-trained tree. Living, evergreen sculptures come into their own in the winter, standing out through the mist and rain against a backdrop of bare branches. If you can, place topiary where it can be seen from a window, or french doors where you sit and view the garden, to create a restful view from inside the house all through the year.

Living sculptures made of willow and hazel can be used to create interesting features such as a rustic seat or a willow arbour. If your vegetable garden is close to the house, a simple hazel wigwam for runner beans or sweet peas can create a wonderful focus. In fact, even in the distance, a little further down the garden, the top of it peeking through the shrubs indicates an area worth wandering down to for a closer look. Keep in mind that if you intend to have a distant focal point, it should not conflict with another one. Create as many as you like, but they should only be viewed from different areas or angles so that they do not confuse the eye.

Water

Water in a garden, indeed water anywhere, helps to settle the mind. Water is about cleansing, relaxing and enjoyment, so to have the opportunity to make the most of it in a garden is wonderful. A favourite way is to create naturalistic still ponds, planted with rushes, grasses and water lilies that appear from the banks, merging softly into the water.

Suspending a simple bridge, a jetty or even a deck over water takes you to the centre of its magic. These stopping places allow you time to linger and contemplate the

▲ Fresh and tactile fern blocks soften the stone pathway and lead the eye through to a perfect round spy hole with beautiful views beyond. The wall stops you from seeing everything all at once and the round window concentrates the eye for optimum aesthetic.

◄ A shaped evergreen hedge creates the feeling of a soft backrest for this aged and elegant stone seat; a protected cosy place for solace and relaxation.

◄ A shady row of trees guides you down to a sunny retreat, but the mystery of what lies at either end of the path that crosses over is even more inviting. The perfectly trimmed Box hedges and the straight lines of the grass path further increase the sense of direction.

▲ The zigzag stones across the water are an irresistible path to a cool shady courtyard. The polished surface makes you want to throw off your shoes and feel the cool stone under foot.

▶ Strong lush planting opens out into a small stone courtyard with a simple squirting water feature. The splashing water brings freshness and serenity, while colour from flowers and foliage soften the stone and gently scent the area.

◀ The dappled shade over these elegant stepping stones and soft colourful planting create a tranquil setting and the perfect garden to escape to after a long hard day. The strong symmetrical stones create a formality that contrasts with the cottage-like planting and the simple waterfall brings harmony.

▶ This beautifully constructed pond illustrates how even a small water feature can add to any size garden. Cut out and finished in stone. It is set among planting that will shade fish from the glare of the sun. Installing a pond creates a brand new area for growing a whole new set of plants.

peaceful atmosphere of your surroundings, helping to relieve those external pressures. To sit on the edge of a deck and dangle your feet in the water in a Huckleberry Finn-type way completes the image.

Sound in the garden

All our senses are important to our ability to relax, and equally vital as soothing the eye is comforting the ear. This may take many forms – one day you may wish to listen to your favourite music, and another to the sound of the wind rustling through the trees. It is easy to create a number of sounds in the garden to enhance the serenity of the space.

Still water can create a focal point for contemplation and relaxation, but the sound of running or falling water has long been favoured as a soothing sound. In smaller gardens, simple water features such as water bubbling out of a stone sphere and gurgling into an underground reservoir, or running from a hollow bamboo into a Japanese stone basin, are easy and inexpensive to create. They can add a sense of tranquillity to a seating area or patio, or to a hidden corner where a seat has been tucked away to provide a clandestine escape.

If you have a little more space, a stream or rill can run through a patio, under a deck or simply disappear off into the garden, creating soothing sounds, as well as having a cooling effect in summer and, of course, a visual impact. Water running down a vertical surface, such as a wall or a tall, rough, standing stone, creates a similar sense of peace as horizontal water. Many of these features rely on pumps to move the water; they do not need to run constantly, however, which means that you also have the option of silence.

The wind can create many different sounds, too, as it rustles the leaves of trees, rushes through bamboo or tinkles chimes. Wind chimes come in many shapes and sounds, but a well-chosen chime that makes a relaxing sound can really place you in a peaceful, meditative frame of mind.

► In the evening, the breeze-block screening in this garden is reinvented through the simple but dramatic placement of night lights – tiny candles that illuminate and dramatize what is essentially a simple utilitarian wall. The scene is completed by the dramatic uplighting of standard trees.

▲ A dramatic and inviting low-slung outdoor living room. Rubble walls, massive wooden beams, built-in seating and a huge fireplace, which is the focus of the room, create a gathering point outside the house, while side openings frame views of the garden.

▥ Lighting effects

Lighting a garden adds a wonderful dimension and brings it to life when it would otherwise be unusable. Summer evenings spent in the garden watching the daylight fade have their own special magic, and that feeling can last well into the night with some well-appointed lighting.

A relaxing ambience can be created by low, soft lighting. The process of lighting the garden should begin at the design stage, because this is when forward planning of the position of cables will pay off. The cable of each light should be long enough to allow its position to be changed to a certain extent, but there should not be so much that it is difficult to hide, which may impede your gardening work.

If you do not wish to wire up the garden and would prefer a more environmentally friendly option, solar powered lights are widely available. They give a good soft light and have the added advantage of being easy to move anywhere in the garden. Be mindful of particularly shady places where there may not be enough light to charge them up during the day.

Another environmentally sensitive option is to use candles. Garden candles are usually quite sturdy and can withstand a breeze. Alternatively, place nightlights in glasses for a twinkling effect.

Up-lighting trees is a clever way to broaden the night-time view, and accentuates the beauty in the structure of the tree. In this way, you can create nocturnal focal points, which will retreat into the background in the daytime garden. Be careful to place the light correctly so that the crown of the tree is lit up. If the light source is too close to the base of the tree, with the beam almost vertical, the effect will be entirely lost and you will simply light up the trunk.

Lighting with water is obviously a dangerous combination but, in professional hands, it can make a hugely successful contribution to a relaxing garden. If you decide to install a water feature or pond, make the most of the opportunity to light it, too. In a still, reflecting pond, lights placed at the base will create absolute magic. Moving water takes more skill to light effectively, but it can beautifully effective.

Furniture and Soft Furnishings

Relaxing in the garden would be limited to sitting or lying on the ground if you had no garden furniture, so it is an essential component of any outdoor space. The choice is overwhelming – not just in style but function, too. Would you prefer to spend the afternoon in a reclining chair, on a lounger or flat out on a sunbed? Speaking of long summer days and moments of peaceful solitude, one favourite notion of relaxation is almost a cartoon cliché: two palm trees on a beach with a hammock swinging between them. Simple and inexpensive, hammocks are the perfect means of creating the right atmosphere for the escape from the rat race.

As an immediate extension to indoor space, french doors should open onto a patio or deck, furnished with comfortable loungers or a collection of throw cushions and small tables – another simple method of creating the right ambience for relaxing. The flow from inside to outside is seamless and inviting, while the injection of colour and texture from furniture and soft furnishings can enliven an otherwise dull scene. Make sure that the furniture is durable, or not too heavy or unwieldy to store easily during the winter months or inclement weather.

An outdoor dining room can be highly designed and permanent, however, with adaptable seating made from solid, sculptural materials – cubes of rendered and painted breeze blocks, for example – softened by carefully placed cushions. If you introduce integrated water bowls and candleholders, you can evoke an altogether more exotic atmosphere. It is inviting and stimulating all at once.

Away from the house and deeper into the garden, there is nothing more enticing than a hint of something beyond to lead you to a space that promises rest. A wonderful device is to create a strong line, which could be a row of simple rectangular slabs, that winds through a heavily planted plot and ends up at a semi-secret retreat. As a picture from the house, this seems to suggest reward for a journey taken. In the back of your mind, you know that when the chores are done or when visitors arrive, walking through the theatre set of your planting will offer the ultimate reward of relaxation, food and drink.

Occasionally, seats that signal rest and relaxation are used for a different purpose – posing as sculpture. An arrangement of two outdoor armchairs nestling symmetrically beneath two small garden trees creates an air of formality and suggests that this is a place where one should stop, take stock and admire the surroundings. While acting as a focal point, the chairs indicate that this is a place to be admired from afar.

▲ At the edge of a pond, a patio jetty stands over the water, safely corralled behind simple wooden fencing. A grouping of director's chairs allows for a gathering at the water's edge.

▼ A serpentine seat, supported by an intriguingly light framework, curves itself gracefully around a tree. The arrangement becomes the focus in a very simple garden.

Planting

The planting in your garden will ultimately dictate your mood, but keep in mind that nature itself is soothing and plants have a relaxing effect on people by just being there, so you really cannot go too wrong.

Ornamental grasses have become popular in gardens for their relaxing qualities. The soft, flowing flowerheads of *Stipa tenuissima* can create a dreamy quality, while taller, more upright grasses, such as *Calamagrostis* x *acutiflora* 'Karl Foerster', catch the breeze higher up. Combining grasses with tall perennials gives the double effect of hearing the grass blow in the wind and seeing little blobs of colour bobbing around with the flowing plumes of the grass. A great combination for producing this effect is that of *Miscanthus sinensis* and *Verbena bonariensis*.

Bamboos are wonderful for catching the wind, but also for creating hidden areas where you can escape to. Aside from this, they are beautiful plants, and the stems of some varieties are stunning colours. *Phyllostachys nigra*, for example, has wonderful black stems, which contrast with the green leaves, while *Phyllostachys aurea* has cheery yellow canes.

Staying with architectural plants but going for a completely different effect, a couple of banana plants can transform any garden into a relaxing tropical paradise. *Musa basjoo* is probably the most well known and is quite hardy. *Ensete ventricosum* is another lush banana, but it may need a cover of fleece in the coldest months. If you have a conservatory to keep it for the winter, it is worth growing *Ensete ventricosum* 'Maurelii' in a large pot for its

wonderful purple leaves, which really catch the light. Bananas need a spot sheltered from strong winds or the leaves will tear. A similar lush green effect can be achieved by growing sweetcorn, with the added bonus that you have an edible crop at the end of the summer.

Trees can make a relaxing garden. The rustling of leaves is a soothing, natural sound that people instinctively find calming. Birch trees rustle gently in a breeze, and if you plant *Betula utilis* var. *jacquemontii*, you get the added bonus of the smooth white bark that picks up all available light on dull winter days. *Populus tremula* is so named for its trembling leaves, and if your garden is very large, this is the ultimate rustling tree. Eucalyptus trees, such as *Eucalyptus gunnii*, quickly mature into good-sized specimens that create a rustling sound in a stiff breeze, as well as flowing with the wind – a soothing sight on a breezy summer's day.

Ultimately, we love to see flowers in our gardens. On a patio or decking area, some well-placed terracotta pots, glazed pots or metallic-finish containers can be filled to bursting with trailing plants and flowering annuals, creating a feeling of softly overflowing abundance. If you usually plant geraniums, why not try a scented one to achieve that extra dimension. Heliotropes are a classic container plant, which provides the most deliciously sweet scent, while trailing surfinia petunias are extremely free-flowering, as well as being wonderfully scented. The containers can provide earlier interest, too, if you plant some bulbs, such as early tulips and scented hyacinths and daffodils, which will delight you in spring.

There is nothing like relaxing in the garden after a day's hard work on the land. Aside from the satisfaction of looking at the fruits of your labours, many gardening tasks are gentle and therapeutic. The repetitive nature of pricking out seedlings, dead-heading or mowing allows you to concentrate solely on what you are doing and let your troubles fade away. Pruning and planting are opportunities to be creative. Planting seeds and watching them germinate and grow brings you closer to nature. So relax in your garden, nurture your plants and they will nurture you.

▲ All the planting in this sea of grasses and perennials is relatively low, with structural hedges kept to the far distance. Suggestion is key to the design, with the scene allowing the mind to relax, even if the body never reaches this oasis.

◄ Just a hint of what may be beyond creates the message of destination: two chairs, their backs peeping above a swathe of grasses, the simple view framed dramatically with flame-like licks of eremurus.

◄ A rustic wooden plank pathway leads to a floating deck set at an angle. The deck could be a place to stand and view from, a resting point on a journey or, with some temporary seating like these chairs, it could be the final destination, all the time lost in an ocean of colourful perennials.

◄ These cage-like pronged spheres of differing dimensions appear to have been rolled into place, as if part of a giant game of boules. Photographed on a hazy day and nestling in a rural idyll, this odd but quite timeless collection achieves both serenity and drama.

▶ From top to bottom, bonsai scissors, a two-pronged weeder, a folding pruning knife, secateurs and garden string – some of the essential tools of a gardener's trade.

Practical

How to Plan a Garden

Like a mass said in Latin, the idea of planning a garden is full of mysteries to the layperson. This wonderful notion implies that the designer is knowledgeable and cultured on a well-regarded subject: there is a certain awe that travels with the territory. On visiting renowned gardens throughout the world or appreciating classic styles whether through books or television, the intimidation is often heightened further.

This vast subject touches many different disciplines, from science, including chemistry and botany, through laws of proportion, mathematics, architecture and engineering, to meteorology and geology – sometimes touching on theology. It is exhausting thinking about it. The reality can be, of course, much simpler. Having a knowledge of the evolution of garden styles, why, where and how they came about, together with an appreciation of nature, is a good start. These days, because there are so many sources of inspiration, mostly immediately available through television and magazines, we tend to have a little knowledge about a lot of things. Through the Internet even more information, some extremely detailed or even inaccurate, is at our fingertips.

Remember though, garden styles have evolved in many different places for many different reasons and the innovators and the perfectors of individual styles often only knew their way around their particular genre. The many different types of garden did not just arrive in the last century or the century before. Many have been thousands of years in their development and evolution and the practitioners would not have had a clue about what was happening elsewhere, what was in vogue elsewhere – they dealt within

their arena. So the modern age can be deeply confusing. But relax the awe and increase the enjoyment. Understand that unless you decide to become a scholar it will be nigh on impossible to appreciate the history and intricacies of even one style. As with our other senses of appreciation and taste, what appeals to you will bubble to the surface. Understanding what you like and also appreciating that the original innovators were human, just like you, is a great help. Of course if you are a professional, a working knowledge of many garden traditions and styles is a necessity, and is accumulated through the years.

Planning your own garden is a difficult subject to talk about in broad strokes. We come from many different starting points. Also the book on garden design is not yet closed and never will be. It is still evolving and still being written; the leaps in understanding of new plots, different materials and the new gardener over the last fifty years have been more dramatic than in any period before.

But back to this book: previous chapters have given evaluations of different garden styles. We should have a good idea of what we like, an idea of what we want and given our situations – budget, climate, landscape – the two will link together to encompass our dreams.

▥ Your Plot

Examine what you are dealing with: what is your situation? What is your budget? What is your passion? Will you really want to garden or just create something that looks good? What is your timeframe – how long until you move house? Will you create an instant garden? Or would you like to see it grow over time with you and see it evolve from seeds and cuttings and grow into a mature

paradise? Is your garden appropriate for all members of the household? Are your dreams and ambitions for it too high? Are you getting the right knowledge for the location that you live in? Are you aware of the possibilities, the limitations and the styles that are out there?

There is nothing wrong with instant gardens – pay no heed to the highbrow detractors – it is a millennia-old tradition, and obviously suited to today's fast lifestyles. But if you do have time and dedication a lot can be achieved for very little and even very elevated dreams can be realised. It all comes down to a reality check and understanding what you have, so start analyzing gently, without being intimidated, and see where your inspiration takes you.

▥ Different types of plots

How do you form a relationship with the plot? How do you get to know it? Many people are stuck because their garden seems problematic – it may be on a slope, or it goes across the back of the house instead of running away from it, or it is to the front of the house and not the back, or it is a mess, or full of rubble or maybe it is just a beautiful old garden, one that you can appreciate but one that also inspires guilt because it is just not you. Relax and live with it for a while. Observe it; sometimes for a year. Get to know it, look out, go out and see where the sun is during different times of the day. See how warm or cold it is at different times of the year. Are there times when the exterior conditions are hostile, months that you never venture out because of extremes of heat or cold? If your house is a new build this observation can be easy as you may have been left with a small patio and a spanking newly rolled out lawn, but remember this could be

hiding a multitude of builders' sins – compacted soil, dumped rubble and drains in unexpected places.

Also cast an eye on what you live in – what is your house like? Because of intensive house construction, a lot of people live in boxes of little or no architectural merit. But you may benefit from an interesting style. Remember as well as working against defined boundaries, you will also be working against the architecture of your house and trying to blend in your living space, melting the indoors into the environment beyond or contrasting one with the other.

▥ Soil

This mix of organic matter, minerals, air and water plays a massive part in the success of your garden's growth. Getting to know your soil is one of the most important aspects of understanding what you have to work with. Check your pH level. Is it limey or acidic or is it neutral? Is the soil heavy, do puddles form after rain and drain away slowly or is it light and sandy, a composition that leaches water and nutrients too fast? Is it chalky or full of shale or rock? It may be a big job but these conditions can be altered or changed to improve the gardens ecology and the success rate of the plants. Or, knowing what you have, you can choose plants that will thrive in your conditions.

A good soil would be dark in colour and light by touch, much like chocolate-coloured bread-crumbs, which can be easily rolled up into a sausage shape but then will fall apart under pressure. Another sign of a good soil is the abundance of earthworms and insects. Teeming soil can only show that the mass is jammed pack full of all the nutrients that a plant will need to grow strong and healthy.

▥ Chalk

Pale, shallow and usually stony it is quite free draining, which is good, as it does not get waterlogged, but it will lose nutrients quite quickly. Its pH is always alkaline.

▥ Clay

A bit like Playdough – it is sticky and can be moulded into shapes and heavy to cultivate. It may be full of goodness and nutrients, but the drainage is bad; it gets sticky and floods in the wet and dries to be rock hard in the summer. Clay tends to take longer to heat up in spring.

▥ Sand

This soil feels gritty – this means that water will drain very quickly from it, which is good, but so too will all the nutrients, which is not good. This can be improved by adding organic matter – sand needs frequent irrigation and feeding. In the spring months it warms up quickly.

▥ Silt

Halfway between clay and sand, this retains water better than sand and is more fertile, but it tends to get compacted like clay because its structure is weak, leading to bad drainage.

▥ What do you need?

To create a garden that works well for you, at the earliest stages of planning it is vital to have an understanding of your particular requirements. These differ from one person to the next depending on lifestyle, family size and background. It is important to understand who will be using the space, what the space will be used for and when it will be used, before any construction work takes place. A family with three children who love cycling will need somewhere accessible to store their bikes, whereas a professional couple may need a sophisticated space that fits in

with their lifestyle. These initial questions will safeguard the success of the final design and gradually, a picture of the lifestyle begins to emerge. Only then can you start attacking a blank piece of paper with design ideas.

You may decide that a practical, low-maintenance garden will suit you and your lifestyle best. Of course there is nothing wrong with this choice, it is a sensible option if you want to take on other jobs inside the house or have no available spare time for doing a bit of weeding or mowing the lawn. However you may see the garden as a hobby rather than a chore and may never be happier than when pottering around the plants and

attending to your self-grown wilderness. Whichever side of the fence you may sit, gardening should be about enjoying yourself, enjoying the space and losing yourself within an environment that is brimming full of life and fresh vibes – enhancing our spiritual mood and encouraging us to take in a bit of nature's goodness.

Take control
It is important to take control of the space and to clarify in your own mind what you are after. Take gradual steps, laying down lines, creating shape, and designing the planting scheme. Treat it as if you were decorating the interior of your home: start by picking an initial

concept and then add to it until reaching the desired effect, much as you do when choosing a paint colour and soft furnishings.

Remember that style should be followed through with good design and be presented in a clear, concise way. The architecture of your home, the kind of life you lead and the landscape features you choose should all work together as part of the big picture.

Lines and Shapes
Producing a quick rough sketch of your boundaries and any fixed features will help to develop a good understanding of what the space has to offer. Following that it would be wise to go out with a 30-metre tape

and take more accurate measurements of your plot. Refer to your sketch and use a scale rule to draw the space to plan. Photocopy the plan a few times so you can play around with different shapes and styles and throw away any designs that you are not happy with. Just getting a few shapes on to paper will give you a general feel of what looks good in the space, but will also start to translate into different elements of the garden like the lawn and patio.

Some of the best garden designs are based on strong lines and shapes, which determine the style, proportions, and movement in the garden. The line of a garden usually refers to a path or route that leads the eye and directs you through the space. Lines impose order and offer clarity, helping to create an overall look of the garden, while shapes and volumes fill the areas between them. Shapes also provide definition and pattern, and create places for you to stand at a distance and appreciate the different features of your garden, but they also make the most of the available space.

Shapes and lines signify the style of your design. Curved lines and oval shapes usually give a garden an informal appearance, while straight lines, squares and rectangles confer formality. Lines and shapes can also divide up a garden into smaller spaces, with proportions that feel more comfortable. To create a sense of proportion, shapes need to have a relationship with one another; when you have a combination of various small shapes within a larger plan it looks fussy and over-detailed.

Curved lines – whether full circles, a simple 'c' curve or a more complicated 's' shape – may form some excellent base lines around which to build up a garden. The lines will create a visual pathway through the garden, and will lead you to

walk down the space. Use broad strokes – big blocks of planting tend to look much more impressive and are easier to maintain than lots of smaller beds.

Straight lines in the garden often follow the notion of clean informality or allude to ordered, formal gardens. They are great for leading the eye to the end of the garden or a special feature, but can also form the basis of informal, asymmetrical design. Providing an excellent framework for almost any garden, straight lines, interlocking squares and rectangles can create movement through the garden – experiment by shifting central lines to create asymmetry for interest and unpredictability.

Balance and proportion
Well-designed gardens all have a unifying principle, a central, understated idea that creates a cohesive, integrated look. Some contemporary designers purposely set out to create slight discord by building gardens that are off balance, but most of us want our outdoor spaces to offer a peaceful sanctuary. Broad, flowing borders that sweep gracefully through the space, or wide, straight flowerbeds flanking a pool, create order and immediately relax you, whereas dotted flower beds make a garden unbalanced and chaotic. The size of the shapes must be in proportion to the size of the plot that you are dealing with. Conflicting shapes will create a disjointed design.

You can draw on tracing paper laid over photos of your garden to give an idea of how features and planting will look in situ, and it's a good way to check sizes and proportions. When you have something you like, transfer your ideas onto your paper plan, and then, when you have a well-balanced, confident design you will be ready to put the plan into action.

The Role of a Garden Designer

Should the prospect of planning your own garden prove too daunting there is always the option of employing the services of a professional.

While the role of garden designer or planner has always existed, it has only been in recent years that it has well and truly joined the ranks of mainstream creative disciplines. Despite a long heritage, it is still an area that in the public's mind is in its infancy. To have your garden planned or designed was, until a couple of decades or so ago, an expensive luxury out of the reach of average working men and women. Happily, with today's relative prosperity, the profession is now widely accessible, but it is one that still causes confusion in people's minds. This will naturally clarify itself when, given time, garden design will become another commonplace service.

The ultimate aim of designers working in the garden is to help produce beautiful spaces which are practical to maintain, that have achievable installation and that take account of budget. Because there is an inevitable romance associated with the notion of gardens, definitions of the role and qualifications to undertake the profession are vastly varied – many of the best gardens that have been created privately or professionally have been undertaken by unqualified people who have not an iota of college learning. Indeed many of the best gardens have slowly evolved and experience and observation is definitely the best teacher. Garden design is an artistic pursuit. A good eye is all important, but add to that a sense of proportion and understanding of space, an understanding of climate and ecology, a knowledge of hard landscaping and an encyclopaedia of plant reference – you see that the combination of skills either learnt or practically acquired can be daunting.

The garden design profession – a background

Defining who is who and who does what in the gardening world can be quite difficult for the garden owner or even the careers teacher. Many of the professional models contain elements of each other and are often interchangeable. The profession extends from the aloof landscape architect to the humble general gardener. And in between there are garden designers, landscape designers, garden contractors, design and build practitioners, garden draughtspeople; the list goes on. What is a necessity is an understanding of how gardens work, how plants grow, why they grow and where they love to grow. But also the knowledge and understanding of who your client is – who you are creating gardens for.

Choosing the right professional

In the same way as people ask what is the difference between a psychiatrist, a counsellor, psychologist or therapist, the profession of garden design can be similarly confusing. People want to know the definitions to find out what they are looking for and what is suitable for them. But it is also handy to examine in case you are thinking of entering any area of this great profession or even if you are just planning a garden, major or minor, to understand the role of the professional, what each area has in common and what you will have to master to take logical steps.

Once the decision is made regarding which category of the profession you need to employ, take time to find your most appropriate collaborate. Personal recommendation will always be best but remember to check out the professional's work. Your brief will be different to anybody else's and you have to be sure that the party that you hire is up to the job. Always remember the old maxim about hiring or working for friends or family.

Landscape architects

Landscape architects tend to spend many years in college, learning the academic theory of how to design layouts for schemes from roadside planting to theme parks and everything in between. Their practical experience will vary hugely, depending on the facilities available to them at college. They deal with computers, reams of paper and acres of specifications. They go on site to instruct, never to dig, and they have huge influence over how our towns, cities, and prominent landmarks look. As with every other garden-related profession landscape architects range in excellence from the good to the bad to the ugly. They will mostly be recommended by architects. So check out their work – not just one scheme – and when you do commission a firm of landscape architects, make sure that you are benefiting from the skills of the principal or most talented and that you are not being fobbed off into the arms of an eager intern.

Garden designers

Garden designers are probably the most precious of the species. They are an open book as a group, often ego mad. Remember this is the species (and this writer among them) who put themselves forward at annual flower shows and scream the loudest for attention. Anybody can define themselves as such, it does not take a college qualification, but there are many such courses available and it is worth checking credentials. In recent times, if you introduce yourself as a garden designer, let's say at a cocktail party, the term can invoke a sense of haughtiness and awe. It is a mysterious title which in some ways leaves no room for challenge; it can be adopted by ladies who lunch, or by stockbrokers looking for an escape route. But it is certainly an area that inspires fascination in other people. And being a garden designer is like being a doctor at a party: you are very popular and everybody has a query. It is a profession that tends to attract practitioners who try many different things in their lives, flitting from one occupation to another. Personal recommendation is key, as the diverse range of work and the competency of the practitioners varies wildly. Websites are good, but try and visit completed gardens and, after admiring the view, ask the client whether they were listened to and how did the relationship travel.

Design and build

Design and build, for some, is the bedrock of the industry. For many it is what you have to do to get established – offer a complete, often no-nonsense service, tailoring your product to the client's needs. It can be uncomplicated but can also suffer from a lack of imagination. This species of garden creator will advertise through notices on pick ups, vans and trucks. They will often be associated with local garden outlets, have websites and advertise in the local directory.

Professional gardeners

Finally, the humble gardener. I hope there is a bit of the humble gardener in all of the above professionals. Because if you do not understand soil, and if you do not understand how and why plants grow, not just in

theory but with hands-on experience, you have no business being part of this business. The gardener, again, is a loosely defined role. There is a very attractive sense of freedom attached to the notion of being a gardener and most can probably do a little bit of everything. Many work for institutions such as botanic gardens, parks or stately homes. These people will have a clearly defined job and continue an age-old tradition of garden craft. They often deal with some form of planning and are accountable to curators or estate managers, and they may deal with ordering materials, labels and budgets.

But the self-employed gardener who works in the private sector is harder to pin down. Increasingly they assume the air of a wizard: elusive and all-knowing of mysterious ways forgotten by mere mortals. This is partly because of a recent lack of good teaching skills, but more due to the lack of desire in young people to become gardeners when being a designer has been seen as a much sexier option. Now, of course, the wizards are the

▼ Diarmuid at work in his garden design studio.

ones that are increasingly held in awe because they hold the answers to your gardening woes and, for a price, they will arrive and make everything in the garden rosy. Grab one if you can and try to build a relationship. Their prices are creeping up but they are worth their weight in gold. Always look at other work and check with their other clients if possible. You'll find this clan by word of mouth or you can seek them out by detective work – ask at your local garden centre if they know of people who work in your area who appear passionate. There are plenty of cowboys around with a slash-and-burn mentality and no knowledge, so beware.

The client/professional relationship

The relationship that you will have with your service provider is a two-way contract. They obviously have a job to do, but you have a huge part to play and the success of a design project depends on it. You must prepare and you must develop a line of communication that is open and clear. Although your instinct might be to 'get someone in quickly, just sort it, create something beautiful', in

general that will not work. Firstly, you have to define who you want and you have to find them. Once identified, you have to see if there is a personal chemistry – did you click, do you bond, do you get on? Are they sweet or arrogant? Remember, you are hiring somebody who is full of knowledge but they have to see beyond that knowledge and listen to you. Not only listen but take it in. We all know the wedding planner who befriends bride and mother, charms them to the high nines and proceeds to create his vision. As a group we are nearly as bad, marching in, dictating orders to an imaginary work force: chop down those trees, move the pond... but have they listened to the client? Look out for the breed who feel the need, often through lack of experience, to change everything, and try to blind or seduce you with their 'vision'.

Once you have made your match and feel you have a connection or an understanding with your professional, draw up the rules of engagement. There are many different ways of working. With garden designers and landscape contractors, there will generally be a written contract; fees and stage payments will be decided and there may well be amounts held back until all snagging has been completed or unsuccessful planting has been replaced. It is much better that everybody knows where they stand from the outset. Pricing, as with any other profession, varies from city to suburbs to country, from practice to practice. As the client you must decide on your budget – you should have an understanding of the costs of employing the designer and the designer in turn has an obligation to design to the scale of your garden and your construction budget.

Relationships break down through misunderstanding and bad communication. If you are commissioning a new garden through representatives, clarify the methods of communication with your service provider. Time frames are often vital but remember designing a garden is a creative process. Allow the practitioner time to dream (for a little while). When using contractors, there are standard forms of contract available, much as in the construction world. Monitor progress, ask questions all along and, if possible, retain the garden designer as a consultant right through the building process. Ask for regular reports, be they written or verbal and get involved, whether in the choice of sandstone or size of plants. It is this collaboration between client and designer that will generate a truly individual garden that reflects your likes and dislikes.

The initial development of the garden is simply the beginning. Gardens are living things – they change on a daily basis. You must have an understanding of what is being created, or it can be like waking up one morning and finding a squealing baby in a cot abandoned on your doorstep. Get a maintenance plan (for up to five years), to be carried out by you or your gardener, and take interest in and be rewarded by your new addition.

Planting in Design

▥ Structure

Albizia julibrissin f. *rosea*
H 10M; **S** 10M

The elegant leaflets and almost clear, fluffy pink flowers of the silk tree bring a rich beauty to the garden. The slender, layered stems can be used to great effect if you want a slightly unusual boundary.

Aralia elata
H 10M; **S** 10M

Tall spindly stems create an open, relaxed shape and beautifully fine foliage perfects the Japanese angelica tree. A striking specimen tree and fantastic when under planted in groups, particularly in autumn when the leaves turn golden yellow and red.

Betula utilis var. *jacquemontii*
H 15M; **S** 10M

This white-barked birch is a fabulous structural element when planted in close groups or as a specimen tree. Small, serrated, apple-green leaves create a light, airy shade perfect for any size garden. The multi-stemmed forms have become extremely popular.

Carpinus betulus 'Fastigiata'
H 10M; **S** 10M

This member of the hornbeam family grows fabulously upright in the shape of a flame. Its slenderness enables the tree to get to great height without taking up much room on the ground. A perfect punctuation mark in any garden design and a superb autumn colour change.

Cynara cardunculus
H 1.5M; **S** 1.2M

With its deeply cut, silvery leaves this architectural perennial is hard to ignore. Although it is worth growing for the foliage alone, in summer, the cardoon bears large purple flower heads on hefty stems. Give it a sunny spot and plenty of space.

Dicksonia antarctica
H 10M OR MORE; **S** 4M

The exotic tree fern's stout, dark brown, hairy trunk contrasts with the most glorious huge green fronds, making it one of the most dramatic of all trees. The grand unfurling of its whorls is the ultimate in garden theatrics.

Fatsia japonica
H 3M; **S** 3M

A member of the Araliaceae family, the fatsia is splendid for its large, deeply lobed, shiny leaves. The plant's rounded habit makes it useful as a specimen shrub, but its evergreen nature means that, in numbers, it creates a rich depth to larger borders.

Gunnera manicata
H 1.8M; **S** 2.2M

One of the most spectacular architectural plants to have landed in our gardens. With its enormous, textured leaves and curious flower spike, this architectural perennial is the most primeval of plants and lends real drama to any planting scheme. It will thrive in full sun or partial shade in moist, boggy soils. When grown en masse, cut away some leaves to form a mysterious and exciting tunnel under the umbrellas of foliage.

Paulownia tomentosa
H 15M; **S** 15M

This fascinating tree is huge at full size, but can be pruned back hard and kept multi-stemmed so that it produces the most scary, outsized, velvety leaves. The leaves and robust trunk are a complete contrast to the lilac foxglove-like flowers produced in spring.

Phormium tenax - Purpureum Group
H 3M; **S** 1-2M

Distinctive, deep purple sword-shaped leaves grow straight out of the ground and stand beautifully upright to form this classic specimen shrub. Stout flower stems carrying deep red flowers add to the effect in summer.

Phyllostachys nigra
H: 6-8M; **S**: INDEFINITE

Outstanding bamboo with ebony black canes that make fantastic verticals and soft rustling green leaves bringing movement and sound to the garden. The distinctive mottling on young canes disappears as they mature.

Pseudosasa japonica
H 6M **S** INDETERMINATE

If you have the space to let it spread, this vigorous bamboo will produce many olive-green canes that will form a marvellous architectural screen. It does not mind slightly shaded conditions, so it can be grown as a specimen plant in a woodland setting.

▥ Texture

Acanthus spinosus
H 1.2M; **S** 60CM

The more upright choice of the acanthus family. Beautiful for its deeply cut, dark green foliage, but known for its spiky spires of mauve and white flowers that add excitement and glamour to planting.

Clerodendrum bungei
H 3M; **S** 3M

Deeply serrated, heart-shaped leaves carried on deep purple stems make this a very strong looking shrub. Fantastic domed clusters of deep pink flowers that burst out of purple buds in late summer and autumn give off the sweetest fragrance. A favourite at Great Dixter.

Euphorbia characias subsp. *wulfenii*
H 1.5M; **S** 1.5M

The most fabulous plant to bring in the spring, this euphorbia is covered in the biggest, most luminous yellow flowers all the way through to summer. Beautiful around the base of a tree and will quickly grow to fill the most awkward spaces in the garden.

Hosta 'Frances Williams'
H 60CM **S** 1M

Huge, glaucous leaves are comfortably quilted and form large clumps, which are topped by short spikes holding white, bell-shaped blooms. I love this and other varieties, but unfortunately, so do slugs and snails.

Ligularia dentata 'Desdemona'
H 1.2M; **S** 60CM

The colours of mahogany and purple enrich the undulating, leathery foliage of this ligularia. Dark brown flower stalks bear vivid, daisy-like clusters of orange flowers from mid- to late summer. Wonderful in shady, moist areas with other bog-loving plants.

Miscanthus sinensis 'Silberfeder'
H 1.2M; **S** 45CM

This graceful, arching perennial grows in clumps of deep green, grassy leaves like fountains. It displays long-lasting, light purple silky flower plumes late in the summer and is perfect when grown either as a single plant or massed in great swathes.

Onopordum nervosum
H 2.5M **S** 1M

Plant the cotton thistle and stand well back – huge, brooding branches erupt from the clusters of fabulous, silver spiny leaves and in summer, are topped by clusters of vivid purple thistles. Ideal grown in gravel.

Platanus x *hispanica*
H 30M **S** 20M

An indispensable tree for a large garden, the London plane can put up with all sorts of climates and will even thrive in highly polluted areas. Grow it for the bark, which falls off in big plates to reveal a camouflage effect on the trunk.

Sambucus Black Lace TM (*Sambucus nigra* 'Eva')
H 6M; **S** 6M

The most beautiful, deep green to black, feathery foliage makes this shrub fabulous for contrast, texture and the perfect foil for brightly coloured leaves and flowers. Adds elegance and movement to a border.

Santolina pinnata subsp. *neopolitana* 'Sulphurea'
H 75CM; **S** 1M

This elegant, mounding plant has the most gorgeous scented, feathery leaves and is adorned with masses of pale yellow flowers throughout the summer. Imagine an evergreen pin cushion.

Zantedeschia aethiopica
H 90CM **S** 60CM

It is worth growing the arum lily for its huge, quilted leaves alone, but from late spring until the end of summer, it produces gorgeous white flowers on long stems. Its clean looks are perfectly suited to an architectural garden.

▥ Form

Alchemilla mollis
H 80CM; **S** 45CM

One of the most versatile and attractive infillers. Apple green, felty leaves that grow in softly rounded clumps provide the perfect background for the hundreds of tiny lime-coloured flowers that appear in early summer. Alchemilla complements other perennials and grasses alike.

Allium cristophii
H 60CM **S** 19CM

This is one of the most dramatic bulbs you can grow. In late spring, massive rounded heads of pink/purple flowers are held aloft on stout stems,

◄ A maze-like path on different raised levels creates a sense of mystery and intrigue by snaking around tall stems of bamboo.

providing a garden with a floral firework display - the dead flower heads will often remain well into winter, providing useful structure. A perfect bulb to thread through perennials.

Buxus sempervirens
10 YRS: H&S 1.5M; **20 YRS: H&S** 2.5M

The definitive evergreen shrub. Clipped into shapes and hedging, box sits beautifully in both contemporary and traditional gardens. Superb as a specimen, backdrop or boundary. Fabulous for creating low-growing hedges to divide beds and borders in the kitchen garden. Slow growing and well behaved, it loves to be kept tightly clipped and retains its shape well to provide structure to the garden throughout the year.

Hebe pinguifolia 'Pagei'
H 15-30CM; **S** 60CM-1M

Slightly tumbling, evergreen mini-shrubs that form soft mounds when mature. Short white flower spikes appear in from spring to summer, which perfectly complement the silvery green foliage. Their mounding habit is best used if grown as the lone species within a border.

Heuchera micrantha var. diversifolia 'Palace Purple'
H 45CM; **S** 45CM

A tidy habit, strong leaf shape and a deep red wine colour make this heuchera indispensable to the flower border. Fine sprays of white flowers on long purple stalks add to the effect. Great in sun and partial shade, it will even grow vertically on the side of a building.

Hosta fortunei var. albopicta
H 75CM-1M; **S** 1M

The most favoured shade plant of all. The fantastically stout, bronze-green shoots quickly heighten into pale green and creamy yellow, arching leaves that grow in solid clumps. Pale lilac flowers add more in summer.

Hydrangea arborescens
H 2.5M; **S** 2.5M

A glorious specimen shrub with robust leaves and heavy globes of creamy white flowers in summer. Fantastic in a white garden.

Kniphofia caulescens
H 1.2M **S** 60CM

In summer huge red and yellow club-like blooms are held on stout spikes above clumps of glaucous, evergreen leaves. This red hot poker can be grown among cottage garden plants or in a town garden and makes a good specimen in a gravel garden, where devoid of competition, it can develop and be seen fully.

Osmanthus heterophyllus
H 2.5M; **S** 3M

With a dark green colour and holly-like leaf shape, the osmanthus is strong and dependable as an infiller and border foil.

Phlomis fruticosa
H 1M **S** 1.5M

Vibrant grey colour leaves smother the mound-forming Jerusalem sage, an ideal shrub for Mediterranean-style gardens thanks to its tolerance of drought conditions. In early summer, hooded yellow flowers appear in whorls on top of erect stems.

▥ Vertical Interest

Akebia quinata
H 10M OR MORE

An elegant climber known as the chocolate vine because of its deep, dark purple flowers that emit a spicy vanilla scent in late spring. Beautiful, twining cover for a garden pergola.

Cardiocrinum giganteum
H 1.5-3M; **S** 75CM-1M

Enter the giant lily. This huge bulb produces a stem up to 3m in height, which carries great white trumpet flowers with deep purple-red streaks and a fragrance to die for. You may have to wait a good few years for a bulb to flower, but it is well worth the wait.

Cynara cardunculus
H 2M; **S** 1M

Huge, spiky silver clumps of arching, frond-like foliage make this perennial stand out a mile. The giant purple thistle-like flowerheads complete the drama in summer.

Delphinium Summer Skies Group
H 180CM **S** 75CM

Skyrockets of stately blue emerge from great clumps of foliage in mid summer to add strong form and colour to my borders. The beautiful spikes, made up of dozens of single flowers, are good for cutting, too.

Digitalis ferruginea
H 90CM **S** 45CM

Dangerous-looking spikes of golden brown flowers stand aloft deep green rosettes of leaves in midsummer. Foxgloves are ideal for a shady border. The spikes make good cut flowers.

Echium lusitanicum subsp. Polycaulon
H 1M

The echium plant is made up of fantastical bristly leaves that grow in huge rosettes. In complete contrast, spikes of pale blue flowers hang on soft hairy stems in the spring.

Eremurus robustus
H 2.2M; **S** 1M

Magnificent and tall, the slender flower spires soar above the strappy green foliage of this stunning perennial. Plant through a border of contrasting perennials for height and splendour.

Eremurus stenophyllus

H 1M **S** 60CM

Architectural wands of dark yellow sparkle in the garden and punctuate the border with colour during mid summer. There are many other varieties of foxtail lily worth seeking out with pink, white and blazing orange blooms.

Rheum palmatum 'Atrosanguineum'

H 2M; **S** 2M

The ornamental rhubarb has extremely large, deeply jagged leaves that start off red-purple and mature to a deep green. The striking foliage effects are joined by fluffy red flower spikes that tower up to 2m high in summer.

Verbascum bombyciferum

H 1.8M **S** 60M

Huge spikes of flowers erupt from dense rosettes of woolly leaves, putting on an impressive show of summer fireworks. The mammoth, 1.2m flower spikes are clad in large, sulphur yellow blooms. Perfect in a flower border or gravel garden.

Verbascum olympicum

H 2M; **S** 1M

The large, grey velvety leaves of this verbascum form a rosette up to half a metre across before sending up a magnificent spike of bright yellow flowers from mid-summer to September. The finest plant of the genus.

▦ Scent

Brugmansia suaveolens

H 5M **S** 3M

Native to Brazil, this variety of angels' trumpet needs protecting in less mild regions although it is ideal grown in a pot, which can be removed indoors for protecting over winter. The large, yellow, bell-shaped flowers that hang from the branches of this shrub are heavily perfumed and fill my conservatory with a heavenly, heavy scent from summer to autumn.

Cosmos atrosanguineus

H 60CM; **S** 45CM

Loved by children, this cosmos has tall dark stems with the deepest maroon-brown flowers, which give off the most amazing chocolate fragrance. They will need protecting over winter.

Galium odoratum

H 15CM; **S** 30CM

The elegant lupin-like leaves and tiny flower stars of this plant are all beautifully fragrant. Wonderful when grown near the patio for an extra special scented carpet!

Lathryus odoratus

H 2.5M **S** INDETERMINATE

For swags of colour and scent all summer long, sweet peas are hard to beat. There are loads of different varieties of this climbing annual and we grow dozens of them all over the garden. Ideal for cutting and perfect for attracting wildlife.

Lavandula angustifolia

H 1M **S** 60CM

The true lavender, beautifully aromatic foliage and flowers. Place it where you can touch it, brush past it, pick it or just take it all in.

Lavandula angustifolia 'Hidcote'

H 60CM **S** 75CM

In summer, lavender is hard to beat. The fabulous silver foliage oozes its essential oils in the heat of the sun infusing the air with its scent, while the beautiful purple flowers appear in profusion. A great plant in a Mediterranean garden and for attracting bees and butterflies into your space.

Lilium regale

H 2M **S** N/A

There is nothing subtle about the regal lily, a stately flowering bulb, which boasts massive white blooms, flushed with purple. The summer flowers have an overpowering scent, and look great in a border or on their own in a large pot.

Monarda 'Prärienacht'

H 1.2M; **S** 45CM

The crazy-looking monarda flower will brighten up any corner. The hallmark flower whorls are dense and rich purple in colour and this cultivar, in particular, is brilliant for additional height.

Nepeta nervosa 'Blue Carpet'

H 35CM; **S** 30CM

Grown essentially for its clumping, scented foliage, this catmint is awash with pale blue flowers all through the summer months. Best planted in good-sized blocks.

Pittosporum tobira

H 6M; **S** 4M

A beautiful, large shrub with lustrous, leathery leaves and creamy white flowers that have a fantastically orangey fragrance. Superb.

Santolina chamaecyparissus

H 75CM; **S** 1M

Elegant, tactile and aromatic; this rounded shrub is a perfect ornament in the garden all year. Bright lemon-yellow flowers, like buttons, adorn this mini-globe in summer.

▦ Colour

Achillea millefolium 'Cerise Queen'

H 60CM; **S** 60CM

This gorgeous upright yarrow adds texture with its feathery foliage and brilliant colour in its large plate-like heads of deep pink. A definite injection of colour, which lasts all summer long.

Agapanthus africanus

H 1M; **S** 50CM

The African lily is one of the most beautiful plants to add colour to the garden. Imagine deep blue fireworks that burst out and last for weeks. The broad, strappy leaves provide handsome evergreen cover at ground level.

Allium hollandicum 'Purple Sensation'

H 1M; **S** 10CM

Dense purple flower globes on robust green stalks make alliums unforgettable. Fantastic when grown among other plants so that they pierce through from nowhere.

Fritillaria persica

H UP TO 1.5M; **S** 10CM

An exquisite spring-flowering bulb valued for its deep brown-purple bell-shaped flowers that have a dusty grey bloom. The silver-green foliage complements this unusual flower colour beautifully.

Ipomoea indica

H 6M **S** INDETERMINATE

The blue dawn flower is a wonderful climber for quickly covering a bare wall or eyesore. When its large purple, funnel-shaped blooms smother its stems from spring to autumn, it lifts the spirits like no other flower. It likes a sunny spot, but is tender and needs a sheltered garden to do well.

Lobelia 'Cambridge Blue'
H 10CM **S** INDETERMINATE

A tasteful, well-behaved bedding plant. This quickly makes compact mounds of green foliage which are cloaked in sky-blue flowers throughout the summer months. Perfect for temporary edging or used in pots.

Muscari aucheri
H 15CM **S** 5CM

Planted en masse, the grape hyacinth makes a dramatic carpet of blue for a few weeks in spring. We have planted this diminutive bulb in a large basin and the effect is quite dazzling.

Myosotis sylvatica
H 30CM **S** 15CM

A carpet of forget-me-nots can be a breathtaking sight in spring and this biennial with tiny blue flowers makes wonderful ground cover in my garden, where it is mixed with alpine strawberries.

Papaver orientale 'Patty's Plum'
H 90CM **S** 90CM

The true divas of the plant kingdom, oriental poppies provide blowsy colour all summer long and this has decadent, deep purple blooms with papery petals. A show-stopping perennial for a sunny garden.

Rosa 'Iceberg'
H 80CM **S** 65CM

Perhaps the ultimate in flower power. Masses of beautiful white flowers are borne prolifically from summer into the autumn, almost concealing the emerald green foliage of this large shrub rose.

Salvia patens
H 45-60CM; **S** 45CM

One of the most striking blues of all the salvias. A few plants will quickly spread to produce a carpet of gentian-blue. The dark green foliage is, of course, deeply aromatic.

Sedum spectabile
H 45CM; **S** 45CM

From spring through to summer, the fleshy, silver-green leaves of this sedum grow in perfect mounds, providing form and contrast to other planting. Pink flowers arranged in flat heads in late summer bring welcome late-season colour.

Verbena bonariensis
H 1.5M; **S** 60CM

The amazingly popular verbena grown for its tall, wiry stems that carry tufts of tiny purple-blue flowers all through summer and into autumn. Plant as a clear screen or among other perennials for an added dimension and colour.

▍▍ Boundaries and Screening

Buxus sempervirens
10 YRS: H&S 1.5M; **20 YRS: H&S** 2.5M

Its compact growth and small, glossy leaves make the box plant perfect for creating decorative, low hedges within the garden while maintaining views across the garden as a whole. Used as screens, divisions or to frame flower beds.

Carpinus betulus
H 25M; **S** 20M

Hornbeam quickly establishes into a classic beech-like hedge, which retains its brown, crispy leaves through the winter. It grows beautifully straight so that it can be used to form a perfect pleached hedge.

Clematis montana
H 14M **S** 3M

A rampant climber with fabulous starry white flowers that are borne prolifically over the stems from late spring and well into summer. Ideal if you have a large, bare patch of wall that needs covering quickly.

Corylus maxima 'Purpurea'
10 YRS: H 4M; **S** 3.5M; **20 YRS: H** 4M; **S** 6M

An attractive boundary shrub for its toothed, dark purple foliage and bushy habit. It

produces edible brown nuts in winter, which are a bonus for the local squirrels.

Fagus sylvatica
H 25M **S** 15M

Common beech is the quintessential English landscape tree, but it is as a hedge that it is most useful. Grow as a clipped formal boundary to enclose the garden – the pale green leaves take on a darker hue before turning brown in autumn. Unlike most deciduous hedges, the leaves hold well into late winter.

Griselinia littoralis
H 6M; **S** 5M

The griselinia is particularly useful in coastal areas as it is fantastically resistant to wind and salt. It has bright, leathery, apple-green leaves and there is a variegated form for extra colour.

Hydrangea paniculata
H 7M **S** 2.5M

Clouds of confetti-like white flowers shroud a wall of my house in late summer, when this deciduous shrub comes into bloom. It is an ideal plant for lighting up an area of dappled shade in a woodland garden.

Phyllostachys nigra
H 6-8M; **S** INDEFINITE

The fabulous black bamboo with soft green, rustling leaves can be kept thinned out for a fine screen or allowed to clump up for a stronger boundary. The bamboo creates a wonderful atmosphere in the garden.

Prunus lusitanica
H 6M; **S** 6M

The Portuguese laurel has a dense, bushy and spreading nature with glossy green foliage that makes it an elegant hedging plant. A wonderful deep green backdrop that is not as overwhelming as yew or box.

Taxus baccata
10 YRS: H 2M; **S** 1.5M; **20 YRS: H** 4.5M; **S** 4.5M

An ancient tree of the English landscape, the very darkest,

dense foliage of yew makes it perfect as a hedge, backdrop or shaped specimen. It is slow growing so probably worth investing in larger, more established plants at the outset. Yew forms the structural backdrop to many of our finest gardens, where it is grown as a tightly clipped hedge – used to enclose or divide spaces, or as a dark screen for displaying riotous displays of perennials. Its ability to respond well to regular clipping means it is a classy alternative to box as a topiary plant.

Thunbergia alata
H 2.5M **S** INDETERMINATE

Black-eyed Susan is a fast-growing evergreen climber with stunning golden-yellow flowers with a distinctive chocolate brown 'eye'. I grow it up tripods, where the twining stems cling firmly to deliver a wonderful display of summer colour.

Wisteria floribunda
H 9M **S** INDEFINITE

A stunning climber that makes a cloud of blue and white on the front of my house in mid-spring. The pendant racemes of flowers drip from the plant and provide a magical scent in the evening.

▍▍ Autumn Interest

Anemone x hybrida 'Honorine Jobert'
H 1.5M **S** 60CM

Pure white flowers on wiry stems, each with a spongy green ball in the middle, prolong the flowering season. Japanese anemones spread quickly and are beautiful when established in large, swaying drifts.

Kirengeshoma palmata
H 1M **S** 60CM

Distinctive and lush foliage feature most on this alternative shady perennial. Unusual sprays of shuttlecock-like flowers last right through to October.

Liriope muscari
H 30CM; **S** 45CM

The liriope's evergreen, strap-like leaves are a splendid feature all year, but in autumn, the fabulous violet flower spikes appear, looking like tiny purple balls on sticks. The perfect garden plant.

Liquidambar styraciflua
H 30M; **S** 22.5M

The glossy, lobed leaves of the liquidambar develop the most stunning of all autumn colour changes. Shades of brilliant red, orange and purple adorn the tree all at the same time. You have to stop and stare.

Rhus typhina 'Dissecta'
H 5M; **S** 6M

Graceful and arching, the velvety shoots of R. typhina are fantastic in themselves. The deeply cut foliage carries out the most stunning orange-red colour change in autumn. Picture a giant, luminous red fern!

Viburnum opulus 'Roseum'
H 4M; **S** 4M

This handsome native shrub has a double attraction in the autumn. Its maple-like leaves turn a fantastic red and its flower panicles develop the brightest, translucent berries to be found. So worthy in the garden.

▍▍ Winter, early season

Catalpa bignonioides
H 15M **S** 15M

In a large space, the Indian bean tree comes into its own, spreading out its wide branches to provide lovely dappled shade below. It is a graceful tree, covered in clouds of yellow flower during the spring, followed by curious long seedpods that drip from the branches in autumn.

◀ Maintaining a well-clipped shape is the secret behind this impressive expanse of interweaving box hedge.

Erythronium dens-canis
H 15-25CM; **S** 8-10CM

An absolutely exquisite bulb with mottled leaves which give rise to drooping, pink flowers with fantastically reflexed petals. Beautiful in groups and naturalised in woodland gardens.

Helleborus Orentaris 'Harvington Shades of the Night'
H 30CM; **S** 30CM

We are so fortunate that such a wonderful evergreen as this will flower so early in the season. When most plants are still dormant, this hellebore produces large dark purple to almost black flowers with creamy yellow stamens. Velvety and rich against stark borders.

Darmera peltata
H 1-1.2M; **S** 60CM

Fascinating perennial that sends up ominous-looking, hairy brown flower stems straight from the ground in spring. The pink and white flower clusters are only joined by the foliage in summer.

Epimedium x versicolor 'Sulphureum'
H 30CM; **S** 30CM

Delicate, low-growing plant with fine, heart-shaped leaves tinted red and exquisite sulphur-yellow flowers in Spring. Fantastic underplanting for trees in sunny or shady areas.

Helianthus 'Lemon Queen'
H 1.7M **S** 1.2M

A proliferation of bright and cheery pale yellow daisy flowers smother the lanky stems of this statuesque, back-of-the-border perennial. An excellent plant for bringing late colour to the garden.

Melianthus major
H & **S** 2-3M

Strangely arched, deeply serrated leaves in blue-grey make the melianthus

totally unique. Strong, deep red-brown flower spikes are on display until summer. Pinch the leaves for a fresh peanut smell.

Fritillaria meleagris
30CM **S** 5CM

With chequer-board-patterned flowers, the snake's head fritillary is an unmistakable bulb that is ideal for naturalising in meadow gardens. It is my favourite spring flower, and the pendent blooms, sitting demurely on short stems, beg for closer examination. Sometimes, the flowers are pure white.

Hamamelis x intermedia 'Jelena'
H 4M **S** 4M

Delicate, spidery, orange flowers are borne in profusion on the naked stems of the witch hazel in early winter, when the still air is infused by their mysterious scent. Before leaf fall, the foliage of this deciduous shrubs puts on a firework display in the autumn, turning bright orange and then red.

Prunus serrula
H 10M **S** 10M

Wonderful for its luxurious copper-red, peeling bark throughout the year, this prunus is at its most beautiful when it displays a fine, white blossom in the spring. During winter the trunk of this ornamental cherry holds your attention, as the shiny copper bark sparkles when backlit by the low sun. Simple white flowers cover the branches in spring and herald in the gardening year, soon to be followed by red fruits. A highly decorative tree.

Salix alba var. vitellina 'Britzensis'
H 25M **S** 25M

Backlit by the sun, this willow has bare scarlet stems that almost sparkle in winter,

providing much-needed colour when there is little else around. It can grow tall, but is best coppiced to about 5ft (1.5m) which keeps it manageable and helps it produce plenty of colourful young stems.

▥ Containers

Agapanthus campanulatus
H 1.2M **S** 45CM

Thick clumps of leathery, strap-like leaves gradually emerge from the soil in early spring before this perennial – a variety of African lily – puts on its bravura performance in mid summer, when classy, dark blue flowers explode from a robust stalk. Perfect when grown in a container and kept slightly pot-bound.

Agave americana 'Variegata'
H 1-2M; **S** 2-3M

A commanding succulent with sharp, sword-shaped leaves, which are striped yellow. Fabulous at the edge of a shaped lawn or in ornamental patio planters, the agave provides texture and drama.

Hakonechloa macra 'Aureola'
H 40CM; **S** 45-60CM

A robust, spiky grass with yellow and green striped leaves on deep purple stems. The leaves age to a bright red-brown colour late in the season. It is slow-growing and fantastically unusual as a potted plant.

Miscanthus sinensis 'Gracillimus'
H 1-2M; **S** 45CM

This cultivar has much finer, arching grassy leaves, which develop into a deep bronze. White spiky flowers spray out like feathers in autumn. Let it clump up on its own to fill a pot for all-year beauty.

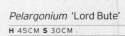

Pelargonium 'Lord Bute'
H 45CM **S** 30CM

Most varieties of pelargonium, with bright red, white or pink blooms are redolent of window boxes found across the Mediterranean, but 'Lord Bute' is in a class apart with large, rich purple flowers. Essential for summer containers.

Petunia x hybrida 'Blue Daddy'
H 30CM **S** INDETERMINATE

Planted in containers, the flowers of this petunia are essential for quick summer colour. The gorgeous, ruffled flowers with a bluish hue are huge and distinctively marked with violet veins. In my garden they keep going all summer long.

Rosmarinus officinalis
H 1.5M; **S** 1.5M

This fantastically drought-resistant herb is tactile, fragrant and indispensable in the kitchen. Small blue-lilac flowers grace the evergreen foliage in summer. Grow in free-draining pots where it can be accessed easily.

Tulbaghia violacea
H 45-60CM; **S** 30CM

Elegant, strap leaves which give rise to long-stalked clusters of lilac pink flowers from summer through to late autumn. Fabulous in smaller pots, which can be taken indoors over winter.

Astelia chathamica

H 1.2M; **S** 2M

Steely, spear-shaped leaves covered in tiny hairs contribute to this wonderful perennial. Astelias have amazing presence in colour, texture and shape. Brilliant when established across large border areas.

Bergenia 'Abendglut'

H 23CM **S** 30CM

The leathery, crinkly maroon leaves of this bergenia make wonderful ground cover and contrast to adjacent planting. This cultivar bears dense clusters of deep magenta flowers on longer-than-usual flowering stalks.

Sasa veitchii

H TO 1.5M; **S** INDEFINITE

Extremely useful as a slow spreading bamboo, the slightly broader leaves develop striking white edges along purple canes. This is a strong and distinctive, low-growing bamboo.

Viburnum x carlcephalum

H 6M; **S** 6M

This viburnum is a beautifully open, yet rounded shrub that produces tightly packed balls of deep pink buds, which open into white, highly scented flowers. It looks exquisite when the pale green foliage peeps through its skeleton of twigs in the spring.

▥ Edible Garden

Allium tuberosum

H 25CM **S** 8CM

A great choice if you prefer just a hint of garlic! The flavour of this garlic chive is half-way between ordinary chives and full-blown garlic. Slightly broader leaved than chives, it has white summer flowers and is perfect in leafy salads or simply as a garnish sprinkled on top of cooked vegetables.

Atriplex hortensis var. rubra

H 2-2.5M; **S** 45CM

The self-seeding atriplex is rich for its dark purple leaves and seed heads. A wonderfully tall, slender plant, which is perfect when peeking through other foliage plants. The leaves are an unusual addition to salads.

Capsicum annuum 'Apache'

H 60CM; **S**60CM

This Mexican chilli is prolific in growth and produces long, bright red chillis, which get hotter as they mature. A superb plant for pots indoors or outside in a sheltered, sunny position.

Cymbopogon citratus

H 1.5M; **S** 1.2M

The lemon grass of oriental cuisine is a tall miscanthus-like grass with an amazing, zesty lemon twist. It looks magnificent in pots, which can be taken indoors for the winter.

Cynara scolymus

H 1-2M; **S** 1M

The globe artichoke is fantastically noble, having deeply serrated leaves and huge, purple, thistle-like flowers. The boiled flowerheads provide the ultimate hors d'oeuvre.

Ficus carica 'Brown Turkey'

H 2.5M; **S** 3M

Wonderful against a warm wall, the unmistakable lobed fig leaves are a joy in the growing season. The fat, chunky figs are a fabulous brown colour when ripe.

Foeniculum vulgare

H 1-1.5M; **S** 60CM

Fennel's fantastic tall and feathery foliage provides texture and vertical structure to the edible garden. For different colours, grow the bronze form which perfectly complements brightly coloured flowers.

Cydonia oblonga

H 5M **S** 5M

The golden-coloured fruit which are borne on the common quince in the autumn are exquisite. They can be turned into wonderful preserves, but have a lovely perfume and we put them in the linen cupboard to scent clothes. This large, deciduous tree also has pretty white blossom in the spring, but needs plenty of space to thrive.

Fragaria vesca 'Semperflorens'

H 30CM **S** 30CM

Hundreds of tiny, gleaming red jewels smother the alpine strawberry, which forms tidy clumps of foliage to make an ideal ground-cover plant. The fruits are delicious, but it is back breaking work gathering them.

Mespilus germanica

H 6M **S** 8M

The fruit of the medlar is only ready to be picked after the first frosts of autumn, but then, when they are slightly rotten, they are delicious eaten with cream and port. Apart from the fruit, this spreading specimen tree has pretty white flowers and fabulous autumn colour.

Tropaeolum majus Jewel of Africa

H 240CM **S** INDETERMINATE

Nasturtiums are grow-anywhere annual climbers, which give a splash of colour and provide masses of delicious honeyed petals for salads. This mixture has a variety of orange, red, white and yellow flowers that are produced prolifically over marbled green leaves.

▥ Wildlife Friendly

Buddleja davidii

H 3M **S** 5M

An untidy shrub that more than earns its keep in the garden as a magnet to wildlife. Butterflies and bees are drawn to the legion of pendant flowers that drip from its lax branches, while small birds will feast on the pollinating insects. There are many fine varieties of butterfly bush, in many shades, that are worth seeking out.

Corylus avellana

H 5M **S** 5M

An essential ingredient of the native hedge, hazel has lovely, pretty green catkins in spring, followed by masses of edible nuts later in the year. These are delicious, if you can beat the squirrels to them.

▥ Low Maintenance

Amelanchier lamarckii

H 10M; **S** 12M

The most perfect tree for the smaller garden, elegant as a single or multi-stemmed specimen. Elliptic leaves that start bronze move through to green and then turn a brilliant red in autumn. Tiny creamy blossom stars produced in spring develop into purple black fruits with the autumn colour change. Reasonably slow growing, it needs hardly any looking after at all.

Materials in Design

Designing and creating gardens has always involved a mixing a concoction of elements. Ideas come together, plans are formed and subsequently gardens are created. By definition, for most people, a garden is all about plants. It is about green, lush growth and colour. We mean a controlled landscape – not fields, forests, savannah, mountain or lakeside, and within the boundaries it is taken for granted that there will be pathways, patios, contained water, walls, structures, steps, furniture – the hard materials that add to gardens in either practical or beautiful ways. Gardens are full of things that make green spaces work; we need paths to walk on; dry areas to stand on, places to sit, and structures to hide ugly or practical features and for storage.

Contemporary gardens are often dominated by structure and bought materials. This obsession is not necessarily either positive or negative – it is simply a reflection of the influence from different disciplines, such as architecture and art, on our green spaces. We live in an era where affluent societies get excited by design. With financial security, living has become easier and more luxurious, allowing people to make choices about their surroundings, expressing their taste in and around their homes. We live in a forward-thinking world, where new ideas, surprises and unexpected juxtapositions are enjoyed and appreciated.

So there has been a reassessment in post-modernist design of almost all materials (some that have been used for centuries), a re-evaluation of their physical qualities. We have the luxury of looking again, of re-examining every type of material such as wood and stone, metal and glass, plastic and acrylic, reinterpreting, using them in a different ways. Technology creates completely new materials and offers exciting possibilities for brand new ways of using old materials.

Materials and Tradition

Traditionalists and the old-school gardeners have been up in arms about the new vogue of concentrating on materials and non-green features in gardens, but gardens have always been such. The great classical traditions – Italian, Islamic, Persian, French or Japanese – have always relied on a careful balance of hard and soft landscaping. Terraces, walling, statuary, irrigation, dramatic water features, intricate carving, seas of gravel, pavilions and tea houses are admired by every garden lover and their relevance to historic tradition never questioned. The simpler type of garden using rustic materials is epitomised in the English cottage garden. The dividing line between these two traditions is financial: where there was money and power, plenty of ornate features were introduced, where there was little, one looked much more to the naturalistic and relied on a heady mixture of plants and improvisation with whatever was to hand. When these humble English cottage gardens began to be appreciated by the likes of Gertrude Jekyll they too became grander, the idea evolving in some cases into dramatic herbaceous borders, with larger gardens divided up into rooms and earthy-type materials such as clay brick and York stone being used in conspicuous quantities to create tasteful edifices.

Materials in the Modern Garden

But today we are in a situation where the appreciation of contemporary design and materials is common, yet the space available for each garden is limited. And along with this there exists a demand for gardens to offer more drama for less maintenance, as time is at a premium. So the re-evaluation of our gardens continues apace and the balance between hard and soft, introduced and planted features in gardens, has shifted. Materials and how they are used are important to the contemporary gardener.

With the rush to be new and on the cutting edge, contemporary designers have engaged in a race to be the first to try new materials whether reinterpreting the use of everyday objects or using materials designed for one purpose in another context. Glass is good in some applications – toughened glass for instance can make excellent balcony surrounds in gardens, creating a safe barrier on terraces without impinging on a view. Plastics, while looking good initially, can suffer through exposure to ultra-violet light and can deteriorate over time. Rubber, recycled or tailor made, has a number of applications in gardens, most notably for shock-absorbent, colourful flooring in playground areas.

Structures and Buildings

In traditional gardens, buildings and structures were made from a limited range of materials – wood and stone, often with slate roofs. There was also a great tradition in Russian, European and French gardens of creating wrought iron structures. Many garden buildings of the past would have been ornate places for people to rest, possibly for taking tea, and then to act as focal points in the landscape.

Outhouses such as tool sheds and lakeside boathouses in large gardens would generally have been constructed from wood. This material has the great advantage of being relatively cheap, easy to use, and naturalistic in its appearance. In the recent past the wood of choice has been a selection of fast-growing pines or other softwoods, while many traditional English garden features would have been made of oak. In contemporary times there has been a move towards the large-scale use of teak and other imported hardwoods, but now the disastrous effect of harvesting on their native environment is well known and pressure from the ecological movement is making its mark. Around the world there are various schemes which monitor the harvest, export, sale and use of endangered species or species whose removal from their place of growth can have a negative effect. So the gardener and the designer have moral responsibilities to face.

Similarly with stone, its past use in grand gardens was all about power and money. Whether marble or limestone, garden owners could afford to commission wonderfully carved, ornate statues and structures and often did so in celebration of an event in life – a marriage, a birth, a death, the winning of a war. Stone was a much favoured material, with the hope that the memories associated with the memorial would last as long as the material. Today, our own native stone is expensive and quarries are subject to environmental and health regulations. But in less developed parts of the world cheap labour costs combined with lax safety and ecological laws have led to a flood of stone arriving for the construction of patios and pathways from places like India and China, not all of which is suitable for use in our climate. There is a healthy trade in architectural salvage with contractors rescuing old building stone, brick and wood from demolished sites and selling it for very good prices where its use can often be seen in the creation of naturalistic or old-fashioned type gardens.

Flooring

The ground, whether it be hard or softly landscaped, is one of the most important elements of the garden as it acts as a framework to the entire composition. Paving of various kinds will provide paths, steps, ramps, driveways, areas for seating and dining as well as other garden features. The choice should be determined by the overall design and character of the garden, which will, in turn, be influenced by the style, location and age of the house that it adjoins, as well as the owner's desires and lifestyle. Using the same material that the house is built from to lead out into the garden helps to connect the areas with an easy flow. Indeed, try to limit the number of hard materials that are used in a space to avoid a disjointed and cluttered finish.

Hard-standing areas are essential to make a garden usable, for example for setting out tables and chairs and general navigation through the garden. Natural stone looks good in both traditional and contemporary settings. It can be expensive but will last, and displays a great range of subtle colours and textures. It is possible to get reclaimed natural stone from street pavements or the floors of old mills and factories, which can bring a wonderful, aged effect, but check the stones carefully for damage or oil stains. Portland stone, sandstone and slate are particularly beautiful. Many great gardens in the past were made from local stone as to import stone was so expensive. As a result the gardens seem to fit in with their environment as they had an inherent link. In addition, they would often construct all the garden features from the same stone so that coherence and integration was achieved through the use of a single material. If local stone is available in your area it is probably the best choice.

◄ This bespoke garden
canopy extends outwards
from the house and
provides welcome shade
from the heat of the day.

Slate is also an ideal material for paving. The dark colour associates well with planting or lawns and it looks even better when it gets wet. It is an extremely adaptable material as it can be sawn into crisp rectangles or broken into random pieces or even laid loose as ground cover.

Decking is an extremely popular choice and with good reason – it is easy to construct, is durable and relatively cheap. It is important to ensure that all woods are obtained from a renewable source, so look for the Forest Stewardship Council (FSC) and Programme for the Endorsement of Forest Certification Scheme (PEFC) labels when you purchase. Decking can be particularly useful when the garden slopes away from the house, enabling a series of decked terraces, but it also great to form barbeque areas and boardwalks. Decking feels comfortable and warm to walk on barefoot so it is fantastic around wet areas like swimming pools and hot tubs, soaking up the water from your feet almost immediately. It does have the greatest advantage of being able to be cut, with relative ease, into virtually any shape to fit the most awkward areas – even allowing trees to grow happily through the surface. It does, however, have the disadvantage of being slippery in damp climates and will need cleaning and re-oiling periodically, a factor to bear in mind when making your choice.

The largest part of your garden floor may be given over to lawn, ground cover or planting. Chamomile and thyme can be used as lawns, but grass is still the most cost effective and useful flooring. It is tough, easy to lay and if well maintained, can look gorgeous. There are various grass mixes to choose from to grow a hard-wearing lawn for the domestic home or a fine bowling lawn where needed. Lawns can be sculpted into the most exciting three-dimensional shapes and ground forms, an art-form perfected by Charles Jencks in the Garden of Cosmic Speculation near Dumfries in Scotland.

Steps

Various materials are suitable to create steps, but they must be safe and practical to use. In these days of liberal litigation, garden design and building is well regulated and attention is generally paid to creating safe access from one level to another, or through slopes.

Stone or brick is the obvious material to chose, sometimes used in combination for the treads and risers. Brick can be susceptible to frost damage – soft house-bricks will flake and disintegrate if they are used on a horizontal plane, and slate treads on top of brick risers can be an excellent choice. Over the past forty years railway sleepers have often been used set in slopes informally to create steps but they can have the disadvantage like decking of being slippery when wet. Metal has its place, both traditional wrought iron and contemporary metals such as galvanised grille, but these are not suitable for all footwear especially stiletto heels and bare feet in summer.

Walls/Screens/Fences

Walls, screens and fences are all boundaries, either visual or actual. We mark our territory to protect our families, our friends and our property. Generally our outer boundaries are determined, but different parts of the world have different local traditions. In Britain and Ireland, for example, most front as well as back gardens will have real boundaries, defined by a wall, fence or hedge, whereas in parts of America the front garden just does not exist. In eastern countries the house itself is the outer boundary with the gardens being internal courtyards.

The cheapest type of boundary to establish can take some time - rows of plants used as formal or informal hedging. Traditionally box, beech, holly, hawthorn, yew, privet, griselinia and Leyland cypress are plants that are all suitable for planting while young and establishing relatively fast to heights of 2-3 m (6-10 ft) or more. Laws and regulations certainly govern their use and in the UK, the fast-growing Leyland cypress has been the cause of much argument between neighbours as it climbs so high that it blocks out light and starves the soil. So agreement with your neighbours on a suitable boundary is often a good first step. Hedges are reasonably inexpensive and also make excellent windbreaks. Essentially they also provide a lush green backdrop for planting and more colour if you plant a flowering hedge. In addition, a mixed native hedge offers local wildlife a place to inhabit and berries and nectar to feed on.

Brick walls, rendered painted concrete, trellis, glass-brick walls, chain-link wire are just a few examples from a great number of options open to us today. Brick or stone walls can make a natural continuation from a building of the same material so creating a link to the garden, but for many, a timber-panelled fence will be the most cost-effective solution. Some self examination and understanding of what you are trying to achieve will give the answers for what choice to make.

Dividing your garden into different areas or rooms makes it a much more interesting space. Well-positioned dividers create a sense of mystery and surprise that will not fail to attract you into a garden - you have to find out what lies beyond that hedge, trellis or wall. The style of the surrounding garden will determine the choice of divider and it is that, with an appreciation of scale and positioning, which will add real depth to your overall garden design.

Furniture

It seems to be every architect's desire to express his qualities as creator by producing at least one new chair in a life's work and history over hundreds of years can certainly be charted in the creation of these everyday objects. But this rich history has until relatively

recent times been concerned with furnishing inside a dwelling. Outside we have been limited again to stone, wood or iron. In medieval gardens turf was used to create mounds akin to sofas, or a combination of stone, soil and plants such as chamomile or thyme was used to create wonderfully scented places to sit. But with prosperity for the masses has come a desire to create different ranges of outdoor furniture. Philippe Starck has designed polyethylene sofas, and you can get creations in glass, steel, wood, wicker, plastic, acrylic and fabric. We are in the middle of a time of real change in the way we that we lounge around outside. No longer is the wooden bench the ultimate in garden furniture. Good designers are paying

attention to the fact that people require all-weather suites of furniture – loungers, tables, chairs, and sofas – pieces that do not have to be stored, and look good, are comfortable and reflect an aspirational life style. The great change in recent times as with garden design in general has been the emergence of choice.

Art in the Garden
Sculpture and art in the garden is highly subjective. Many artists at the moment are experimenting with different media, particularly ephemeral materials. Andy Goldsworthy, the best-known of these, makes fleeting constructions out of natural materials such as leaves, twigs, stones and even snow. For traditional sculptors, materials have been chosen for

longevity, using stone, particularly marble, and cast bronze. In earlier times, wood was used, for example for totem poles. Often, salvage pieces and driftwood will find their way into gardens, offering something unique with an aged appearance. Wood will blend into most settings as there is so much choice in the type and finish that can be selected. A single piece of sculpture can define a period in time; imagine the impact of a white marble Michelangelo or a Damien Hirst – they are completely of their time. It is worth investing in a good and interesting piece of sculpture as it is often the perfect full stop for a garden of any style or age.

In contemporary gardens illusions of art and sculpture are created by visual

projections and of course there is great tradition of mural frescoes. Antoni Gaudi has been been responsible for nations of amateur tilers, inspired by his mosaics in Barcelona. The stunning waterfalls, sculptures and ceilings all combine to create a one-off garden experience at Parc Guell in Barcelona. Your choice of material can emphasise the classical or contemporary statement you are trying to make.

Plant Supports
Plant supports are a wonderful addition to a garden to add a bit of height and extra interest to the flower borders. There are smart new ranges of obelisks and frames on the market that enable you to create really beautiful botanical sculptures, having elegant proportions and detailing. Decorative plant supports in bamboo cane, heavy duty steel or wood are a way of focusing your climbing plants in one area so that they look much stronger and neater. A run on supports arranged into a zigzag line allow you to flow one plant into another so that contrasting foliage and flowers can be shown off.

A large pergola structure can be used to make a much bigger statement. Pergolas are at their most beautiful when set over a patio for dappled shade. They look most effective when painted with a complimentary paint colour so as to meld the structure into the whole garden design. A flowery arbour is also very romantic, especially if it leads you through to a new garden area – somewhere slightly hidden from your immediate view.

Water in the Garden
Water can entertain, soothe, exhilarate and relax; it can transform the atmosphere in all types and styles of garden, from a small rooftop space to a grand stately home's formal garden. The most important

consideration is to choose a feature that suits the existing style of garden or the design that you have in mind. In our crowded cities, water can create a pleasing new sound that serves to distract you from the background noise and bring peace to the garden. Flowing water can focus your attention within the garden.

Consider the effect that you want to create and always look out for new ideas that will enliven the space. Misting machines that are popular in modern Japanese gardens produce spectacular effects with lighting, and dancing jets of water that bounce and disappear into the ground are just delightful. They will not fail to make a garden extra special and to lift the spirits of all who visit.

Ponds increase the feeling of space in a garden as they reflect the sky on the water's surface and those with running water can create a peaceful and serene atmosphere. Straight edges of a pond or pool are formal where curves are more relaxed – ensure that whichever you choose fits in with the rest of the garden. Before embarking on any pond project, the safety aspect should be considered first as even the shallowest ponds can be dangerous for young children. A bog garden or upright water feature can be a fantastic alternative.

Water features with no standing water are wonderful if you have limited space, no time for pond maintenance or if children are around. A wall fountain, a pebble pool or a vertical surface of rippling water all have the benefits of a water feature without the hard work of maintaining a pond. A dramatic wall of water can be a great focal point for the end of the garden, finished off with strong lines of structured planting such as Fatsia japonica or Phormium tenax and lush, green, arching species like ferns.

▥ Advice

Arboricultural Advisory and Information Service
Alice Holt Lodge
Wrecclesham, Farnham
Surrey GU10 4LH
www.treehelp.info
Wide-ranging advice on trees

Composting Association
3 Burystead Place
Wellingborough
Northamptonshire NN8 1AH
www.compost.org.uk
Promotes composting as sustainable organic waste management practice

Garden Organic
National Centre for Organic Gardening
Ryton-on-Dunsmore, Coventry
Warwickshire CV8 3LG
www.gardenorganic.org.uk
Promotes organic gardening methods

Dry Stone Walling Association of Great Britain
Westmoreland County Showground
Lane Farm, Crooklands
Milnthorpe
Cumbria LA7 7NH
www.dwsa.org.uk

Gardening for the Disabled Trust
Hayes Farm House
Hayes Lane, Peasmarsh
East Sussex TN31 6XR
Provides advice, grants and information

Health and Safety Executive
Information Centre
Broad Lane, Sheffield
South Yorkshire S3 7HQ
www.hse.gov.uk
Concerned with gardening health and safety

Horticultural Therapy
Goulds Ground
Vallis Way, Frome
Somerset BA11 3DW
Provides advice and information

National Inspection Council for Electrical Installation Contracting (NICEIC)
Warwick House
Houghton Hall Park
Houghton Regis, Dunstable
Bedfordshire LU5 5ZX
www.niceic.org.uk
Produces a list of approved electrical installation contractors

Permaculture Association
Hollybush Conservation Centre
Broad Lane, Kirkstall
Leeds
West Yorkshire LS5 3BP
www.permaculture.org.uk
Encourages the practice of permaculture, the use of ecological, organic and bio-dynamic principles for sustainable cultivation

Royal Caledonian Horticultural Society
28 Silverknowes Southway
Edinburgh EH4 5PX
www.royalcaledonianhorticultu
ralsociety.org
Advice, publications, events, membership benefits

Royal Horticultural Society
80 Vincent Square
London SW1P 2PE
www.rhs.org.uk
Advice, publications, events, membership benefits

Royal Horticultural Society of Ireland
Cabinteely House
The Park, Cabinteely
Co. Dublin
Ireland
www.rhsi.ie
Publications, events, membership benefits

Soil Association
South Plaza
Marlborough Street
Bristol
Avon BS1 3NX
www.soilassociation.org
Promotes sustainable relationship between plants, soil, animals, people and the biosphere to protect and enhance the environment

▥ Garden Design Courses

English Gardening School
Chelsea Physic Garden
66 Royal Hospital Road
London SW3 4HS
www.englishgardeningschool.c
o.uk

Harlow Carr Botanical Gardens
Crag Lane, Harrogate
North Yorkshire HG3 1QB
www.rhs.org.uk/harlowcarr/har
lowcarreducation.asp

Royal Horticultural Society Education Department
RHS Garden Wisley
Woking
Surrey GU23 6QB
www.rhs.org.uk

Many horticultural/agricultural colleges, universities and adult education centres also offer garden design courses

▥ Garden Designers

The Society of Garden Designers (SGD)
Katepwa House
Ashfield Park Avenue
Ross-on-Wye
Herefordshire HR9 5AX
www.sgd.org.uk
List of Full Members, whose work has passed an assessment. Full Members number around 60 but account for less than 10 per cent of the Society's total membership

The Garden & Landscape Designers Association (GLDA)
PO Box 10954
Dublin 18
Ireland
www.glda.ie
List of Full Members

Diarmuid Gavin Designs
Studio 4, Folly Mews
223a Portobello Road
London W11 1LU
www.diarmuidgavindesigns.
co.uk

▥ Garden Contractors

British Association of Landscape Industries (BALI)
Landscape House
Stoneleigh Park
National Agriculture Centre
Warwickshire CV8 2LG
www.bali.co.uk
List of approved members

Association of Professional Landscapers (APL)
C/o The Horticultural Trades Association
19 High Street
Theale, Reading
Berkshire RG7 5AH
www.landscaper.org.uk
List of approved members

▥ Garden Structures

Agriframes
Tildenet Ltd.
Hartcliffe Way
Bristol BS3 5RJ
www.agriframes.co.uk
Steel pergolas, arches, arbours, bowers, obelisks

Alitex
Torberry farm
South Hartiing, Petersfield
Hampshire GU31 5RG
www.alitex.co.uk
Aluminium glasshouses

Amdega
Faverdale Industrial Estate
Darlington, DL3 0PW
www.amdega.co.uk
Softwood conservatories and summerhouses

Appeal Blinds
6 Vale Lane
Bedminster, Bristol
Avon BS3 5SD
www.appealblinds.com
Conservatory blinds

Deckor Timber
PO Box 296
Harrogate
North Yorkshire HG1 5WE
www.deckortimber.co.uk
Softwood retaining structures, gazebos, pavilions, pergolas, decking, trellis, planters, seating

Anthony de Grey Trellises
Broadhinton Road
77A North Street
London SW4 0HQ
www.anthonydegrey.com
Trellis, pavilions, gazebos, pergolas, arbours, decking, planters

English Hurdle
Curload
Stoke St Gregory, Taunton
Somerset TA3 6JD
www.hurdle.co.uk
Willow hurdles, summer-houses, arches, arbours, bowers, seats, benches, chairs, tables, plant climbers

Good Directions
8 Bottings Industrial Estate
Hillsons Road, Botley
Southampton
Hampshire SO30 2DY
www.good-directions.com
Cupolas, clocks, weathervanes

HLD
The Old Shipyard
Gainsborough
Lincolnshire DN21 1NG
www.hld.co.uk
Hardwood and softwood retaining structures, bridges, gazebos, pergolas, decking, trellis, fencing, planters, seating

Haddonstone
The Forge House
East Haddon, Northampton
Northamptonshire NN6 8DB
www.haddonstone.co.uk
Reconstructed stone architectural components for balustrading, pergolas, pavilions, steps, etc

Jacksons Fine Fencing
75 Stowting Common
Ashford
Kent TN25 6BN
www.jacksons-fencing.co.uk
Specialist supplier and installer of timber and metal fencing and gates

Jungle Giants
Ferney
Onibury
Craven Arms SY7 9BJ
www.junglegiants.co.uk
Bamboo poles, screens, fencing, gates

Lloyd Christie
Greystones
Sudbrook Lane
Petersham TW10 7AT
www.lloydchristie.com
Hardwood and softwood conservatories, summer-houses, gazebos, pavilions, decking, pergolas, trellis, planters, seating

M&M Timber Co
Hunt House Sawmills
Clows Top, Nr Kidderminster
Worcestershire DY14 9HY
www.mmtimber.co.uk
Softwood retaining structures, bridges gazebos, pavilions, pergolas, decking, trellis, fencing, gates, planters, seating

Marston & Langinger
192 Ebury Street
London SW1W 8UP
www.marston-and-langinger.com
Conservatories

Raffles Thatched Garden Buildings
Laundry Cottage
Prestwold Hall, Prestwold
Loughborough
Leicestershire LE12 5SQ

Redwood Decking
Bridge Inn Nurseries
Moss Side. Formby
Liverpool L37 0AF
Hardwood and softwood retaining structures, bridges, gazebos, pavilions, pergolas, decking, trellis, planters, seating

The David Sharp Studio
201A Nottingham Road
Somercotes
Derbyshire DE55 4JG
www.david-sharp.co.uk
Reconstructed stone components for balustrading, pavilions, steps, etc

The Swimming Pond Company
Carpe Diem, Common Road,
Bressingham, Diss
Norfolk IP22 2BD
www.theswimmingpondcompany.com

Stuart Garden Architecture
Burrow Hill Farm
Wiveliscombe
Somerset TA4 2RN
www.stuartgarden.com
Hardwood gazebos, pavilions, pergolas, bridges, decking, trellis, gates, planters, seating

Thatching Advisory Services
The Old Stables
Redenham Park Farm
Redenahm, Andover
Hampshire SP11 9AQ
www.thatchindadvisoryservices.com
Thatched sunshades, prefabricated thatch tiles, split cane screening, peeled reed screening, heather screening, reed panels, willow and wattle hurdles, bamboo fencing

▥ **Paving, walling & stone**

Atlas Stone Products
Westington Quarry
Chipping Campden
Gloucestershire GL55 6EG
www.b-c-l.com/sites/atlas/atlas.html
Paving slabs and walling

Baggeridge Brick
Fir Street
Sedgley, Dudley
West Midlands DY3 4AA
www.baggeridge.co.uk
Clay pavers and accessories, facing and engineering bricks, plus specials

Bardon Fyfe Natural Stone
Bardon Hill
Coalville
Leicestershire LE67 1TL
Granite and sandstone cubes, setts and paving, plus rockery and walling stone, boulders, feature stones, cobbles, and decorative aggregates

Blanc de Bierges
Eastrea Road
Whittlesey
Peterborough
Cambridgeshire PE7 2AG
www.blancdebierges.com
Modular creamy buff concrete paving slabs and setts, plus seats and planters information

Blockleys Brick
Sommerfield Road
Trench Lock, Telford
Shropshire TF1 5RY
www.michelmersh.com/blockleys
Clay pavers and accessories, and facing bricks, plus specials

Border Hardcore
Buttington Quarry
Welshpool
Powys SY21 8SZ
www.borderstone.co.uk
Natural stone boulders, cobbles/pebbles, large rocks, rockery stone, obelisks and decorative aggregates

Civil Engineering Developments (CED)
728 London Road
West Thurrock, Grays
Essex RM20 3LU
www.ced.ltd.uk
Natural stone paving, setts, boulders, cobbles/pebbles, mosaic cubes, large rocks, rockery stone, aggregates

Freshfield Lane Brickworks
Freshfield Lane, Dane Hill
Haywards Heath
Sussex RH17 7HH
www.britishbricks.co.uk
Clay pavers and facing bricks, plus specials

Ibstock Building Products
Leicester Road
Ibstock
Leicestershire LE67 6HS
www.ibstock.com
Hand-made and machined clay pavers and accessories, facing and engineering bricks, plus specials and ceramic tiles

Marshalls
Birkby Grange
Birkby Hall Road, Birkby
Huddersfield HX3 9SY
www.marshalls.co.uk
Concrete paving, block and sett paving and accessories plus clay pavers and accessories, facing and engineering bricks, and specials

Michelmersh Brick
Hillview Road
Michelmersh, Romsey
Hampshire SO51 0NN
www.michelmersh.com/mich.html
Hand-made and machined clay pavers and facing bricks, plus specials

Silverland Stone
Holloway Hill
Chertsey
Surrey KT16 0AE
www.silverlandstone.co.uk
Natural stone paving, walling, rockery stone, imported stone, decorative aggregates, plus reclaimed materials and man-made paving and walling

Stone Heritage
Portaway Mine
off Dudwood Lane
Elton, Derbyshire DE4 2BD
www.stoneheritage.com
New and reclaimed natural stone paving, setts, boulders, walling, rockery stone

Stonemarket
Old Gravel Quarry
Oxford Road
Ryton-on-Dunsmore
Warwickshire CV8 3EJ
www.stonemarket.co.uk
Reconstituted stone paving, edging, walling

The York Handmade Brick Co
Forest Lane, Alne
North Yorkshire YO6 2LU
www.yorkhandmade.co.uk
Hand-made clay pavers and accessories, facing brick, specials and terracotta tiles

▥ Lighting & Irrigation

City Irrigation
Bencewell Granary
Oakley Road, Bromley Common
Kent BR2 8HG
www.cityirrigation.co.uk
*Irrigation system design and
installation*

Garden and Security Lighting
Lightscape Projects
67 George Row
London SE16 4UH
www.gardenandsecuritylightin
g.com
*Initial design consultations,
lighting proposals and
demonstrations, product
supply, and installation*

H2O Irrigation
Foxhill Stables, Home Farm,
Foxhill Road, West Haddon
Northamptonshire NN6 7BG
www.h2oplc.com
Automatic watering systems

Hartland Irrigation
Unit 4, Manor Farm Business
Centre
Kingston Lisle, Wantage
Oxfordshire OX12 9QL
*Irrigation system design and
installation*

Leaky Pipe Garden Systems
Frith Farm
Dean Street, East Farleigh
Maidstone
Kent ME15 0PR
www.leakypipe.co.uk
*Supply and installation of sub-
surface or sub-mulch porous
hose system*

Porous Pipe
Cottontree, Colne
Lancashire BB8 7BW
www.porouspipe.co.uk
*Porous hose made from
recycled car tyres*

▥ Furniture & Ornament

Barbary Pots
45 Fernshaw Road
London SW10 0TN
*Hand-thrown Moroccan
terracotta pots*

Humphrey Bowden
6 Park Terrace
Tillington, Petworth
West Sussex GU28 9AE
www.humphreybowden.com
*Sculptures and copper
fountains*

The Bulbeck Foundry
Reach Road, Burwell
Cambridgeshire CB5 0AH
www.bulbeckfoudry.co.uk
*Lead statuary, fountains, pots,
urns, planters*

Capital Garden Products
Gibbs Reed Barn
Pashley Road, Ticehurst
East Sussex TN5 7HE
www.capital-garden.com
*Fountains, urns, pots, planters,
lead cisterns*

Julian Chichester Designs
Studio S
The Old Imperial Laundry
71 Warriner Gardens
London SW11 4XW
www.julianchichester.com
www.westminsterteak.com
Teak seats, benches, tables

Chilstone
Victoria Park, Fordcombe Road
Langton Green, Tunbridge Wells
Kent TN3 0RE
www.chilstone.com
*Hand-made reconstituted
stone statuary, pots, urns,
planters, seating, fountains,
obelisks, columns, balustrading*

Connoisseur Sundials
Lane's End
Strefford, Craven Arms
Shropshire SY7 8DW
www.sun-dials.net
Brass and bronze sundials

The Conran Shop
Michelin House
81 Fulham Road
London SW3 6RD
www.conranshop.co.uk
*Tables, chairs, shades, pots and
planters*

Andrew Crace
49 Bourne Lane
Much Hadham
Hertfordshire SG10 6ER
www.andrewcrace.com
*Bronze sculptures, bronze pots
and urns, gazebos, seats,
benches, tables, umbrellas*

Serena de la Hey
The Willows, Curload
Stoke St Gregory, Taunton
Somerset TA3 6JD
Willow sculptor

Fairweather Sculpture
Hillside House, Starston
Norfolk IP20 9NN
www.fairweathersculpture.com
Hand-made ceramic sculpture

Frolics of Winchester
82 Canon Street
Winchester
Hampshire SO23 9JQ
*Ornamental trellis, trompe
d'oeil, silhouettes, seats,
benches, chairs, tables,
planters*

Forsham Cottage Arks
Goreside Farm, Great Chart
Ashford
Kent TN26 1UJ
www.forshamcottagearks.com
*Dovecotes, poultry and
waterfowl housing, aviaries*

Garden Heritage
Heritage House
Swallow Drive
Milford-on-Sea
Hampshire SO41 0XD
www.garden-heritage.co.uk
*Carved granite, marble and
sandstone statuary, water
basins, Japanese lanterns,
bamboo poles, screens and
water features*

Gaze Burvill
Newtonwood Workshop
Newton Valence, Alton
Hampshire GU34 3RT
www.gazeburvill.com
*English oak seats, benches,
chairs, tables*

David Harber Sundials
The Sundial Workshop
Valley Farm, Bix
Henley on Thames
Oxfordshire RG9 6BW
www.davidharbersundials.com
Sundial maker and restorer

Ironart of Bath
Upper Lambridge Street
Bath
Avon BA1 6RY
www.ironart.com
*Wrought-iron and steel seats,
benches, tables*

Vanessa Marston
Gorwell House,
Goodleight Road, Barnstaple
Devon EX32 7JP
www.vanessamarston.com
*Bronze and bronze-resin
sculpture*

Minsterstone
Pondhayes Farm
Dinnington, Hinton St George
Somerset TA17 8SU
www.minsterstone.ltd.uk
*Stone seating, planters, staddle
stones, balustrading, paving,
tiles*

Pearson/Lloyd
117 Drysdale Street
London N1 6ND
www.pearsonlloyd.com
Furniture and industrial design

Pots and Pithoi
The Barns
East Street, Turners Hill
West Sussex RH10 4QQ
www.potsandpithoi.com
*Cretan pots, antique
Mediterranean pots*

Christine-Ann Richards
Chapel House
The Street, Wanstrow
Shepton Mallet
Somerset BA4 4TB
www.christineannrichards.com
*Ceramic vases, planters, water
features*

Rusco Marketing
Little Faringdon Mill
Lechlade
Gloucestershire GL7 3QQ
*Wrought-iron, teak and iroko
furniture, umbrellas,
hammocks*

Sandridge House Sculpture
Sandridge Hill
Melksham
Wiltshire SN12 7QU
Hand-carved natural stone ornaments

Sundialman
The Smithy
Pentrefoelas, Betws-y-Coed
Gwynedd LL24 0HY
Brass and slate sundials

Rupert Till
The Martens Court
Postlip, Winchcombe
Gloucestershire
GL54 5AJ
www.ruperttill.com
Lifesize wire sculptures

Whichford Pottery
Whichford
Shipston-on-Stour
Warwickshire CV36 5PG
www.whichfordpottery.com
Hand-made terracotta pots and urns

||||| **Specialist Nurseries**

Apple Court
Hordle Lane
Hordle, Lymington
Hampshire SO41 0HU
www.applecourt.com
Ferns, grasses, hostas, South American plants

Anthony Archer-Wills
Hawks Haven
109 N Mountain Road
Copake Falls
NY 12517
USA
www.archerwills.com
Aquatics. Also specializes in water garden design, construction and maintenance

Architectural Plants
Cooks Farm
Nuthurst, Horsham
West Sussex RH13 6LH
www.architecturalplants.com
Foliage plants, hardy exotics

David Austin Roses
Bowling Green Lane
Albrighton, Wolverhampton
Shropshire WV7 3HB
www.davidaustinroses.com
Over 900 varieties of antique, climbing, rare and unusual roses

Peter Beales Roses
London Road, Attleborough
Norfolk NR17 1AY
www.classicroses.co.uk
Over 1,000 varieties, especially old-fashioned and climbing roses

Blooms of Bressingham
Bressingham, Diss
Norfolk IP22 2AB
www.bloomsofbressingham.co.uk
Herbaceous perennials, alpines, conifers

British Wild Flower Plants
Burlingham gardens
31 Main Road
North Burlingham
Norfolk NR13 4TA
www.wildflowers.co.uk

Eucalyptus Nurseries
Allt-y-Celyn
Carrog, Corwen
Denbighshire LL21 9LD
www.eucalyptus.co.uk
Eucalyptus and acacias

John Chambers Wild Flower Seeds
15 Westleigh Road
Barton Seagrave, Kettering
Northamptonshire NN15 5AJ

The Beth Chatto Garden
Elmstead Market
Colchester
Essex CO7 7DB
www.bethchatto.co.uk
Unusual perennial plants

The Citrus Centre
West Mare Lane
Pulborough
West Sussex RH20 2EA
www.citruscentre.co.uk

Coblands Nursery
Trench Road
Tonbridge
Kent TN10 3HQ
www.coblands.co.uk
Bamboos, grasses, ferns

Countryside Wildflowers
Chatteris Road
Somersham
Cambridgeshire PE17 3DN

Deacon's Nursery
Moor View
Godshill
Isle of Wight PO38 3HW
www.deaconsnurseeryfruits.com
Soft fruit and fruit trees

Drysdale Garden Exotics
Bowerwood Road
Fordingbridge
Hampshire SP6 1BN
Bamboos, foliage plants, Mediterranean plants

Emorsgate Seeds
Limes Farm
Tilney All Saints
King's Lynn
Norfolk PE34 4RT
www.wildseed.co.uk
Native wildflowers and grasses

Fibrex Nurseries
Honeybourne Road
Pebworth
Stratford-on-Avon
Warwickshire CV37 8XP
www.fibrex.co.uk
Ferns, ivies, hellebores

Global Orange Groves
Horton Road
Horton Heath
Wimborne
Dorset BH21 7 JN
www.globalorangegroves.co.uk
Over 30 varieties of citrus, including lemons, mandarins and kumquats

Hoecroft Plants
Severals Grange
Wood Norton, Dereham
Norfolk NR20 5BL
www.hoecroft.co.uk
Grasses, foliage plants

Iden Croft Herbs
Frittenden Road
Staplehurst
Kent TN12 0DH
www.herbs-uk.com
Herbs, wildflowers

Jekka's Herb Farm
Rose Cottage
Shellards Lane, Alveston
Bristol
Avon BS12 2SY
www.jekkasherbfarm.com
Medicinal, culinary and aromatic herbs, wildflowers

Langley Boxwood Nursery
Langley Court
Rake, Liss
Hampshire GU33 7JL
www.boxwood.co.uk
Over 50 varieties of box, topiary

Mattocks Roses
C/o Notcutts Nurseries
Woodbridge
Suffolk IP12 4AF
www.mattocks.co.uk
Over 350 varieties, especially new and old ground-cover and shrub varieties

Ken Muir
Honeypot Farm, Rectory Road
Weeley Heath, Clacton on Sea
Essex CO16 9BJ
www.kenmuir.co.uk
Soft fruit and fruit trees

The Palm Centre
Ham central Nursery
Ham Street
Ham, Richmond
Surrey TW10 7HA
www.thepalmcentre.co.uk
Palms for interior and exterior use, bamboos and cycads

P W Plants
Sunnyside
Heath Road, Kenninghall
Norfolk NR16 2DS
www.hardybamboo.com
Bamboos, grasses

Reads Nursery
Hales Hall
Loddon
Norfolk NR14 6QW
www.readsnursery.com
Citrus, fig and other fruit trees, vines, yew, box hedging, topiary

The Romantic Garden Nursery
The Street
Swannington
Norwich
Norfolk NR9 5NW
www.romantic-garden-nursery.co.uk
Topiary including holly, box and yew

Stapeley Water Gardens
London Road
Stapeley, Nantwich
Cheshire CW5 7LH
www.stapeleywg.com
Aquatics, fish, filters, fountain jets, pool liners, preformed pools

ACKNOWLEDGEMENTS

The publisher would like to thank the following photographers, agencies and designers for their kind permission to reproduce the following photographs:

Endpapers: Claire De Virieu/ Inside/Photozest (Owner: Pierre Berge, Provence); 1 Sanei Hopkins Architects Ltd; 4-5 Helen Fickling; 6-7 Sculpture: 'Na Hale 'O Waiwai', 2003 by Patrick Dougherty, photo Paul Kodama, courtesy of The Contemporary Museum, Honolulu, HI, USA.; 8 Marion Brenner (Designer: Andrea Cochran); 10-11 Philip Bier/View (Designer: Paul Archer); 12 Andrea Jones/Garden Exposures (Designers: David McRory & Roger Raiche); 15 Robin Matthews/ Diarmuid Gavin Designs; 17 J C Mayer - G Le Scanff (Garden: Jardin de Berchigranges 88 France); 18-19 Mads Mogensen; 20-25 Andrew Montgomery/ Conran Octopus; 26 Guy Hervais (Designer: Andre Le Notre); 28 J C Mayer - G Le Scanff (Garden: Jardin de Berchigranges 88, France); 28-29 Jerry Harpur/Harpur Garden Images (Designer: Steve Martino, Phoenix, AR, USA); 29 above Helen Fickling (Designer: Raymond Jungles, FL, USA); 29 above Helen Fickling (Designers: Debra Yates, Raymond Jungles Inc., FL, USA); 30 above J C Mayer - G Le Scanff (Designers: Coignet & Sereo, Festival des jardins de Chaumont sur Loire 41 France); 30 centre Yann Monel; 30 below Andrew Lawson (Docton Mill, Devon); 30-31 Jerry Harpur/Harpur Garden Images (Designer: Steve Martino, Phoenix, AR, USA); 31 above Jerry Harpur/ Harpur Garden Images (Designer: William Martin, Victoria, Australia); 31 below J C Mayer - G Le Scanff (Designers: Ossart - Maurieres, Jardin de L'Alchimiste a Eygalieres-en-Provence 13, France); 32 Nicola Browne (Designer: Daniel Ost, Belgium); 32-33 Marianne Majerus (Designer: Jessica Duncan); 34 above left Andrew Lawson (The Dillon Garden, Dublin); 34 above right Jean-Pierre Gabriel (Designer: Dominique Lafourcade); 34 centre Edwina

von Gal; 34 below Christian Sarramon; 35 above left Andrew Lawson (Designer: Kathy Swift. Morville, Shropshire); 35 above right Marianne Majerus (Designer: Jessica Duncan); 35 below John Glover (Designer: Alan Gardener); 36 left Jerry Harpur/Harpur Garden Images (Designer: Jenny Jones, IOW); 36-37 Nicola Browne (Designer: Steve Martino, USA); 37 above left Jean-Pierre Gabriel (Designer: Denis Dujardin); 37 above right Nicola Browne (Designer: Dan Pearson); 37 below J C Mayer - G Le Scanff (Designers: Pascal Cribier, Lionel Grubert, Patrick Blanc, Jardin de Mery sur Oise); 38 above J C Mayer - G Le Scanff (Pheasant barn garden, UK); 38 below John Glover/Gap Photos (Designer: LandArt); 39 Nicola Browne (Mount Usher Gardens, Ireland); 40-43 J C Mayer - G Le Scanff (Designers: Ossart - Maurieres, Sculptor: Pierre Baey, Jardin de la Noria, pres d'Uzes 30, France); 44 Jerry Harpur/Harpur Garden Images (Designers: John & Pauline Trengrove, Christchurch, New Zealand); 44-45 Jean-Pierre Gabriel (Designer: Philippe Renac, Summer house designer: Daniel Libbrecht); 46 John Glover (Designer: Fiona Lawrenson); 46-47 above Andrew Lawson (Shute House, Dorset); 46-47 below Leigh Clapp/Gap Photos; 47 Jerry Harpur/Harpur Garden Images (Designer: Rosemary Alexander); 48 above Andrea Jones/ Garden Exposures (Designer: Piet Oudolf); 48 below Yann Monel; 49 above left Jan Baldwin/ Narratives; 49 above right Yann Monel; 49 below left Helen Fickling (Petersham House, UK); 49 below right Marianne Majerus (Designer: Piet Oudolf); 50 Yann Monel (Chateau de Beauregarde, France); 51 above John Glover; 51 below Yann Monel (Designer: Yves Gosse de Gorre, France); 52-55 Jerry Harpur/Harpur Garden Images (Designer: Ulf Nordfjell, Sweden); 56-57 Yann Monel (Designer: Jef Cools, Belgium); 58 Jerry Harpur/Harpur Garden Images (Designer: Topher Delaney, San Francisco, CA, USA); 60 left Marianne Majerus (Designer:

Aileen Scoular); 60 right Marianne Majerus (Designer: Charlotte Rowe); 61 Michael Wee; 62 above left Marianne Majerus (Designer: Claire Mee); 62 above right Helen Fickling (Designer: Patrick Blanc, Festival des jardins de Chaumont sur Loire, France); 62 below left Eugeni Pons/ RBA; 62-63 Mark York/Red Cover; 63 left Clive Nichols (Designer: Wynniatt-Husey Clarke); 63 right Helen Fickling (Designer: Wynniatt-Husey Clarke); 64 above Jerry Harpur/Harpur Garden Images (Designer: Peter Nixon, New South Wales, Australia); 64 below Marianne Majerus (Designer: Michelle Osborne); 65 above Jerry Harpur/Harpur Garden Images (Designer: Cilla Cooper, Auckland, NZ); 65 below Andrea Jones/ Garden Exposures (Designers: Joe Swift/Sam Joyce); 66-69 Jerry Harpur/ Harpur Garden Images (Designer: Christopher Bradley-Hole, London, UK); 70 above Ripple Lawn, Ben Wrigley/ Designers: Taylor Cullity Lethlean; 70 below Nicola Browne (Designer: Bernard Hicks); 71 Johnny Bouchier/Red Cover; 72 above Helen Fickling (Designer: Christopher Bradley-Hole, Italian plaster by Perucchetti); 72 below Marianne Majerus (Designer: Julie Toll); 72-73 above Jerry Harpur/ Harpur Garden Images (Designer: Sam Martin, London, UK); 72-73 below Jean-Pierre Gabriel (Designer: Jacques Wirtz); 73 Jerry Harpur/Harpur Garden Images; 74 above Marianne Majerus (Designer: Declan Buckley); 74 below Marianne Majerus (Designer: Jane Brockbank); 75 Jerry Harpur/ Harpur Garden Images (Designer: Sitio Roberto Burle Marx, Rio de Janiero, Brazil); 76 above Desert Garden, Trevor Fox/Designers: Taylor Cullity Lethlean; 76 below Marianne Majerus (Designer: Jinny Blom); 76-77 Jerry Harpur/Harpur Garden Images (Designer: Declan Buckley, London, UK); 77 above Jerry Harpur/Harpur Garden Images (Designer: Vladimir Sitta, NSW, Australia); 77 below Marianne Majerus (Designer: Jane Brockbank); 78-79 Eugeni

Pons/ RBA (Architect: Antonio Jimenz Torrecillas); 80 Jerry Harpur/ Harpur Garden Images (Designer: Luciano Giubbilei, London, UK); 81 Henry Wilson/Red Cover; 82 Robin Matthews/Diarmuid Gavin Designs; 82-83 above Marianne Majerus (Designer: Diana Yakeley); 82-83 below Clive Nichols (Designer: Stephen Woodhams); 83 Jerry Harpur/Harpur Garden Images (Tim and Dagny Du Val); 84 left Deidi von Schaewen (Designer: Olivia Putman); 84-85 Deidi von Schaewen (Designer: Andrée Putman for Pearl Lam, Shanghai); 85 above Jerry Harpur/Harpur Garden Images (Designer: Ulf Nordfjell); 85 below Nicola Browne (Designer: Ross Palmer); 86-89 Jerry Harpur/Harpur Garden Images (Designer: Vladimir Sitta, NSW, Australia); 90 Melanie Acevedo (Designer: Judy Kameon); 92 Simon McBride/Red Cover; 92-93 Marc Capilla/RBA; 94 Clive Nichols (Designer: Wynniatt-Husey Clarke); 95 Sharrin Rees (Designer: Brian van der Plaat Design); 96 above Jerry Harpur/Harpur Garden Images (Designer: Steve Martino, Phoenix, AR, USA); 96 below Giulio Oriani/Vega MG; 96-97 above Helen Fickling (Designer: Wynniatt-Husey Clarke); 96-97 below Marion Brenner; 97 above Jerry Harpur/Harpur Garden Images (Designer: Topher Delaney, San Francisco, CA, USA); 97 below Kristian Septimius Krogh/ House of Pictures; 98 Denise Bonenti/Vega MG; 98-99 Helen Fickling (Designers: Terence Conran & Nicola Lesbirel, RHS Chelsea 2004, UK); 99 D, Chatz/Inside/Photozest; 100 Jack Merco/The Garden Picture Library; 100-101 Marianne Majerus (Designer: Claire Lewis); 101 above Clive Nichols (Designer: Wynniatt-Husey Clarke); 101 below Simon McBride/Red Cover; 102-103 & 104 above left Nicola Browne (Designer: Kristof Swinnen, Belgium); 104 above right Maayke de Ridder (Designer: Kristof Swinnen); 104 below & 105 Nicola Browne (Designer: Kristof Swinnen, Belgium); 106 above Richard Powers (Architects: Marmol

Radziner & Associates); 106 below Richard Powers (Architect: Koning Eizenberg); 107 above Geraldine Bruneel, courtesy of Vladimir Djurovic Landscape Architecture; 107 below Tim Street-Porter; 108 Jerry Harpur/Harpur Garden Images (Designer: Vladimir Djurovic, Beirut, Lebanon); 108-109 Jerry Harpur/Harpur Garden Images (Designer: Vladimir Djurovic, Beirut, Owner: Jimmy Bassil, Faqra, Lebanon); 109 above Marianne Majerus (Designer: Claire Mee); 109 below Marianne Majerus (Designer: Declan Buckley); 110 above Simon Upton/The Interior Archive (Designer: Antonia Hutt); 110 below Simon McBride/Red Cover; 110-111 above Denise Bonenti/ Vega MG; 110-111 below D. Vorillon/Inside/ Photozest; 111 Robin Matthews/ Diarmuid Gavin Designs; 112 above Thomas Stewart/Conran Octopus; 112 below Undine Prohl; 113 Ray Main/ Mainstream (Designer: Diarmuid Gavin); 114 Marianne Majerus (Designer: Claire Mee); 114-115 above Jerry Harpur/ Harpur Garden Images (Designer: Vladimir Djurovic, Beirut, Owner: Jimmy Bassil, Faqra, Lebanon); 114-115 below Marianne Majerus (Designer: Claire Mee); 115 Robin Matthews/ Diarmuid Gavin Designs; 116-119 below Undine Prohl (Landscape Architect: Russ Cletta); 120-121 Geraldine Bruneel, courtesy of Vladimir Djurovic Landscape Architecture; 122 Jonathan Buckley (Designer: Christopher Lloyd); 124-125 Marianne Majerus (Designer: Piet Oudolf); 126 above & 126-127 Andrew Lawson (Designer: Jill Walker); 127 above left Marianne Majerus (Designer: Bunny Guinness); 127 above right Marianne Majerus (Aldenhaeve, NL); 127 below J C Mayer - G Le Scanff (Les Jardins d'Yves Gosse de Gorre a Sericourt 62 France); 128 above Marianne Majerus (Designer: Chris Marchant); 128 below Jonathan Buckley (Designer: Maureen Sawyer); 129 Nicola Browne (Blackenham Wood); 130 above Jerry Harpur/ Harpur Garden Images (Designer: Margot Gaywith, Cape Town, South Africa); 130 below Andrew Lawson (Fence by Tim

Neville); 130-131 Nicola Browne (Designer: Ben Fogey, USA); 131 above Andrew Lawson (Designer: Iam Hamilton Finlay, Little Sparta); 131 below J C Mayer - G Le Scanff (Jardin de Berchigranges 88 France); 132 Marianne Majerus (Designer: Pamela Lewis, Sticky Wicket); 133 Andrew Lawson (Designer: Pamela Lewis, Sticky Wicket); 134 & 134-135 John Glover (Designer: Pamela Lewis, Sticky Wicket); 135 Andrew Lawson (Designer: Pamela Lewis, Sticky Wicket); 136-137 Andrew Lawson (Designer: Tom Stuart-Smith); 138 above Marianne Majerus (Aldenhaeve, NL); 138 below & 139 above Marianne Majerus (Designer: Joanna Crane); 139 below Andrew Lawson (Wollerton Old Hall); 140 above Marianne Majerus (Designer: Miranda Holland Cooper); 140-141 Andrea Jones/Garden Exposures (Designer: Daniel Lloyd-Morgan); 141 above Francesca Yorke; 141 below Marianne Majerus (Designer: Claire Lewis); 142 above Richard Felber; 142 below Helen Fickling; 142-143 above Jane Sebire (Designer: Richard Pim, Westonbury Water Mill); 142-143 below Marianne Majerus (Designers: Chris & Toby Marchant); 144 Nicola Browne (The Clock House); 145 above Clive Nichols (Designer: Clare Matthews); 145 below left Jonathan Buckley (Designers: Wendy & Leslie Howell); 145 below right Nicola Browne (RHS Wisley, Designer: Piet Oudolf); 147 above left Torie Chugg (Designer: J H Hewitt. RHS Hampton Court 2005); 147 above centre Clive Nichols; 147 above right Andrew Lawson; 147 centre left Marianne Majerus (Designer: Hans Carlier); 147 centre Marianne Majerus (De Bikkershof, Utrecht); 147 centre right Jerry Harpur/ Harpur Garden Images (Designer: Ulf Nordfjell, Sweden); 147 below left Andrew Lawson; 147 below centre Nicola Browne (Designer: Dan Pearson); 147 below right Torie Chugg (Designer: Stephen Hall. RHS Chelsea 2004); 148 below & 148-149 Marianne Majerus (Designer: Wim Kanbier, Oase, Netherlands); 149-151 Jane Sebire (Designer: Wim Kanbier,

Oase, Netherlands); 152 Kim Sayer/Red Cover; 154 Andrea Jones/Garden Exposures (Designer: Siegfried Speckhardt); 154-155 Helen Fickling/Conran Octopus (Designer: Wayne Hemingway); 155 above J C Mayer - G Le Scanff (Designers: NB Architectes: Elodi Nourrigat, Jacques Brion. Festival des jardins de Chaumont sur Loire 41 France); 155 below Helen Fickling (Designer: Out of Orbit Design, Italy, Festival des jardins de Chaumont sur Loire, France); 156 above Maayke de Ridder (Designer: Jacques van Leuken); 156 below Marianne Majerus (Designer: Alastair Howe Architects); 157 Robin Matthews/ Diarmuid Gavin Designs; 158 above Sanei Hopkins Architects Ltd; 158 centre Jerry Harpur/ Harpur Garden Images (Designer: Tania Compton); 158 below Jonathan Buckley (Designer: David Rosewarne); 159 above Jerry Harpur/ Harpur Garden Images (Architect: Piet Boon, Landscape Architect: Piet Oudolf, Netherlands); 159 below Mads Mogensen; 160 above J C Mayer - G Le Scanff (Le Vallon du Villaret 48 France); 160 centre S. Laurenz/ H&L/ Inside/Photozest; 160 below Marianne Majerus (Designer: Claire Mee Designs); 161 Jerry Harpur/Harpur Garden Images (Designer: Topher Delaney, San Francisco, CA, USA); 162 Andrew Lawson (Designer: Dipika Price); 162-163 Marianne Majerus (Designer: Julie Toll, Sculpture by Simon Percival); 163 Marianne Majerus (Designer: Roberto Silva); 164-167 Helen Fickling/Conran Octopus (Designer: Wayne Hemingway); 168-169 Helen Fickling (Petersham House, UK); 170 above J C Mayer - G Le Scanff (Festival des jardins de Chaumont sur Loire 41 France); 170 below Andrew Lawson (The Manor House, Blewbury, Oxon); 170-171 Marianne Majerus (Designer: Alastair Howe Architects); 171 Robin Matthews /Diarmuid Gavin Designs; 172 above Marianne Majerus (Designer: Roberto Silva); 172 below Francesca Yorke; 172-173 Marianne Majerus (Designer: Tom Stuart-Smith);

173 Jerry Harpur/Harpur Garden Images (Designer: Topher Delaney, San Francisco, CA, USA); 174 Marianne Majerus (Designer: Adam Caplin); 174-175 Jerry Harpur/Harpur Garden Images (Designer: Topher Delaney, San Francisco, CA, USA); 175 left Marianne Majerus (Designer: Helen Pitel); 175 right Marianne Majerus (Designer: Del Buono Gazerwitz); 176 left Marianne Majerus (Designer: Claire Lewis); 176 right S. Anton/ Inside/ Photozest; 176-177 Marcus Harpur/Harpur Garden Images; 177 Dook/House & Leisure/ Inside/ Photozest (Architect: Sean Godsell); 178 above Ken Gutmaker (Designer: Andrea Cochran); 178 below & 179 Holly Stewart (Designer: Andrea Cochran); 180 Ken Gutmaker (Designer: Andrea Cochran); 180-181 Helen Eging (Designer: Andrea Cochran); 181 above & below Ken Gutmaker (Designer: Andrea Cochran); 182-183 Verne/OWI (Designer: Piet Boon); 184 J C Mayer - G Le Scanff (Jardins de Villandry 37 France); 186 above J C Mayer - G Le Scanff (Designers: E. Jalbert & A. Tardivon, Festival des jardins de Chaumont sur Loire 41 France); 186 below Clive Nichols (Designer: Clare Matthews); 187 Andrew Montgomery/Conran Octopus; 188 above J C Mayer - G Le Scanff (Designers: J.P. Collaert & J.M. Wilmotte. Festival des jardins de Chaumont sur Loire 41 France); 188 below Andrew Montgomery/ Conran Octopus; 188-189 J C Mayer - G Le Scanff (Les Jardins du Prieure N.D. d'Orsan 18 France); 189 Clive Nichols (Designer: Amir Schlezinger/My Landscapes); 190 above J C Mayer - G Le Scanff (Restoration House and Gardens, Rochester, UK); 190 below left Marion Brenner; 190 below right J C Mayer - G Le Scanff (Restoration House and Gardens, Rochester, UK); 191 above Andrew Montgomery/Conran Octopus; 191 below Stellan Herner (Stylist: Lotta Noremark); 192 above Jean-Pierre Gabriel; 192 centre Hugh Palmer/Red Cover; 192 below Andrew Montgomery/ Conran Octopus; 192-193 Juliette Wade/ The Garden Picture Library; 193 above Marianne

Majerus (Designer: Bunny Guinness); 193 below Clarisse/ Inside/ Photozest (Designer: Dean Riddle); 194 J C Mayer - G Le Scanff (Restoration House and Gardens, Rochester, UK); 195-203 Andrew Montgomery/ Conran Octopus; 204 J C Mayer - G Le Scanff (Designers: Ossart-Maurieres, Jardin de L'Alchimiste a Eygalieres-en-Provence 13 France); 204-205 J C Mayer - G Le Scanff (Jardins de Villandry 37 France); 205 Jo Whitworth/ Gap Photos; 206 above Jerry Harpur/Harpur Garden Images (Designer: Mark Brown, Varengeville, France); 206 below JS Sira/Gap Photos; 207 John Glover/Gap Photos; 208 left Claire de Virieu/Inside/Photozest (Designer: Madison Cox); 208 right Clive Nichols (Designers: Claire Warnock/ Rachel Watts); 209 left Andrea Jones/Garden Exposures (Designers: Terence Conran & Nicola Lesbirel, RHS Chelsea 2004, UK); 209 right Helen Fickling (Designers: Terence Conran & Nicola Lesbirel, RHS Chelsea 2004, UK); 210 & 213 Marianne Majerus (Designer: Paul Gazerwitz); 214-215 Andrew Montgomery/Conran Octopus; 216 J C Mayer - G Le Scanff (Le Baqué 47 France); 218 Chris Tubbs for Elle Decoration; 219 Helene Toresdotter/House of Pictures; 220 above George Logan courtesy of Ecospace; 220 below Painted Pavilion; 220-221 Marianne Majerus; 221 Marianne Majerus (Designer: Sally Brampton); 222 Steven Wooster; 222-223 Paul Smoothy (Architect: Sarah Wigglesworth); 223 Kim-CUC/ Inside/Photozest; 224-227 Floribunda/The Garden Picture Library (Designer: Diarmuid Gavin Designs); 228 above Roger Foley (Designer: Bill Bauer); 228 below James Balston/ Grand Designs Magazine/ Media 10; 229 Andrew Lawson; 230 left J C Mayer - G Le Scanff (Designers: Serge Rodrigues & Jean Hubert Chow); 230 below Chris Tubbs/Red Cover; 230-231 Andrew Drake; 231 Andrew Lawson (Daluaine, Scotland); 232 above Jerry Harpur/Harpur Garden Images (The Garden

House, Hyannis Port, Mass., USA); 232 below J C Mayer - G Le Scanff (Les Jardins du Mirail 72 France); 233 Jerry Harpur/ Harpur Garden Images (Greywalls, E. Lothian, Scotland); 234 left J C Mayer - G Le Scanff (Designer: Fernando Caruncho); 234 above Andrew Lawson (Designer: Tom Stuart-Smith. Broughton Grange); 234-235 Andrew Lawson (Heronswood, USA); 235 above Jerry Harpur/Harpur Garden Images (Designer: Richard Hartlage, Seattle, WA, USA); 236 Marianne Majerus (Designer: Claire Mee Designs); 237 Ken Hayden/Red Cover (Architect: Andrzej Zarzycki); 238 Andrew Lawson (Designer: Piet Oudolf, Scampston Hall); 239 above left Nicola Browne (Designer: James van Sweden); 239 above right Steven Wooster; 239 below left Gianni Basso/Vega MG; 239 below right Christian Sarramon; 240 above Andrew Lawson (Designer: Piet Oudolf, Scampston Hall); 240 below J C Mayer - G Le Scanff (Jardin de Berchigranges 88 France); 241 Andrea Jones/Garden Exposures (Designer: James Hitchmaugh); 242-243 Nicola Browne (Designer: Cleve West, France); 244 Clarisse Inside/ Photozest; 247 Marianne Majerus (Designer: Judith Sharpe); 248-249 Courtesy of Diarmuid Gavin Designs; 251 Nicola Browne (Villa Medici, Rome, Italy); 252 Marianne Majerus (Designer: Declan Buckley); 253 J C Mayer - G Le Scanff (Pheasant Barn Garden, UK); 255 Jerry Harpur/Harpur Garden Images (Designer: Peter Latz, Germany); 256-257 Marianne Majerus (Elton Hall); 259 Graham Atkins-Hughes/ Red Cover; 260 Steven Wooster (Designer: Bill Dixon & Matt Baxter); 261 Helen Fickling (Designers: Catherine Baas & Jean-Francoise Delhay, Festival des jardins de Chaumont sur Loire, France); 272 Gregg Segal

Every effort has been made to trace the copyright holders. We apologise in advance for any unintentional omissions and would be pleased to insert the appropriate acknowledgement in any subsequent publication.

Dedications

'To my little flower, darling Eppie'— DG

'To darling Vicki my heart of Oak and also Jonathan my athletic gardener who grows the best vegetables in the world'— TC

Published in 2007
by Conran Octopus Limited,
a part of
Octopus Publishing Group
a Hachette Livre UK Company

2–4 Heron Quays,
London E14 4JP
www.conran-octopus.co.uk

Publishing Director Lorraine Dickey
Consultant Editor Martyn Cox
Managing Editor Sybella Marlow
Project Editor Rae Spencer-Jones
Copy Editor Galiena Hitchman
Proofreader Helen Ridge

Art Direction and Design Jonathan Christie
Picture & Location Researcher Liz Boyd

Production Manager Angela Young

ISBN: 978 1 84091 483 2
Printed in China